Shaykh and Effendi

Harvard Middle Eastern Studies, 14

ROBERT A. FERNEA

Shaykh and Effendi

Changing Patterns of Authority Among

the El Shabana of Southern Iraq

HARVARD UNIVERSITY PRESS

Cambridge, Massachusetts 1970

© Copyright 1970 by the President and Fellows of Harvard College
All rights reserved
Distributed in Great Britain by Oxford University Press, London
Library of Congress Catalog Card Number 70-88804
SBN 674–80585–2
Printed in the United States of America

In remembrance of my father, George Jacob Fernea, 1887–1947

Preface

This book is based on field work in southern Iraq, where for eighteen months, between 1956 and 1958, my wife and I lived in a tribal settlement near the small town of Daghara. The research results were originally analyzed in a dissertation prepared in 1959 for the Department of Anthropology at the University of Chicago. At that time my major interest lay in the relationship between irrigation and political authority. Had tribal leadership become centralized because of its association with the localized administration of irrigation systems? I did not find this to be so, insofar as I was able to study the situation in its traditionally tribal setting.

At the same time I became interested in several related problems. Older tribal practices and newer national policies concerning land and water resources had social and ecological consequences that invited comparative analysis. Within the tribe itself, historic variations in land tenure and use had apparently led to basic modifications in traditional tribal organization with attendant contemporary contradictions between the cultural ideal and the socio-economic reality. Although irrigation systems seemed more the product of traditional tribal organization and authority than the reverse, by 1956 overall control of water distribution was one of the most important local functions of the national government. Thus irrigation administration could be seen as a significant variable in the shift of local interests and loyalties from tribe to government bureaucracy. In this context, comparing the roles of the tribal shaykh and the effendi irrigation engineer became a means of understanding some of the changes which were taking place.

In attempting to achieve that always uncertain metamorphosis from dissertation to book, I have expanded and rewritten the study with these broader, more descriptive concerns in mind. Further, given the lack of published ethnographic data from southern

Iraq and the difficulties of undertaking new research, I have included general information where relevant.

I have visited the scene of the original research twice since 1959, and interviewed informants from Daghara as recently as 1967 during a visit to Baghdad. Studies published since the completion of the dissertation have also aided me, and my perspective has been enlarged, I hope, by six years of further research and teaching in the Middle East from 1959 to 1965.

I held a graduate fellowship from the National Science Foundation while in Iraq and I received a Danforth Graduate Fellow stipend while writing the dissertation in Chicago. This book was largely completed while I was a postdoctoral fellow at the Center for Middle Eastern Studies at Harvard University during 1965–1966. I gratefully acknowledge this institutional support.

In expressing gratitude to all the members of the faculty of the Department of Anthropology at the University of Chicago who helpfully read and criticized my original formulation of this work, I must especially thank Robert McC. Adams. He provided the original guidance and assistance which led me to southern Iraq, and over the years has helped me reexamine many of the problems discussed in this book; his example and friendship have been a constant source of encouragement and personal satisfaction.

As with most social anthropologists, the greatest yet most difficult debt to acknowledge is to those friends we call "informants." It is a sad reflection on the state of the world that I hesitate to mention many Iraqis in Daghara, Diwaniya, and Baghdad who provided valuable assistance a decade ago, for fear that they might now suffer for my expression of gratitude. The traditional hospitality of the Arab world was at all times extended to my wife and myself in Iraq but nowhere more generously than in Daghara, where we were guests of Shaykh Mujid Atiyah El Sha'lan. He and his son Kamal could not have done more to help us in every possible way. Sayid Karim Abd el Abbas, the irrigation engineer in Daghara played a vital role in my research and became a close friend in spite of his deep antipathy toward American foreign policy in the Middle East. His death in an auto accident was a great personal loss, as well as a loss to his own society.

A number of Americans were extremely kind to us in Iraq, particularly the Sheldon Turners, the Gordon Lovelesses, and the

Harold Davenports. No less hospitable were our many Baghdadi friends, and I wish in particular to thank Fakhri Shehab, who provided much valuable advice and assistance.

It was Derwood Lockard, Associate Director of the Center for Middle Eastern Studies at Harvard who insisted this book should be written and whose initiative and encouragement made it possible. I am most grateful to him. My thanks go also to Thomas Stauffer, a graduate student in economics at the Center in 1965, who provided much help in the analysis of agrarian economic data. At least six secretaries have typed drafts of the study and I thank them all for their patience.

Finally, and with great affection, I must thank my wife, Elizabeth, who not only helped me in every possible way to write this book, but also wrote her own version of our Iraqi experience, to which I suggest the reader refer when he wonders about the people and experiences around which this analysis turns.

Robert A. Fernea

Austin, Texas
March 1969

A Note on Transliteration

Transliteration from classical Arabic to English is at best a compromise, and several systems coexist. In this book, the problem is further complicated because practically all the transliterated words and phrases are from the southern Iraqi dialect of Arabic, which differs significantly from the classical language and from other dialects of the spoken Arabic. Inasmuch as this is not a linguistic study and the questions raised do not hinge on an exact transliteration, I have attempted to provide an approximate, consistent spelling of Arabic terms that at the same time will not render them unpronounceable for the reader unacquainted with Arabic. For example, the name of the community most discussed in this book is دغّارة in Arabic. I have spelled this "Daghara" in the text, although a more exact transliteration would result in "Daghghārah." (The "gh" represents a sound similar to the French "r" as pronounced in Paris — a voiced uvular fricative.)

Perhaps the other most common proper name in the text is El Shabana, the name of the tribal group near Daghara. A more exact rending of this name would be el Āl Shabānah, "the Shabana people," but this longer form did not seem necessary.

I have tried to provide a more exact transliteration of the Arabic words in the glossary, using standard diacritical marks. The differences from the spellings in the text are not so great as to hinder the reader in using the glossary, however. Plural forms of Arabic words in the text have been created by adding "s" as in English. For those interested in the phonemes and structure of spoken Baghdadi Iraqi Arabic, the best source is probably *Spoken Iraqi Arabic,* by Merrill Y. Van Wagoner, New York: Henry Holt and Co., 1949.

Contents

Illustrations

(following p. 62)

Shaykh and Effendi

Introduction

The problems of becoming a nation after a history of foreign rule
have been repeatedly illustrated since the Second World War as,
one after another, African and Asian territories have joined the
ranks of independent nations. Iraq is an old new nation; the
British mandate in Mesopotamia, established after four centuries
of Turkish domination, ended in 1932. Here in Iraq, just as clearly
as in parts of Africa, one sees the stresses and strains which arise as
a nation emerges from within borders established as administrative
conveniences. The struggle in Iraq is not yet over. Today the
Kurdish region of northern Iraq is in open rebellion and it is not
yet certain that the period of political violence which began with
the revolution and regicide of 1958 has passed. No social institution, no group in the country has remained untouched by the
process of making into a nation a diversity of peoples whose most
common political characteristics at the time of independence were
their dislike of alien domination and their distrust of and antipathy for one another.

The tribes of southern Iraq have been particularly adamant in
their refusal to submit to a central authority. In fact, their apparent subjugation in the early decades of this century marked the
end of nearly half a millennium in which the people of southern
Iraq essentially governed themselves. Today, as this long period
of tribalism begins to end, the most fundamental kind of social
revolution is in progress; for the first time, the people of this region
are accepting the state as the primary focus of political loyalty.
This process has not been completed, and the tribal and town
people here, as in other regions of Africa and Asia, exhibit many
of the disruptive symptoms of rapid social and cultural change.

This book is an attempt to explore certain aspects of the Iraqi
social revolution, using as a case in point one tribe, the El Shabana,

1

and to a lesser extent its neighbors, who live near the town of Daghara, along the central reaches of the Euphrates river, roughly one third of the way from Baghdad to Basra. The term "revolution" is not lightly used, for the penetration of this tribal area by the full force of central government could never have been accomplished without the preempting or fundamental changing of local patterns of political authority. It is this problem area which is of particular interest. What was the nature of traditional authority here? What did it accomplish? How has it changed and what has replaced it?

For a new nation like Iraq, it is far easier to join the United Nations and establish diplomatic relations with other countries than to come to terms with the nonbureaucratic, traditional and local patterns of authority within its own boundaries. What is happening among the El Shabana, the rural tribal people of Daghara, as they adjust to new patterns, the patterns of bureaucracies, of the urban middle class effendis?

These questions cannot, of course, be answered by isolating political phenomena from other aspects of social life. The answers will require several related analyses. To grasp the nature of traditional authority we must understand the environmental conditions in which it developed and the tribal system of which it was a part. To discuss the accomplishments of traditional authority, it is necessary to look at the ability of tribal leadership to respond to the problems confronting the tribe at various points in time, and to understand the changes which have taken place requires an analysis of the political alternatives which have been offered. The questions are, of course, closely interrelated; so must be our responses to them.

The nature of the present study requires that it be concerned with the past almost as much as with the present. Accounts of travelers and analyses of historians provide general outlines of policies and general shapes of institutions for the periods with which we are concerned, but there are many points at which the detail is lacking for the level of analysis attempted here. Fortunately the past and the present of this study span a relatively small number of years. The era of tribal autonomy lies within the memory of living informants, a number of whom took active part in the last battles against the military forces of central authority.

2

These informants provide an important amount of specific information which helps fill in the outlines of recorded history.

More important still, the institutions of the past have not yet completely disappeared. Though participation is less widespread than in the past, though the consequences of participation may be less significant, nevertheless little is said about past customs and institutions in the pages that follow which, to some degree, cannot be directly inferred from present practice. In a sense, of course, one thereby finds oneself reasoning inductively about the past through familiarity with contemporary details, and deductively about the present through a general knowledge of the past. The ultimate test, in such methodologically questionable circumstances, must remain overall plausibility.

Perhaps another, rather tangentially related point may be raised in this respect. In discussing a problem which centers around the replacement of a traditional set of institutions by more modern political and administrative machinery, the rhetorical circumstances of the discussion often seem to lend credence to the charges that social anthropologists are opposed to "progress" and that they would prefer, if they could, to maintain the status quo of tribal or peasant peoples. Let it be said, then, that this is neither an attack on nor a defense of tribalism; both orientations seem quite inappropriate when the objective of a study is dispassionate analysis. If one were speaking of national development on the level of the State, the successful incorporation of all rural peoples into the administrative systems of the government would seem to be applauded as a legitimate and necessary goal of political modernization. At the same time, from a local or tribal level of analysis, the same process seems to involve the destruction of local, independent political systems. Neither point of view necessarily means one approves or disapproves of what is taking place.

For most of the last five centuries, all problems were solved locally in the region which is the object of this study: a limited area of southern Iraq occupied by tribal cultivators on the farmland, and merchants and government employees in the small towns and villages. The area has become of serious interest to the central government only since the turn of the century. Today, governmental involvement in the rural south of Iraq is not merely limited to maintaining law and order; a frank concern with the social welfare of the population has been expressed. Misdirected or mistaken as this interest may sometimes seem, the seriousness of the intentions of Iraq's postrevolutionary government to improve rural welfare cannot be doubted.

Since this study was undertaken between 1956 and 1958 the author has briefly revisited the Daghara region twice, the last time in 1966. Ten years ago, an automobile journey between Daghara and Baghdad required six or more hours over dirt roads; the trip now takes about two hours on paved and graded roads. Daghara enjoys frequent connecting bus service with the provincial capital of Diwaniyya; no longer must one ride an uncomfortable passenger truck or buy an expensive seat in an old taxi and wait for it to fill with passengers. Intermediate and secondary schools have opened and the number of primary schools in the immediate region of Daghara has tripled since 1957.

Underneath the obvious changes others have taken place. Some local residents say less land is under cultivation than before the revolution because each month more farmers desert their unproductive holdings and move to the city to find work. Yet Daghara itself, a town of around 3,000 persons before the revolution, appears to have grown and expanded. The new public buildings exceed in size and number the older structures and the streets of the town are full of newly arrived government employees who are employed in the public buildings. The market has responded to the ready cash of the new arrivals and also seems more prosperous than before.

However, this appearance of prosperity may in part be illusionary. The activity of the marketplace is undeniable. Yet the money which flows through it does not seem to come from local agricultural production but rather from northern production of oil, the revenue of which pays the salaries of the government employees and which is the basis of the current and long-overdue investment in social overhead.

Whether the fundamental agricultural problems of the Daghara region can be solved — the salination of the soil being of primary importance — remains to be seen. Unquestionably, however, social change as described in the following chapters, whereby local and national institutions are becoming more and more interrelated *within local contexts,* is even more pronounced than was the case at the time of this study. The city is moving to the country in the myriad forms of social services now regarded as the responsibility of the central government. At the same time, the country moves to the city as thousands of cultivators find that even the lowest levels of urban life are materially more rewarding than life in the tribal hamlets, where the tides of modernization have yet to flow.

The chapters which follow, then, present tribe and village midstream between the locally oriented tribalism which dominated the first three decades of this century and the urban-oriented nationalism which became so important in the last decade. Perhaps the traditional elements in this situation have been given somewhat greater stress, yet this was my predilection. I make no apology for my preference, believing that if the elements of tradition are clearly modeled and filled in, one can see more accurately, thrown into high relief by the contrast, the changes which have taken place. Even as I write, the pace of change seems to be accelerating still more rapidly in this troubled and ancient land.

I

The Setting: Southern Iraq

Tradition places the Garden of Eden in southern Mesopotamia, on the alluvial plains between the great Twin Rivers, the Tigris and Euphrates. But the traveler to contemporary Iraq will find little to remind him that he is viewing an ancient paradise. Flat and brown, the plain seems to stretch away, scarcely unbroken, to the horizon, under the cloudless sky. The vastness and dullness of the landscape is varied only slightly by the action of the rivers and by human endeavor.

The fertile land of southern Iraq consists of alluvial plains created by the two rivers over thousands of years.[1] The process of silt deposition appears to have pushed the delta of the rivers further southward even since the geologically recent days of Babylon, and has left a large area (some 4,000 square miles during flood season) of marshland and shallow lakes in which the waters linger and merge before collecting finally as the Shatt el Arab, whose waters feed the Persian Gulf. Today in southern Iraq, the traveler, seeing only bits and pieces of the fragmented rivers and canals, may forget he is viewing two of the world's most important rivers until he sees them, combined in the great Shatt el Arab, flowing by at Basra on the way to the Persian Gulf.

Topographical variations in the landscape are frequently related to the rivers: mounds of earth, sometimes meters high, indicate the presence of irrigation canals, both in use and abandoned; large depressions or wadis are empty river beds or dried-up marshes. The occasional field of growing barley, wheat, or rice provides in its rich green a striking contrast to the unirrigated uncultivated portions of the land, which are sparsely covered with dun-colored grasses and low bushes. White ground-salt crystals, signal of salination, extend over wide areas, forming patches and traceries like half-melted snow on the brown earth. Along the irrigation canals, small clumps of date palms mark the rural settlements, with their flat-roofed, mud-walled, houses clustered around the *mudhifs* or tribal guest-houses. The mudhifs, a distinctive and characteristic feature of the region, are constructed of wide arches of bound reeds and are often as high as the palm trees. The few larger towns boast, in addition to the mudhif and the mud-brick houses, the square garden plots and the baked-brick houses of civil servants. In some places, groves of date palms may stretch along the waterways for miles, accounting for Iraq's position as the world's foremost producer of dates. Yet the trees and settlements are widely scattered and the overall effect of the countryside is one of emptiness. This is not surprising in view of the area's comparatively low density of population: roughly eight and a half million people occupy 5,731,000 arable hectares, leaving Iraq with approximately one third more agricultural land per person than Egypt.

The low population density may be related to the harshness of the environment. Southern Iraq offers no more material resources than Egypt, and the people have been obliged to develop an adequate exploitive technology in a far more demanding and rigorous physical setting.

For despite the sameness of much of its landscape, southern Iraq is in many ways a land of extremes. In addition to an excess of marshland and desert, there is great variation in both the diurnal and annual temperatures. Summer temperatures regularly rise above 100°F., yet on winter nights frosts are not uncommon.[2] In the deserts the relative humidity is low, but in the marsh areas, as well as in regions of intensive irrigation, hot summer days can also be very damp. Rainfall may be occasionally heavy in the winter months, but ordinarily May, June, July, August, September, and October are without any appreciable rainfall at all.

Agriculture, the major source of income in this region, cannot be sustained by the rainfall alone. The generally low humidity, hot sun and lack of cloud cover act, through high rates of evaporation, to minimize the benefits of the unpredictable winter rains. In any case, the rains frequently do not arrive at the crucial points in the agricultural season. Therefore all summer and most winter cultivation is dependent on water taken from the Twin Rivers; the rivers' flood pattern constitutes still another uncongenial extreme of the area.

Unlike the Nile, no great distance exists between the headwaters of the Tigris and Euphrates and the alluvial plain. Thus the flood follows quickly upon the winter rains, the April peak coming too late for the winter crops and too early for the summer planting. Until 1958, when flood control installations were completed at Wadi Tharthar, the Tigris regularly flooded into the streets of Baghdad in flood season and ravaged the countryside between the capital and the Gulf. On the other hand, in midsummer the supply dwindles radically and severely limits cultivation.

Since the flood season does not coincide beneficially with the growing season, the "basin" or "flood" irrigation characteristic of the Nile valley is largely out of the question here. The Twin Rivers do not, like the Nile, rise up to deposit a damp, fertile deposit of silt in the spring, just when the climate guarantees the fast growth of a crop. Rather, before 1958, spring floods regularly threatened to wash out the winter planting.

Furthermore, while the land south of Baghdad is relatively flat, the rivers have a comparatively rapid rate of flow due to the steep gradients and subsequently swift descent from the mountainous headlands. This swift current, plus the fact that, as in most alluvial basins, the rivers tend to be above the level of the surrounding countryside, accounts for the inherent instability of the Twin Rivers regime south of Baghdad. Scouring in one place, depositing silt in another, the rivers follow a braided, bifurcated course, favoring first one and then another path to the marshes above Basra. The Diwaniyya bifurcation of the Euphrates, from which the Daghara canal feeds, all but ran dry in the years before the Hindiyya Barrage was renewed at the beginning of the century, and evidence exists for numerous changes of river beds over the centuries of recorded history.

To add to the uncertainties of irrigation-dependent cultivation, the annual supply of water in the rivers varies widely from year to year. In 1939, for instance, the combined river supply was as low as 22,000 million cubic meters while in 1941 it rose to about 80,000 million.[3]

The historic problem which the river posed for tribal cultivators in this region will be discussed in the next chapter. But even in this century no solution has been found to the basic problem of irregular water supply. Although the disastrous floods which ravaged the countryside have been eliminated, the almost equally disastrous low supply years cannot be avoided.

However, despite these many natural disadvantages, the Euphrates and, to a lesser extent, the Tigris River, have provided through the centuries a reasonably manageable source of water for irrigation. This has been possible without elaborately engineered controls because of the bifurcating, braided nature of the streams which allows small portions of them to be dammed with a minimum of effort.

Until modern irrigation works were instituted, beginning in 1916, tribal groups would block small streams with temporary dams of rolled reed matting reinforced with brush and mud, thus forcing the water through prepared canals or over the land in floods. Presumably such techniques have been employed to utilize water resources in the valley for many hundreds, perhaps thousands of years, watering crops to feed larger or smaller groups of people, depending on the state of the soil.

Today the majority of Iraqis living south of Baghdad still earn their living through agriculture and related activities such as animal husbandry. Techniques of cultivation are simple and suited to subsistence agriculture; cash cropping is a relatively recent innovation. The principal southern crops are barley, wheat, and rice. While wheat is a preferred crop, barley is most generally planted and is increasing in popularity because of its apparently greater tolerance for saline soils. The cultivation of rice is generally limited to the fringes of the marshlands where large amounts of water are naturally available.[4]

All the southern towns, with the exception of Basra, Iraq's only seaport, are designed to serve the rural agricultural area and are essentially local administrative and market centers. Any nonagricultural industry is a recent development.

The El Shabana tribesmen and their neighbors in and around Daghara, with whom we are particularly concerned here, share the tough, demanding environment of southern Iraq. Living in the lower Euphrates valley, about one third the way from Baghdad to Basra, the El Shabana are beset by the extremes of temperatures and precipitation, and by the problems inherent in the ecological setting.

The rains of winter not only may wash out the winter crops,

but, if prolonged, will melt the walls of houses, soaking through the palm mat and mud-plaster roofs, and turning the footpaths and roadways into slippery, sticky, nearly impassable mud. The old proverbs about the impermeability and adhesiveness of Mesopotamian mud are based on fact.

During the periods of heavy rains and cold damp weather, it is nearly impossible for irrigation engineers, police, or other officials to traverse the unpaved roads of the countryside. Farmers cannot make their way into towns for shopping, postal, and medical services. Influenza, bronchial infections, pneumonia, and tuberculosis are at their peak.

With spring comes the *sharqi* or east wind carrying dirt and sand across the land in suffocating waves of heat. After April such disturbances become rarer; the winds eventually subside, and high summer begins: cloudless skies and temperatures reaching as high as 125°F. The water supply radically declines and in many places barely meets the demands of human and animal thirst. Cultivation, totally dependent on canal water, shrinks to one third its winter proportions, and the problems of water distribution and division plague tribe and government alike.

In the summer, pasture also shrivels up, and what little remains is shared by local animals with the flocks of many shepherds, who bring their flocks into the Euphrates valley from the desert in order to have access to a steady water supply.

The intense dry heat of summer brings its special illnesses: sunstroke and heat exhaustion, dysentery provoked by dehydration. Typhoid is also a problem in summer, and the government takes stringent precautions against smallpox, which may be brought in by religious pilgrims traveling to the shrines at Karbala, Najaf or Kadhimain.

I have described the extremes; winter days *are* often dry and sunny, and although summer days are never cool, the nights are justly famous for their comfort. Both village and city come alive after sundown as the people, having napped in the heat of the day, visit back and forth until late at night, carrying on the social and political life of their communities.

But from every point of view, the best seasons of the year are the spring and fall months, March, April to mid-May, and late September, October, and November. These periods constitute the seasons of intense agricultural activity. Rainfall supplements the irrigation system and freshens pasture on fallow land and desert alike.

The physical environment also has influenced patterns of settlement in the Euphrates valley since the marsh-land, dry-land variations have necessitated different technological adaptations. In addition, the Tigris and Euphrates valleys have been subject to two quite different centers of cultural and social influence, through contact and immigration from Persia on the east and from Bedouins of Arabia on the west. The most superficial familiarity with the tribes of the two valleys reveals differences in folk tales and dialect.[5]

The southern Euphrates countryside today is populated principally by sedentary tribal groups who have migrated from the western desert into the valley. Nomad groups, of mixed and diverse origins, are also found. In the Daghara area, members of the El Shabana state that they come from the Nejd and claim relationship with the great tribal confederation of the northern Arabian peninsula, the Shammar.

Fully nomadic sheep-herding pastoralist tribes do not frequently come into the environs of Daghara, probably because the local sedentary population raises as many animals as is possible with the available supply of pasture. However, no ethnic distinction exists between the sheep-and-goat pastoralists and the sedentary cultivators. In one instance, where the shaykh of a small neighboring tribe succeeded in privately registering almost all of the original tribal land or *dira,* the members of his tribe chose to turn to pastoral sheep-and goat-herding rather than sharecrop. They have left their old domain to be tilled by men unrelated to the shaykh. These shepherds maintain their tribal ties and regularly assemble at the guesthouse of the sedentary shaykh not only for religious festivals but also to settle intra-tribal disputes.

In addition to shepherds who travel with their flocks by foot, nomadic tribes or tribal sections, commonly referred to as *shawiya,* follow a pastoral existence on donkey-back; they may venture further into the desert after the rains than their pedestrian neighbors. However, "this distinction is not necessarily either tribal or regional. Though tribes may be wholly nomadic or wholly fellahin, many tribes, particularly the larger, contain sub-sections both of shawiya (and pedestrian shepherds), and of fellahin, and the two

11

ways of life are intermingled within the various regions of the country, though the fellahin are tied to the localities where there is water for irrigation." [6]

More exclusive in nature is the practice of camel herding. The classical pattern of Bedouin camel-herding nomadism is more appropriately discussed in connection with the Arabian peninsula, but such tribes do move in and out of the Euphrates valley quite regularly and have longstanding relationships with some of the sedentary tribes of this region. Some camel-owning groups regularly camp on certain fallow lands each summer and appear at harvest times to haul crops to market on their camels in return for a small share of the grain. Such relations between nomad and sedentary peoples are frequently cemented by marital exchanges between the leaders of the groups involved.[7] In addition to the economic importance of such relationships, interaction between the nomads and the sedentary groups may reinforce traditional Bedouin ideals of conduct and tribal organization originating under nomadic conditions, in spite of the fact that these ideals are not well attuned to the circumstances of sedentary life.

Most of the rural citizens of contemporary southern Iraq were born members of a tribe, but the significance of this for the individual and for the stability of tribal life is by no means uniform. A variety of economic and political conditions have unequally affected subregions of southern Iraq, the most important of which has been land tenure and the nature of land registration. Both Turkish and, later, British policy resulted in the widespread, though not universal, registration of tribal lands in the name of the incumbent shaykh. Where this has happened, tribesmen have frequently left their ancestral lands or have been reduced to the status of sharecroppers, while the shaykhs, in the more extreme cases, have become absentee landlords, residing in the city. In general in these situations tribal organization has been reduced to a collection of named groupings with little or no contemporary function or corporate existence. On the other hand, where land registration procedure allowed individual tribal families to retain ownership of a certain amount of land, one usually observes more of the customary social and economic features of tribal life. The more widely the land has been distributed among tribesmen, the

12

more likely some form of tribal organization will be of contemporary social significance.

Yet the equitable distribution of land cannot be carried too far without also undermining the tribal system. In some areas (as near Rumaytha, on the Hilla branch of the Euphrates below Diwaniyya), the landholdings have been widely distributed among tribesmen and subject to fragmentation through inheritance. Many of the shaykhs have holdings no larger than average, yet little remains of a functioning tribal system. In such cases, the traditional leaders lack economic means to maintain the guesthouses where tribesmen traditionally gather and have lost the political and social standing in Iraqi society-at-large which might make them valuable intermediaries for the ordinary tribesman in dealings with the administration. Thus either extreme—radical equality of land distribution or radical concentration of land in the hands of the shaykh—may be inimical to the contemporary political functions of a tribal system.

Complementing the disintegrative processes set in motion through the loss of tribal lands has been the imposition of administrative and judicial systems from Baghdad and the pacification of the countryside which have robbed the tribal organization of most of its historic purpose. The fact that some aspects of the social life of men in most of southern Iraq still remain tribally organized is probably due in large part to the fact that nothing has yet replaced kinship as the principal mode of social intercourse in this region, and the tribal system is, as we shall see, largely a system of extended kinship.

In southern Iraq as a whole, the El Shabana together with the other tribes of the Daghara region and those of the entire Middle Euphrates region—from Hilla south through the areas around Diwaniyya and Samawa—have maintained tribal forms of social organization to a degree unparalleled, for instance, in the middle and southern reaches of the Tigris, around Kut and Amara. In the latter areas great concentration of landholdings and considerable movement of population early in this century effectively terminated most traditional social organization beyond the family.

The El Shabana and its neighboring tribes have continued to live in hamlets and villages surrounded predominantly by resident kinsmen. Although many of these small landowners cannot support themselves through the cultivation of their own holdings, the homesteads are rarely abandoned completely. Even if the head of the household works elsewhere as a tenant farmer or as a laborer in the city (now more commonly the case) some member of the family remains in possession of the property.

The tenacity with which these tribesmen-farmers cling to their small, often unproductive estates stems not so much from innate affection for the land as from a concern for social standing within the tribal community. To completely abandon one's tribal homeland means giving up all rights and duties with respect to the tribal dira or domain and generally withdrawing from any interest in tribal affairs. When a general population census was announced in 1957, the call went out to all absentee El Shabana tribesmen to return to their homes on census day. It was considered important that the tribe make a good showing on this occasion rather than reveal weakness through a decline in population size.

Many tribesmen realized that the ability to demand social services from the government depended on the size of their communities. At the same time, the attempt to muster as large a showing as possible was entirely consistent with attitudes developed under conditions when tribal strength at arms was the key to individual well-being.

The varying conditions of land tenure settlement patterns and political development have also acted to produce a bewildering variety in nominal expressions of tribal organizations. Within a radius of a few score miles the terms for tribal subdivision may differ, making it difficult to determine whether organizational features found in one area actually exist among tribal groups a short distance away.

The situation is complicated by the presence of numerous families of tenant farmers who are of tribal origin by birth but who no longer live in their own tribal communities. These strangers do not ordinarily participate in local tribal affairs but many of these men and their families regularly return to their own tribal areas for religious holidays and maintain an interest in the political affairs of their own tribal groups.[8]

To judge accurately the relative numbers of tenant settlements versus tribal hamlets or the number of resident versus sharecrop-

14

ping farmers in the valley is almost impossible. Poyck estimated that in the Hilla-Diwaniyya area only one third of the agricultural population was self-employed on small holdings.[9] However, the lands of El Shabana are largely owned by the tribesmen, and even on the sharecropped lands, owned by the shaykh, his brothers and uncles, many El Shabana were employed, together with many outsiders. Therefore, all that can be said with certainty is that, of the mixed tribal and tenant farm settlements throughout the valley, tribal settlements predominated in the Daghara area, among the people upon whom this study is focused. Since the concentration of small farms in the Daghara region was greater than in the total area covered by Poyck's survey, it is probably fair to assume that the proportion of tribesmen resident on their own property is higher here than in the area as a whole.

As one travels through southern Iraq from season to season, the tents and flocks of the nomads—the shepherds and camel herders—move farther from or closer to the settlements and hamlets of the sedentary cultivators. Both tribal and tenant farmers live in such hamlets and homesteads which dot the lands surrounding Daghara town. Sociologically, the two types of settlement are quite different; the homestead is occupied by a kin group but the inhabitants of sharecropper settlements may be largely unrelated to each other. Physically, however, the settlements of tribal and tenant farmers may at first glance appear similar. Settlements, tribal or tenant, are always located near an irrigation ditch which carries water year round and serves both as a source of drinking water and as a sanitary facility. Few settlements of any type are electrified. The houses are the same: walls constructed of sun-baked brick, roofs commonly made of palm leaf mats supported by beams of split palm logs.

Tribal settlements may be differentiated first by the presence of the stately high-arched mudhifs or guesthouses;[10] tenant hamlets seldom have a guesthouse unless the landlord decides to build one for the use of his *wakil* or representative. Individual tribal houses tend also to be larger and more elaborate than those of the tenant farmer, who characteristically carries his wooden roof beams with him and may simply rehabilitate the walls of an abandoned mud hut near his newly assigned plot of land.

The size of a tenant hamlet, which may range from five to fifty

15

families, depends on the amount and quality of the surrounding farmland. Tribal hamlets, by comparison, represent more of an organic growth, which reflects the micro-variations in population size and migration rates occurring from generation to generation. The preference for patrilocal residence after marriage means that a room may be added to the father's house to accommodate a married son and his family. Frequently one finds several married brothers sharing their deceased father's courtyard, though brothers often break up joint households after their father dies. The houses are built close together so that women may slip back and forth without attracting general notice or walking long distances in the sun.

But perhaps it is the stands of palm trees that mark most vividly the tribal hamlets and constitute the most conspicuous difference between the two types of settlement. The trees, privately owned and inherited, are testimony to long habitation. They also signify the inhabitants' long-term investment in the settlements, as do the mudhifs, and the more elaborate homes, courtyards, and outbuildings.

The relatively less elaborate homes found in hamlets of tenant farmers and the absence of palm trees and mudhifs do not necessarily reflect more impoverished circumstances so much as the residents' unwillingness to invest money and effort in property which, at any time, they may choose or be obliged to abandon. Since in this area the larger estate owners have more land than sharecroppers to farm it, tenant farmer settlements tend to shift about from area to area or plot to plot. This is true even when the same family continues to work year after year for the same estate owner, who will alternate cultivation of his lands, following the area's system of fallowing. Here it is generally recognized that the longer a piece of land remains fallow, the better the crop yields when it is eventually cultivated.

The only political office commonly associated with both tribal and tenant hamlets is that of the *surkal*, a functionary required of the hamlet until recently by government law to facilitate the administration of the countryside. The surkal may be called into the police office and questioned about the activities of his neighbors if any problem should throw suspicion on his community, but he has no special standing among his fellow hamlet dwellers

16

and some informants say that men try to avoid, rather than seek the dubious distinction of this job. Among closely interrelated tribesmen, political processes are informal and a matter of consensus; any problems between sharecroppers are likely to be settled directly by the landowner or his representatives.

Both tribal and tenant settlements are incomplete social universes, not even as self-sufficient as the type of community usually called a "village." Little labor specialization exists beyond age and sex differences within the family. Neither shops nor markets are found to facilitate the exchange of goods and, in any case, each family produces approximately the same products.

Thus both politically and economically the hamlets and homesteads are tied to market and administrative centers like Daghara.[11] From every rural settlement, footpaths lead out to canal levees and these eventually to a dirt road which finally passes into Daghara. One can see all of Daghara in a morning walk; the outskirts of the settlement are less than a mile from its center. It is like dozens of other small towns or villages in southern Iraq which are both markets and headquarters of local administration.

Daghara has a population of nearly 3,000 but it serves as the center of an administrative district composed of about 26,000 people.[12] An estimated 10,000 people trade here regularly though they may also go occasionally to the city of Diwaniyya, some fourteen miles away. The village has an electric generator which provides about twelve to fifteen hours of electricity per day for the offices and schools, and for the private houses which can afford the cost. A chlorinated water system, housed in a water tower, is also available to any citizen who can pay nine Iraqi dinars to pipe his house into the system. More than half of the people living in the village proper in 1957 took advantage of these improvements.

The visitor to Daghara finds himself caught up in the constant movement in and out of the village, which may be observed on all but the most inclement days. Traffic comes from the canal, which flows through the village from the Euphrates River in an easterly direction toward the town of Afaq, near the site of the ancient Sumerian city of Nippur. The main road from Diwaniyya passes north and south through the village, crosses over the canal via a new cement bridge, then, as a dirt road, cuts through the tribal settlement to lose itself at last in the surrounding fields. The traffic is varied and mixed: taxis bringing merchants back to the village from buying expeditions in Diwaniyya or Baghdad; women carrying loads of camel thorn on their backs to be sold as fuel; farmers leading camels or donkeys loaded with sacks of grain for delivery to market; an occasional salt caravan from the south; cars of government administrators; herdsmen and farmers from outlying settlements on foot or on donkeyback or horseback come to sell produce or to buy some of the necessities which are not available in hamlets and homesteads. Most of these visitors are bound for the covered suq which lies along the canal, east of the main road. In the suq, farmers wander through the permanent small stalls and shops which offer cloth, canned goods and sundries, spices, tea and coffee, cereals, and other dried foods. Thirty sundries shops and twenty cloth shops are found in this small suq. If the farmer is interested in seasonal fruits and vegetables, he can find sixteen *baqqal* or fruit and vegetable stands under cover, but prices are lower outside the suq, along the road beside the canal, where transient peddlers hawk their wares. Old women sit in the shade of the cottonwood trees with baskets of eggs, a single chicken, or a few tomatoes or cucumbers displayed on a piece of cloth.

The visitor may come to town to have his farm tools repaired at one of the two ironsmiths, or to patch his copper pots and pans at one of the two coppersmiths. Guns and knives can be repaired, or knives made at the shop of the *sayqal*, a man who specializes in this craft. If the visitor is early enough, he can buy fresh meat at one of the two butchershops, where at least one animal (goat, sheep, or cow) is slaughtered daily. The Friday visitor will have more choice, for two or more animals are slaughtered on that day. A prospective bridegroom or a new father may visit the three jewelers, to buy gold for his bride, or silver ankle bracelets and earrings for a new-born child. A woman visitor to Daghara usually goes to the jeweler's, to have a necklace repaired, to sell her jewelry in order to pay for a child's schooling or a medical bill, or simply to look at the finely wrought gold earrings and bracelets for sale.

Visitors do not make the trip to Daghara only to buy and sell produce. Often they come to visit one or more of the government

18

offices, square burnt-brick buildings set down in a row on the west side of the main road, across from the suq. Here is the sarai, housing the police station, the office of the chief administrator, or *mudir nahiya,* and most other government offices. Births and deaths are registered in these offices, complaints made, crimes reported. People are always waiting near the infirmary for medical aid, and the traffic is also heavy at the irrigation office, where farmers come to petition the irrigation engineer for increased amounts of water for their farmland.

The girls' primary school is near the sarai, the boys' primary school around the corner. Two granaries stand on this side of the road, and at the end of the bridge is the taxi stand, hub of the village. Several of the ten coffee shops in Daghara are located near the taxi stand, and during the day they are nearly always full. Men sip a glass of sweet tea, watch the passers-by and play *trictrac* or backgammon as in Baghdad, but in this rural center the shutters come down and the crowd disperses by early evening.

The people of the market and the families of the government administrators live here, on the north side of the canal. Some higher government officials, the mudir nahiya, the doctor, and the irrigation engineer, live in government-supplied houses strongly built of burnt brick and surrounded with walled, tree-lined gardens. Other officials' families, the policemen, the clerks, the school teachers, as well as the market families, live in more traditional mud-brick houses, much like the houses found in the outlying hamlets and homesteads: irregular arrangements of courtyards and rooms, and palm mat roofs supported by beams of palm logs.

Physically, little distinguishes the houses on the north side of the canal from those on the south side. Cottonwood trees line the south side of the canal, too; there are stands of old palm trees. The road winds away toward Afaq following the canal. But here, instead of the fluorescent lights which illuminate the administrative and market side, are old-fashioned street lights and dirt roads. The center of the settlement is the high-arched mudhif, the shaykh's guest-house, for now the visitor is on the tribal side of the canal, a settlement of about 400 families who are part of the El Shabana. The shaykh of the tribe has a large house opposite the mudhif; behind the mudhif are palm groves, fields, and sub-

19

sidiary canals, and radiating out from the mudhif along small alleys and streets are the houses of the tribal families. The Sada live here also, descendants of the Prophet, who are partially supported by the shaykh and the tribe, and utilized as peacemakers in tribal disputes.

The mudhif is the center of traditional tribal political life, and visitors from outside, from other tribes, or even from the administrative center of Daghara itself, are received here by the shaykh. In contrast to the informality of the tea houses and of the visiting within the small mudhifs of the tribal hamlets, strict formality prevails in the shaykh's mudhif, particularly in the presence of the shaykh. No royal court observes finer nuances of precedence and protocol. Coffee is served in traditional Bedouin fashion by the son of a freed slave, the men sit formally on finely patterned rugs and woven reed mats. Yet at the same time fluorescent lights have been installed in the mudhif, and a modern telephone sits behind one of the reed pillars, putting the shaykh into immediate communication with the local heads of government and, occasionally, the ministries of Baghdad.

The people of the tribe cross the canal to visit the suq, to attend the school, to do business at the government offices. But essentially, they are a self-contained unit, not so much a part of Daghara as merely living in its vicinity.

The mosque is the single structure in the village which may be said to be frequented on equal terms by all of the people resident in Daghara and its visitors as well, if they are of the faithful. Standing a little apart from the village, on the administrative side of the canal, the mosque is a modest square mud-brick structure, without a minaret, boasting only a minbar and an inscription above the door, its blue tiles spelling out "There is no God but Allah and Mohammed is his Prophet." On Fridays, a small percentage of men from all sectors of the community attend prayers. On feast days, processions may visit the administrative side as well as the tribal side, but they always end at the mosque.

The great majority of the residents of Daghara are Shi'a, members of that sect of Islam which predominates in southern Iraq. Here it is not possible to provide a detailed discussion of Shi'a history and formal theology, but only to touch upon a few of the regional manifestations of this religious system particularly as they affect the social and cultural ties within the Daghara community.[13]

Commitment to the Sunna or Shi'a sects of Islam divides the northern from the southern half of Iraq roughly at Baghdad. Within the capital itself certain districts are traditionally occupied by Shi'a, others by Sunna; the tomb of Imam el Kadhum, an important shrine for Shi'a pilgrimage, is the center of a large Baghdad Shi'a residential area. In the cities of Najaf and Karbala, which lie south of Baghdad and slightly west of Daghara, are the tombs of the Imams Ali, Hussayn, and Abbas, whose struggles for the leadership of the Moslem world after the death of the Prophet led to their martyrdom. This in turn contributed to a permanent schism between their followers (Shi'a) and the partisans of the Umayyad Caliphate (Sunna).

Pilgrimage to the holy cities of Najaf and Karbala is a duty for all pious Shi'a, and burial in the ground around Najaf is regarded as a means of insuring residence in Paradise. The holy cities annually attract tens of thousands of Shi'a pilgrims, not only the Arabs of southern Iraq but also Persians, Pakistanis, Arabs from the southern Arabian peninsula and the Persian Gulf, and members of Shi'a minorities from practically all sections of the Moslem world. Many of the pilgrims use modern means of transportation which limits their contact with southern tribesmen and villagers, but others travel long distances by animal and on foot, exercising the stranger's traditional right to tribal hospitality.[14]

However, it is the people of southern Iraq who are most easily able to make the pilgrimages to the holy cities. Many of the residents of Daghara make this trip at least once a year, preferably during the ceremonies held in Karbala forty days after the death of the martyr Hussayn. In Daghara, as in other towns and villages of the region, processions and ceremonies are held during the month of Muharram, especially on the tenth day of Muharram, also called Ashura, the anniversary of Hussayn's death. Ashura is marked by the ceremonies of ritual mourning (*matam*) in which groups of men march through the streets, beating themselves with short lengths of chain or striking their foreheads with swords. This self-inflicted, ritualized punishment is performed not so much in a spirit of personal mortification as to demonstrate a group expression of despair and mourning over the martyrdom. Participa-

21

tion in such events is highly formalized; such ʿaza groups of from ten to a hundred or more men, are organized in villages and towns all over Iraq.

Another important public manifestation of the Shiʿa religious life is found in the morality plays. These may be given on the anniversaries of the deaths of any of the first twelve Shiʿa Imams.[15]

The most dramatic features of Shiʿa ceremonialism seem to be those which emphasize grievance against and difference with Sunna orthodoxy. The Shiʿa believe that Imam Hussayn and his family died in order to save their followers from the sinful existence being imposed on them by the Sunna Umayyad rulers, who, by treachery and violence, had deprived Ali and his descendants of their role as leaders of the entire Moslem community.

The Nuri es-Said government tended to discourage public displays and ceremonials of the sect, apparently because they strengthened Shiʿa feelings of opposition to the Baghdad, Sunna-dominated government, and also because they often became occasions for local outbreaks of violence among the participants and observers. Yet in 1958 the rituals and celebrations were still clearly important annual events in the lives of the people in the Daghara region.

In 1958 the residents of Daghara claimed that the village had suffered a serious continuous decline in population and prosperity over the preceding decade; indeed, nearly a fourth of the covered market was empty. The blame for this state of affairs was laid to the increasing salination of the land, and the loss of water in the main canal which had all but eliminated rice cultivation. In 1966 the town of Daghara was physically almost twice the size it was in 1958, and the market had expanded. Yet the local citizens claimed that more than a third of the land under cultivation in 1958 was now unfarmed.

The apparent recent prosperity of Daghara is the direct result of an expansion in government services. Since the 1958 revolution three new schools have been built and a fourth is planned. The size of the local administrative staff has increased by more than two thirds, it is said, and though many men prefer to live in Diwaniyya (now reported to be a city of more than 300,000), traveling to and from work each day on the new bus services and improved roads, enough of them have settled in Daghara and spend their government salaries there to lend a prosperous air to the community. But the tribal settlements seem strangely quiet; even the numbers of animals seem to have diminished—indeed an epidemic of equine fever in 1962 wiped out most of the horse population and since these animals (in addition to being ridden) pulled the plows and turned the water wheels, this disaster was yet another reason for farmers to give up and go to Baghdad.

Between 1956 and 1958, the major period of study, and 1966, the balance of population concentration and activity of all kinds has more decisively than ever shifted from the hamlets of the tribesmen and the settlements of tenant farmers, into the town of Daghara. Farmers who have not gone to Baghdad are, often successfully, seeking jobs with the new bureaucracy of Daghara. Yet, as one tribesmen reflectively put it, "If we don't persuade the farmers to come back and farm the land, the *muwaddafin* (administrators) will soon have no one to serve but each other."

What then is the picture of southern Iraq which emerges from this brief sketch? An alluvial plain, bounded and watered by two great rivers, cultivated over many centuries, the cultivation always subject to the vagaries of the river, the composition of the soil, the harsh extremes of the climate. A people of mixed tribal origin, belonging to the Shi'a sect of Islam, nomads, sedentary tribesmen, whose history is complex, and whose independence from central authority lies in the recent past. Market towns of merchants and civil servants which now serve also as administrative centers of a comparatively new central government.

Yet, as we have seen, the town and the tribe in southern Iraq are more closely intertwined than might be assumed from appearances.

Rivers and plain, fields and canals, nomad herdsmen, tribal cultivators, and town dwellers are today linked inextricably in patterns of economic dependence and authority structure which are of primary importance in the development of the Iraqi nation. These contemporary interrelationships are the objects of this study, yet the social organization of tribe and town, and the ecological setting, predate by centuries the emergence of Iraq as a sovereign state following World War I.

Shaykh and Effendi

Thus, to understand what is being transformed today, we must, in the chapter which follows, briefly examine the Mesopotamian past and, in particular, the history of the Daghara region. During much of this history, the significant relationship has been between tribesmen and land and water, with little or no interposition of outside authority. Nonetheless, the response of this tribal society to its environment was far from a passive acceptance of the status quo or a mindless adaptation of the social to the physical universe; instead the tribesmen of Daghara and other regions of southern Mesopotamia dramatically and creatively molded the resources of the area to their own needs and uses with all the social and technological means at their disposal.

II

Ecological and Social History

The sacking of Baghdad by Hulagu Khan in A.D. 1258 and the collapse of the Abbasid government marked the end of effective central administration throughout most of southern Iraq until the British Mandate period in Iraq following World War I. It is true that the power of the Turkish and Persian rulers, who exercised sovereignty over this area during most of the intervening period, was usually sufficient to protect the cities of Mesopotamia, which at times were important centers of trade and commerce connecting Europe and Asia. It is also true that the military garrisons located in these cities were occasionally strong enough to protect and support the tax collectors in their efforts to provide revenues for the successive overlords. But except for sporadic attempts at tax collection and pacification, the southern Mesopotamian country-side was for nearly seven centuries the home of largely self-govern-ing tribal groups which fought over the land and exploited it without substantial help or hindrance from a central administra-tive authority.

Our knowledge of rural societies after the collapse of the par-ticular empire which bound them together is always seriously limited by the disappearance of the scribes and historians who generally grace more prosperous ages. However, our view of these periods may also be colored by a predisposition to dismiss as chaotic, disordered, and unproductive, life in a countryside which has lost its urban focus. It is a common bias to see in the rise of tribalism and the decentralization of political authority (such as followed the Mongol conquest of Mesopotamia) the antithesis of progress, the beginning of a dark age only lightened finally by the advent of a new strong centralized government.

Iraq is particularly susceptible to this interpretation. For, as has so often been noted, "In perhaps no other country in the world is prosperity so directly dependent on an intricate system of irrigation, demanding the constant attention of the government." [1] The regimes of the Tigris and Euphrates rivers do not lend themselves to simple flood water basin irrigation as was practiced in Egypt for centuries. The floods are more violent in Iraq, the water arrives too early for summer crops and too late to benefit the winter plantings, the amount of sediment carried by the rivers will quickly choke canal systems if not constantly attended, and the levels of water in the rivers vary considerably from year to year. Thus the rise and fall of the rivers must be manipulated with barrages if gravity flow canals are to be fed, fields must be diked to protect them against spring floods, and if the same fields are to be cultivated year after year, drainage canals must be laid to drain away the salts which rise from the impermeable subsoils underlying the fertile alluvial plain deposited by the Twin Rivers.

All of this suggests the necessity of a complex system of perennial irrigation, a system directed by an enlightened administration with resources and authority at its disposal to organize the countryside and prevail against the natural forces which constantly threaten agricultural life.[2] The collapse of the Abbasid government has long been regarded as the beginning of an interregnum in which such an irrigation system decayed and the rural areas of southern Mesopotamia were given over to wandering, rapacious tribes which preyed upon trade, raided town and village, and constantly frustrated any effort to improve the basic conditions of economic and social life.

This point of view overlooks the fact that cultivation based on irrigation has had a virtually unbroken history in the Middle Euphrates area since its cloudy beginnings in pre-Sumerian times. The rise and fall of urban concentrations in Mesopotamia has undoubtedly measured concomitant increases and decreases in the amount of cultivation. Sheep-herding has been common in Iraq from time immemorial and presumably an increase in pastoralism accompanied each decline in the size of areas under cultivation. But at no time have settled communities ceased to exist in southern Iraq and farming has continued at least in the vicinity of such communities.[3] Neither can it be said that irrigation in southern

Mesopotamia suddenly ceased after the collapse of Abbasid authority.

The common view that the ruin of the land was effected in a few years by the destruction of irrigation headworks at the hands of Mongol invaders in the thirteenth or fourteenth centuries, A.D., is certainly false. Some of the Euphrates canals were still in use in the early eighteenth century when Chesney sailed down the Saqlawiya (and beyond) into the Tigris, but all had suffered from administrative neglect and the gradual silting up of both main and branch canals over a period of centuries. It is relatively easy for local cultivators to maintain some head of water in their distributaries by their own efforts and at the expense of weaker neighbours, but when it becomes uneconomical to clear silt from the canal bed because of the increasing height of the banks, a new channel can be cut along-side.[4]

In this regard, however, two questions must be asked: To what extent did "administrative neglect" of the irrigation system limit the agricultural prosperity of southern Iraq during the centuries of weak central government in that region and, conversely, to what extent were the tribes which controlled that region able to cope with problems of agriculture and irrigation successfully?

The problems confronting the irrigating cultivator in southern Iraq are far more complex than those which must be dealt with by the fallahin of Egypt. In addition to the difficulties mentioned above, the more radical gradient of the Tigris and Euphrates, as compared with the Nile, gives rise to a much less stable relationship between the rivers and the riverbeds. The southern Euphrates, between Baghdad and the Persian Gulf, is a braided and irregular stream giving rise to several marshes along its route and capable of shifts of course which may suddenly leave previously prosperous areas of land without a supply of water. Below Baghdad the Euphrates has apparently changed course several times in the last 2,000 years and related marsh areas have varied in size.[5] Major shifts of water have taken place between the Hindiyya (or eastern branch) and Shamiyya (or western branch) of the river. Each of these shifts has seriously disrupted life along the river, but each also has been partially the product of human activity as well as of the natural scouring and silting of the river.

After the Mongol invasion, for example, one major shift of water from the western to the eastern branch of the Euphrates took place. This led to a gradual recovery during the seventeenth century of the lower delta lands along the newly filled eastern branch of the river.

Credit for this land reclamation "belongs to nature, but also to the unremitting but uncoordinated labors of generations of rice cultivators during the post-Abbasid period." [6] The weirs and temporary dams which cultivators had constructed along the western branch contributed to the gradual silting of this natural river-way and its consequent avulsion. Thus, local attention to irrigation works, rather than neglect, precipitated a major change in the river and ultimately, a dislocation and shift in population.

There is other direct evidence for intensive local efforts at irrigation-cultivation in southern Iraq before the modern period of state control. J. Baillie Fraser, traveling on the lower Euphrates between the Daghara region and the Shatt el Arab in 1835, found irrigation works a personal inconvenience:

The ground was cut up by rude water-courses, which held the place of the ancient magnificent system of irrigation, and form very annoying obstacles to the progress of the passenger. I understand that the whole bank of the Euphrates, often on both sides, from Semava [Samawa] to Bussora [Basra] exhibits these evidences of former dense population and cultivation mingled with the spurious and rude attempts of the Montefic [Muntafiq — a tribal confederation] Fellahs, and dotted thickly with the reed villages and camps of the Arabs.[7]

Again the same traveler comments on the activities of tribal leaders in their attempts to cope with natural catastrophe:

. . . we were told . . . that Shaykh Issaw was absent with a party of his tribe, repairing a *sud* or dyke, to restrain the waters of the Euphrates from over-flowing the country . . .

To explain this rather singular occupation of the Shaykhs, I must tell you that among the conditions of tenure by which the Montefic hold possession of the Shamieh [Shamiyya], or western bank of the Euphrates, there is a condition that they shall at all times maintain in good and sufficient order, the dykes from the Semava down to Bussora on both sides, by which the waters of that river are restrained from over-flowing and destroying the country; and this, as on it depends the preservation of their cultivation, they performed for several years. But the great flood of 1830–1 not only rose above, but actually swept away the greater part of the *suds* so that the country behind the river bank became a swamp, down to Bussora; which place from being once remarkable for its healthiness, has since then from the effluvia exhaled by the

28

stagnant waters, become as notorious for disease. The tribes, for their own sakes, are gradually renewing these *suds* but, I believe, in a very inefficient manner, and they, consequently, are always going wrong.[8]

Fraser's surprise that tribal leaders should be concerned with constructive activities such as dike maintenance and his scorn for the quality of their workmanship is, perhaps, typical of urbane attitudes toward the tribes on the part of both Europeans and Middle Easterners. The Turks and later the British reiterated such views each time the tribes rebelled against their regimes of law and order, taxes and military conscription. Yet there seems little reason to deprecate tribal attempts to develop and control natural resources simply because of tribal resistance to the imposition of state authority!

Even the economic historian Charles Issawi, in his otherwise excellent summary of economic conditions in post-Abbasid Iraq, clearly associates tribalism with the rapid fall of population, the soil salination, and the decline of cultivation which followed the Mongol conquest.[9] While noting that the Ottoman government, which recovered the country from the Caucasian Mamelukes in 1831, made little investment in irrigation works, Issawi nevertheless neglects to give the tribes any credit for the substantial rise in agricultural production which took place in the nineteenth century.[10] Rather, increase in cultivation is attributed to the stimulating effects of foreign investment.

The introduction of navigation service on the Tigris in the 1830's certainly provided new markets and better prices for Iraqi agricultural products; it was an innovation "which greatly reduced the duration of the journey to and from the Persian Gulf, cut down freight rates, and made it possible to move the country's rapidly growing volume of foreign trade." [11] This trade was also encouraged by the introduction of a steam navigation line between Bombay and Basra in 1862 and by the opening of the Suez Canal in 1869 which cut the cost and time of transport between the Persian Gulf and Europe. Issawi estimates that "the total volume of Iraqi trade increased eightfold between 1870 and 1914." [12] This trade consisted largely of the export of dates, wheat, and barley— all crops requiring irrigation in southern Iraq. Even granting that part of this increase undoubtedly came from grain grown in areas of northern Iraq, where rainfall suffices for cultivation, there is no reason to believe that the southern region, dependent on canal irrigation, did not participate proportionately in this production growth.

While recognizing that the expansion of foreign trade promoted sedentarization and expanded cultivation within the nomadic sector of the tribal population, Issawi nevertheless fails to point out that it was tribesmen within the traditional framework of tribal society who were responding to the external stimuli of agricultural production in the nineteenth and early twentieth centuries. It was not a rural population reorganized under new political auspices but a tribal society still dependent on local leadership and techniques. Is it not fair to assume that the tribally organized southern region might have increased production earlier in its years of semi-independence had comparable external stimuli developed? The steady upward climb of Iraq's export figures begins well before completion of the Hindiyya barrage in 1914, which helped finally to stabilize the western and eastern divisions of the Euphrates. Had the tribes been encouraged by trade conditions it seems entirely possible that the upward swing in production might have begun much earlier.

In some respects, the response of the southern Iraqi tribesmen to the new economic opportunities of the late nineteenth century seems all the more remarkable when one considers the waves of intermural conflict and the disputation over land tenure and tax collection which originated with the restoration of Ottoman rule in Baghdad. The new government, particularly under the would-be progressive leadership of Midhat Pasha, was anxious to secure a better basis for collecting revenue and conscripting soldiers in the south. Largely to attain this end, the Ottoman Land Code of 1858 was promulgated. This code failed to recognize traditional tribal tenure concepts and practices as totally as did similar land registration laws enforced by the British more than half a century later.

Under the Ottoman Land Code, title deeds (*tapu sanads*) could be granted to those already in possession of the land in return for fees (*mu'ajjala*) paid in advance. Provisions were made for the sale and inheritance of land so acquired, but *tapu* holders had legal rights only to the *use* of the land; the final land ownership (*raqaba*) remained in the hands of the Ottoman government.

Further, tenure depended on constant use of the land; usufruct rights were automatically lost if land was left uncultivated more than three years.

Land reform, so-called, based on such provisions, was bound to cause trouble among tribesmen and in many areas of the south the code was widely and often successfully resisted. As one author notes: "Tribal cultivators of the south, while recognizing tribal allegiance and the state's legal ownership (*raqaba*) of the land, commonly regard their tribal groups as possessors of the soil by immemorial right, whatever the period of occupancy of the land might in fact be." [13]

Under tribal land tenure practices, effective control of lands rested in the hands of tribal confederations or their component parts, and the "territorial holdings of any one group varied in stability with the needs and abilities of rival and associated groups, and their need for land." [14] Cultivation constituted a right to the land cultivated, but tribes were always careful to claim more than the land under tillage in any one year, for cultivation shifted from area to area within the tribal dira to permit long periods of fallowing and to allow for future needs.

Cultivation was not the only basis for tribal land claims. Pasturage rights, unrecognized by the Ottoman code, in association with or exclusive of cultivation rights, were honored by the tribal community as a valid basis for prescriptive claims to land. Such rights were often acknowledged in tribal practice even when many years went by between periods of active use.[15]

The Ottoman code's stipulation which placed tapu rights in the hands of individual tribesmen was also antithetical to tribal practice. Individual tribesmen cultivated parts of the tribal domain by virtue of their good standing in the tribe and, to varying degrees, according to the distribution of land ordained by the shaykh and tribal elders. In contrast, Turkish officials most generally sold tapu rights to townsmen or to friendly shaykhs. Some of the latter eventually sold out to urban land speculators and others reinterpreted their traditional position and retired to the cities, expecting to collect a share of the harvests as landowners, rather than as active tribal leaders.[16]

The code, then, rather than assuring effective allies for the Turks, had exactly the opposite effect. In their efforts to tax and conscript the southern tribesmen, and in providing shaykhs with tapu deeds to tribal lands, the Ottomans effectively stripped many of these leaders of influence over their tribesmen, and created conflicting claims to the land. The Turks sporadically attempted to enforce the misbegotten claims of the tapu holders against strong local tribal resistance, but with small success.

Nevertheless, among the individual tribes, tribal organization stayed firm, and the power of the shaykhs of tribes appears to have grown stronger as the influence of the paramount shaykhs of confederations declines . . . In these conditions it was only by means of their collective strength as members of a tribe that the cultivators were able to protect themselves against government officials and *tapu* holders alike.[17]

Where, as in the Middle Euphrates area, the Ottoman policy of land registration was successfully resisted, the role of less powerful shaykhs and smaller individual tribal units became more important. More than before, perhaps, the tribesmen became "conscious of the tribe as a unity and of their lands as a tribal home or *dira,* held collectively by the whole tribe." [18]

The Ottoman authorities' attempts to collect taxes in the south of Iraq caused further upheaval. In the 1860's, for example, Midhat Pasha appointed his nephew as chief administrative officer for the Hilla district with instructions to dredge canals, reduce corruption among the tax collectors, and collect overdue revenues. This required dealing successfully with the El Khaza'il, the leading tribal confederation in the area, a confederation comparable in strength and size to the better known Muntafiq confederation further south. The pasha's nephew apparently set out to collect revenues while ignoring the canal work, with the result that in 1869 a full-scale battle broke out between government forces and the tribes which finally had to be settled under the direction of Midhat Pasha himself. The pasha dammed the Daghara canal for a time in an attempt to suppress the uprising, but "the government . . . never succeeded in levying taxes . . . or introducing conscription." [19]

The Ottoman land registration and tax collecting policies were not the only disruptive factors in the Euphrates Valley in the late nineteenth and early twentieth centuries, the period preceding the British mandate and subsequent Iraqi independence. The Daghara region and its surroundings provide a good example of the interplay of natural forces which could also upset the established pattern of life in the area.

The present town of Daghara takes its name from the Daghara canal, a natural bifurcation of the eastern branch of the Euphrates, which flows through several towns as well as by the ancient mounds of Nippur before petering out in the marshes beyond Rumaytha. In the early nineteenth century, before being stabilized by headworks, the Daghara canal occasionally carried more water than the Euphrates itself, and it is conceivable that this channel was once the dominant stream of the river.[20] However, when carrying a lesser portion of the Euphrates flow, the Daghara canal provided a relatively manageable stream of water, better suited to traditional methods of irrigation. These included building temporary weirs and dams to force water into smaller canals.[21] "On the Daghara canal and probably elsewhere, the cultivators build a series of dams each of which holds up the water till the fields in the neighbourhood have been flooded, and it is then broken to let the water pass on to the next dam. Dams of the same type are also built by the Arabs to regulate the supply entering canals."[22]

The Daghara canal, however, suffered from the shifts of water between the eastern and western branches of the Euphrates at Hindiyya, and its parent eastern stream suffered a severe loss of water following the disastrous flood of 1867. At that time Midhat Pasha, to stem the flow of water from the Tigris into the city of Baghdad, closed off the Saqlawiyya escape through which excess waters from the Euphrates had customarily spilled into the Tigris. This helped the Tigris carry water away from the capital, but it overtaxed the capacities of the then major eastern branch of the Euphrates, which overflowed into the western stream, cutting a larger channel for itself. Year by year more and more water was drained away from the eastern bifurcation of the river.[23]

Therefore, by the end of the nineteenth century the main stream had already deserted the eastern channel and was back in the western segment of the stream, leaving the Daghara and similar secondary canals woefully short of water.[24] In 1880 the tribes along the Daghara succeeded in diverting such water as remained in the eastern Euphrates into their offtake, leaving the settlement at Diwaniyya, the seat of the district government, practically without water.[25] In 1889, nine years later, the archaeologist

John Punnett Peters was returning to his excavations at Nippur, and reported further loss of water in the Daghara canal: "We found all the canals and marshes dried up and were able to take a straight course to Nippur . . . What water had come down the Daghara canal had been dammed, first by the Daghara Arabs, and then by the el-Bathahtha, and the marshes were dry as bone." [26]

The periodic loss of water in the Daghara canal in the late nineteenth century not surprisingly had a most disruptive effect on the tribes of this region. Furthermore, after the uprising of 1869 the Turkish authorities made every effort to break the power of the El Khaza'il tribal confederation which dominated the Daghara region and had firmly resisted Ottoman tax and land codes. Power being measured by strength at arms, the Turks encouraged sections of the El Khaza'il to leave the region for the better-watered Shamiyya district on the western branch of the Euphrates. The consequent decline of El Khaza'il population opened the door to other tribes who moved in, subjugating, adopting, or forcing out the remaining segments of El Khaza'il origin. Thus, though in the 1850's the El Khaza'il were referred to as the "kings of the Middle Euphrates, owing a merely nominal allegiance to the Turks, and entirely absolved from revenue," [27] by the 1880's they had been largely superseded.[28]

The major tribal alliance replacing the El Khaza'il was the El Aqra confederation of tribes, including among them the El Shabana who presently inhabit the Daghara region. At this time the El Aqra included both sheep herding and cultivating sections and, like the El Khaza'il before them, they traced their origins to the Nejd.

El Shabana tribesmen say that their forebears originally came to the Daghara region as nomads, but that some of their people settled to cultivate as sharecroppers for the El Khaza'il tribes controlling the land. Their success in defeating the El Khaza'il and taking over the area as their own dira is well remembered to this day, as are the periods of drought; the role of the Turks in this episode is, however, largely forgotten or ignored. In fact, though they acquired this land with the blessing, if not the outright cooperation, of the Turkish authorities, the El Aqra were subsequently as implacably resistant to both Turkish and British at-

tempts to establish control over the Daghara region as their predecessors had been.[29]

Judging from the fragmentary evidence available, the final
decade of Turkish rule in the Daghara region was fraught with
strife as tribes from El Aqra confederation, centered near the
present town of Daghara, and the tribes around the town of Afaq,
further downstream, battled for control of land and water.[30] These
disputes have not entirely subsided to this day; the last armed
uprising against government authority (in this case, the Iraq government) was put down by military action as recently as the 1930's.

Tribal wars and resistance to the government did not mean,
however, as one might assume, that agriculture was neglected in
this region. When water returned to the Daghara canal in 1880
then, as now, sheep-herding tribes were found on the land. But
these new occupants of the Daghara banks were as quick as their
predecessors had been to utilize the agricultural potential of the
region. Thus when the British took over from the Turks during
World War I irrigation agriculture was well established. In 1918,
at the time of the British expeditionary force survey, a multitude
of small irrigation canals lined the banks of the Daghara. These
canals were maintained entirely without direction or control from
the Turkish government in Baghdad (see Map 2). A British
intelligence report provides a verbal description of the region at
the outset of British rule:

Of the Daghara: Forms the boundary between Hillah and Diwaniyah
(Liwas) and waters the prosperous district of Agrah (tribes) and Afaj
(tribes) which produce large crops of wheat, paddy, and rice. Navigation is impeded by earth and brushwood dams (hamals) laid in frequent intervals across the canals in order to force the water into distributaries on either side. The whole country is studded with villages
and towns. Daghara village lies 10 miles from the head of the canal, 200
houses, on both banks connect by a quffah ferry. There is a small
bazaar which is the market for all the countryside. The canal is 35
yards wide here. Caravan route leads from Daghara to Bughailah and
Hai [on the Tigris River.] [31]

Undoubtedly the completion of the Hindiyya Barrage in 1914,
the one major investment in Iraqi irrigation made by the Turks,
greatly improved and stabilized agricultural activities in this region, insuring as it did a relatively certain supply of water in the

35

Daghara canal. But here, as elsewhere in southern Iraq, throughout most of the seven centuries between Abbasid and British rule it was local initiative, skill, labor, and leadership which developed the productive resources of the region, largely despite rather than because of the influence of the weak central government.

Only with the advent of British rule in Iraq did effective centralized government begin to include the Middle Euphrates region. The history of this development belongs with our description and analysis of contemporary irrigation and social organization in the Daghara region, for there is considerable continuity between the British experience and the present. As we shall see, control of irrigation has been an important factor in bringing the Daghara region into the framework of the nation's administrative authority.

In summary, locally directed irrigation would seem always to have underlain cultivation in southern Iraq generally and in the Middle Euphrates-Daghara region in particular. The Ottoman administration of Iraq, except for short periods of time, failed to control southern Mesopotamia, particularly the Middle Euphrates area. But irrigation-based grain farming persisted and increased in that area during the nineteenth century. Possibly grain farming became more profitable as a result of a rise in urban population as well as improvements in export facilities; many sheep-herding sections of tribes switched to farming during this time.[32]

The last quarter of the nineteenth century was a period of change in the Daghara region, and no single tribal power ruled. Partly because of Turkish policy, but also because of the shift in the course of the Euphrates which for some years threatened the Daghara region with drought, local groups such as the El Shabana were able to secure direct control of the land and independence from the overlordship of the strong tribal confederacy of the Khaza'il. Groups farming along the Daghara canal took water from the main stream; temporary dams were constructed. The upstream cultivators sometimes blocked the water supply as a punitive measure against their downstream neighbors but some arrangement for joint use of available water may have existed during periods of amicable relations between farming groups. However, no central control of the water supply existed until the arrival of the British; the unanimous report of informants in the Daghara region is that until 1922 water was taken from the canal as the individual cultivator pleased.

All evidence seems to indicate that localized tribal organization was sufficient to sustain and at times extend irrigation-based cultivation in the region over many centuries, in the absence of sustained central governmental administration and investment. Indeed, contemporary study suggests that extensive patterns of decentralized irrigation agriculture as practiced by the tribes may actually have been better suited to the physical environment of southern Iraq than the more intensive patterns of land use which have followed technological improvements in the irrigation systems, improvements developed by modern central government in Iraq.

III

Contemporary Land Use and Income

While the Daghara region is not a microcosm of southern Iraq in terms of the balance of its natural resources, it does include practically every environmental condition to be found in the area. Dry-land grain farming predominates here with a smaller area of marsh where rice is cultivated. Concentrations of date orchards are found around the towns as well as vegetable gardens. Land-holdings are of all sizes from very large estates to small single-family farms. Thus it is a region which provides ample ecological variation for comparative study.

The major agricultural problem of the area today is the progressive salination of the land, the concentration of mineral salts in the soil beyond the tolerance of crops which farmers wish to grow. Daghara cultivators claim that they were obliged first to abandon full-scale cultivation of rice, and then wheat, and more and more in recent years have had to rely on barley which has the greatest tolerance for saline soils. Even so, the point where crop returns do not support the investment of seed and effort has been reached in many places around Daghara.

The effects of salination are clearly visible. Fields glisten with salt crystals, while on lower-lying plots of land are dark, damp patches of soil, indicating poor drainage, a primary cause of salination.

Ironically, improvement in the water supply permitting an increase in summer cultivation in some areas of southern Iraq frequently has only intensified the salt problem. Greater quantities of water are required to cultivate in the heat of summer than in the cooler temperatures of winter; this in itself often accelerates the accumulation of surface salts. Before the increase in the supply of water, the irrigation canals during low-water periods could themselves act as drainage ditches. But once water became continuously in full supply this secondary function was eliminated.

Progressive deterioration of the soil has resulted in a general decline in agricultural activity. Informants report that thirty years ago twice as many men were farming in the Daghara region as there are today. Many men who have not permanently migrated leave the region during the summers to work in Baghdad or to find seasonal employment as agricultural laborers.

This situation has also encouraged farmers to retain animal husbandry as an alternative or supplementary source of income. Today every family maintains a few animals. While not all farmers can afford a horse and some are obliged to hire others to do their plowing, such animals are useful not only for farming but also for transport and, in some areas, for turning water wheels.[1] Cows are common but apparently given to disease in this climate; the water buffalo seem far healthier but are more expensive and more difficult to keep. Several small herds of water buffalo are found in and around Daghara but few families keep individual animals.

Far more common than any other livestock are the goats and sheep which can be seen in the rooms and yards of most hamlet homes. Grazing on the stubble from harvested fields, eating camel thorn and shawk leaves, the ubiquitous goat gives good returns for little expense, providing both a regular supply of milk for the much-favored glass of tea and an occasional kid for the market. Women and children often raise spring kids and lambs from bottles rather than permitting them to nurse their freshened milk animals. The kids and lambs are then sold at market in the fall. Many farmers have sizable flocks of goats and sheep which, as we shall see, constitute an important source of income for most of the cultivators in this region. Frequently a teen-age son takes his father's sheep and those of other neighbors and kinsmen out onto the Jaziira, the area between the main branches of Euphrates and Tigris bordering the Daghara farmlands. In other instances, groups of shepherds unrelated to El Shabana tribesmen, move from hamlet to hamlet offering to take the farmer's animals out onto desert pasture either for outright cash payment or, more frequently, in return for a share of the animals.

Every size of landholding is observable here, from large estates to smallholdings. The shaykh of the El Shabana is one of the larger landholders in the region; many El Shabana tribesmen are smallholders. Sharecroppers who own no land are called *fallahin* (farmers) in contrast to *afrad* (tribesmen), a distinction which is largely of social rather than economic significance. One of the major contrasts to be developed in this chapter is between the economic position of tenant farmers and small independent landholding cultivators, but, as we shall see, this is somewhat blurred. More than half of the approximately 100 sharecroppers on Shaykh Mujid's own land were from his own tribe, the El Shabana. Living in their own hamlets, in most cases they were farming smallholdings of their own in addition to those of the shaykh.

For both sharecroppers and owners of smallholdings, the methods of cultivation are largely the same. Preparation for winter crops begins in October and continues into December, ideally on land which has lain fallow over the previous year. Plowing is done with a horse and straight-tipped, shallow-draft plow which merely loosens the top soil.[2] In order to insure an even distribution of water over the land, the fields are commonly divided into *lowhs*, shallow rectangular basins of land defined by low walls of earth. Small feeder canals run between the lowhs and as a farmer irrigates his field he lets water into one after another of these divisions, thereby insuring that all sections of this plot are watered in spite of variations in height from one end of the field to the other. The borders of the lowh, which vary in size from a few square feet to several meters, may also mark property divisions between one farmer and another and are carefully restored each agricultural season. Lowhs vary in size depending on the limits of the holding and irregularities in the topography of the land.

Seeds are broadcast by hand, often without furrowing or harrowing the freshly plowed ground. The amount of seed sown depends on whether the land is "strong" or "weak." The weaker the land the greater the amount of seed, and the amounts in the case of barley and wheat vary from as little as 15 kilos per meshara to as much as 50 kilos on very poor land. Furthermore, when, as is often the case on smaller holdings, the farmer intends to let his animals graze on the immature barley or wheat, he generally sows a greater amount of seed to strengthen the crop for this purpose. Poorer farmers sometimes rent their fields of immature barley to others with need of pasture, but it is generally recognized that grazing barley grass and then letting it grow again and come to seed results in smaller grain harvests.

After seeding, the fields are flooded, a process which may be repeated from four to eight times during the growing season, depending on the amount of winter rain and the condition of the soil. Broad beans are often planted with the barley. No weeding is done. No fertilizers are applied. Only camel thorn and shawk bushes are cleared off the field and these are in any case regularly gathered by the women for fuel throughout the year. Occasionally a field may be burned clear, particularly if for some reason it has not been cultivated for several years.

Wheat is less commonly grown than in the past, but the methods of cultivating it are the same as for barley. Where an adequate supply of water and sufficiently fertile land makes it possible to grow rice, the fields are sown in May and June, after the stubble has been burned; no plowing is done but rather the earth is covered with several inches of water for a few days. The cultivator tramples the land to achieve a smooth surface and then seed, soaked to the point of germination, is broadcast in the flooded fields. These fields remain covered with water until two weeks before rice harvest time in September or October. Usually the farmer does little weeding, his main job being to guard the fields against the loss of water cover during the growing season.

Intensive cultivation of vegetables is found near the cities of Hilla and, to a lesser extent, Diwaniyya. In the environs of Daghara, however, a more extensive form of vegetable cultivation was observed on a few large estates. Landlords designated and assigned a special piece of land to a few sharecroppers. On this land several ditches were dug five to six feet apart. Egg plant, tomatoes, and melons were planted along the ridges of the ditches, which were periodically flooded with water from the regular canal. Little was done in the way of gardening.

The majority of farmers in southern Iraq, however, who still adhere to tribal standards of conduct, regard vegetable cultivation as demeaning. True, many families maintain small gardens in which tomatoes, cucumbers and some legumes may be grown for home consumption and for modest sales to vegetable peddlers in country towns, but there is considerable resistance to full-time farming of this sort in spite of a ready urban market for vegetable products. Similarly, while fruits and melons can be successfully grown in the region, such farming is still of limited economic importance except on commercial farms near the larger towns.

Except for plowing, no division of labor by sex prevents women from performing farming tasks. While men supervise the work, women and children participate in most phases of cultivation. It is the men, however, who dig and clean canals and who attend to the distribution of water within the fields.

The expenses of cultivation are the responsibility of the farmer, whether freeholder or tenant. Not every farmer has a plow and it is common practice to hire plowing done, even among sharecroppers. On the other hand, every adult agriculturalist owns a spade, as this is essential in irrigation work, and a one-handed sickle used for harvesting the crops. Agricultural tools — plow, harness, spade, hoe, pitchfork, and sickle — have to be repaired regularly and most farmers have a standing agreement with a blacksmith-carpenter in the Daghara market: the artisan keeps the tools in repair and in return receives so many kilos of barley or wheat each year.

Harvesting and threshing are often done cooperatively, the farmers taking turns dumping their grain on the specially prepared threshing ground. Here it is trampled by a string of animals — cows, donkeys, even horses being used for this purpose. The crops are divided in the fields under the watchful eyes of both the tenant farmers and the guards (haras) hired by the landowner. A man from the marketplace, felt to be impartial by both sharecropper and farm owner, measures out the crop, chanting the number of each heaping trayful of grain as he pours it into sacks. When the division is complete the tenants carry their share home the best they can, though some will already have committed all or part of their crop to the landlord or to a merchant in the market for advances in kind or cash.[3] The landlord's grain is often packed into town by the camels of Bedouin, who take payment in kind for this service, the amount varying with the distance.

This, in brief, is the nature of cultivation around Daghara. The tribesmen are anything but committed farmers. One has the impression that many would rather do almost anything else, whether because of distaste for this type of work or through discouragement from struggling in a trying climate with poor land, high rents, and scarce water. The pattern of cultivation is extensive; the skills of intensive cultivation are largely unknown. Farm machinery had just begun to make an appearance on a few large holdings here before the 1958 revolution, as had agricultural extension agents who, with little apparent success, were traveling about explaining the advantages to be gained from planting fallow crops and using chemical fertilizers, or insecticides (which were, in fact, used by some of the large landlords.)

Furthermore, there is every reason to believe that the methods of agriculture described are essentially those of the past: an extensive pattern of cultivation with low average crop production per unit of farmland, the continued fertility of the land depending not on the use of fertilizers but rather on regular fallowing. But in the past several hundred years, even lower densities of population were found in southern Iraq than are typical today. Then, in the absence of land registration, the tribe (or tribal segment) was, as has been explained, the de facto property owner, de jure claims of the Turkish government notwithstanding. Tribal cultivators enjoyed the usufruct of the land insofar as they could defend it. Historically, the areas under cultivation changed from time to time as people moved about. These movements were due to both the fluctuating tribal balance of power and to the changing ecological conditions which resulted from shifts in the natural waterways upon which irrigation depended. Thus, the present *niren-niren* system of fallowing, according to which plots are alternately cultivated one year and "rested" the next, was supplemented historically by overall movements of population which resulted in areas being cultivated for a while and then abandoned for periods of time.[4]

What has changed, therefore, is not the method of cultivation but rather the conditions of land use. With the registration of land, holdings are fixed and owners must do the best they can with land they inherit or are able to purchase; micro-variations in population densities throughout the region cannot be accommodated through expansion or contraction of tribal holdings.

In the Daghara region land registration policies created not only the large estates, but small ones as well, by effectively recognizing the presumptive claims of individual tribal cultivators. This created a balance of landholdings in which roughly 14 percent of the cereal-cultivating population in the Hilla-Diwaniyya

(Middle Euphrates) region owned farms comprising about 18 percent of the fertile farm land, whereas 74 percent of the arable land belonged to large estate owners.[5]

It seems reasonable to ask, then, what have been the economic effects of this change in land tenure, coupled as it was with unchanging methods of cultivation. I will elsewhere examine some of the sociological repercussions. Owing largely to the efforts of others, it is here possible to look at the problem in agro-economic terms.

Shortly after the completion of the anthropological research upon which this book is based, an investigation of agriculture in southern Iraq was undertaken by a Netherlands firm under contract to the Iraq Government. Based on a stratified sample of farm families throughout the Hilla-Diwaniyya region (which in this survey is an area of 1,230,200 mesharas of land), the research produced an impressive array of quantitative information about the agro-economic condition of the lands and people of the region, including the El Shabana and Daghara town. Utilizing the results of this study makes it possible to place an anthropological study of a single tribe and community in wider, economic perspective. Since it is rare to have economic data of dependable quality for a region of comparatively little economic importance, or for that matter, for any region of the developing world, the fortunate co-incidence which results in two different but complementary scholarly investigations being undertaken in the same place would seem to justify a summary of Poyck's reported results in this context. Such a presentation cannot fairly represent Poyck's own multifaceted analysis, however, and the reader is urged to refer to the excellent original report.[6]

Poyck classified the land of the Hilla-Diwaniyya region into six categories according to the size of the holding and whether or not the cultivators were also the owners of the land.

1. Large landholdings — Estates over 4000 mesharas, owned by a landlord, and cultivated by sharecropping tenants.

2. Medium landholdings — Estates of less than 4000 mesharas, cultivated by sharecropping tenants.

3. Farm-owner holdings — Holdings of land 60 mesharas or less in size cultivated by the owners.

4. Communal farms — "Village land . . . owned by the com-

munity consisting of a number of families; land is not divided in any sense. Periodically, usually every two years, the elders of the village re-allot the land in satisfaction of the shares in accordance with crop rotation [sic]. Under this system no cultivator permanently cultivates the same piece of land." [7]

5. Date orchards — Small stands, 5 mesharas or less, of date trees, cultivated by their owners.

6. Date orchards — Large orchards, over 5 mesharas, cultivated by the sharecropping tenants.[8]

The relative locations of these categories of landholdings are shown in Map 8. Daghara lies in the center of the surveyed region. Roughly three quarters of the land in the immediate environment of the village is held by farm owners, one quarter by landlords with medium-sized holdings. The latter belong principally to the shaykh of the El Shabana and his family while the smallholdings are the property of his tribesmen. (The large holdings more distant from Daghara are owned by men unrelated to the El Shabana, who are absent from their estates most of the year.) It is therefore reasonable to assume that much of what follows concerning the average economic conditions of tenants on medium-sized holdings and of small farm owners is characteristic of the El Shabana tribesmen resident in this region.[9]

Table 1 refers exclusively to the rural land areas and to the portion of the total population directly engaged in agricultural work. The total population of the region surveyed (exclusive of Hilla and Diwaniyya cities) was 117,063. Of this number 16,390 persons or 14 percent of the total population were in non-agricultural occupations. Most of the non-agriculturalists are market folk or government employees living in small towns like Daghara, where 84 percent of the population works at nonagricultural jobs.

Poyck estimates that about 50 percent of the entire area surveyed is unproductive, 20 percent due to salination of the soil and most of the rest because of unfavorable location with respect to water. As may be seen from Table 1, however, the wastelands are by no means equally distributed throughout the six categories of landholdings. The small farm owners clearly have the most unfavorable ratio of wasteland to farm land. In addition, among the cereal cultivators, the small owners have next to the highest density of population, the lowest average size of fertile holding and the highest number of persons per holding.

Table 2 reveals something of the owner-cultivator's response to this situation. Because his own property is insufficient as a resource, the independent farmer cultivates an average of six mesharas a year as a sharecropper, in addition to his own land. Furthermore he must yearly cultivate 30 percent of the land which, according to the traditional system here, should be left fallow.

Understanding the situation with respect to fallow land is the key to understanding the agro-economic patterns of this region, for the ability to fallow according to traditional practice is not only crucial to preserving the long-term fertility of land; fallow lands also provide an essential part of yearly incomes, as we shall see. The traditional fallowing system requires that any area of land farmed one year should be left idle the next; only 50 percent of any holding should be under cultivation at any time.[10] As Poyck points out, given the local condition of the land, irrigation and drainage practices, and the almost total absence of artificial fertilizers or nitrogen fixating crops such as clover or alfalfa, the local assumptions about fallowing are largely correct. These assumptions are that fallowing a) reduces the danger of salination, b) helps the soil recover its fertility, and c) combats the growth of the more objectionable weeds which die down without irrigation.[11]

The farmers of Daghara know perfectly well what will happen if they neglect to fallow their land and they break with traditional practice in this regard only out of desperation. For as soon as they try to increase their harvest one year through planting part of the land which should be left fallow, the overall productivity of their agricultural enterprise is reduced, encouraging further encroachment on fallow lands in succeeding years — a vicious circle in which land scarcity or infertility gives rise to ever greater infertility until the property can no longer support its owners and they must abandon it or seek supplemental sources of income.

In Table 3 we see some of the consequences of the greater deterioration of land among the small farm owners. The average yields per meshara of both wheat and barley, the two most important crops, are well under the average per meshara yields of the tenant farms on large estates. Furthermore, the farm owner cultivates a higher percentage of barley in terms of his overall cropping

46

pattern, than do farmers in other categories. This reflects the more saline condition of the small farm owner's soil inasmuch as wheat is less tolerant of salt than barley.

In contrast to the position of the independent farm owner, the tenant farmer rarely is obliged to cultivate land which should lie fallow. It is not in the interest of the landowner to put his tenants on other than the most fertile areas of land, for with the rising tide of migration to Baghdad from rural Iraq, already well under way at the time of this survey, the universal complaint of large landowners is of a shortage of cultivators.

Some landlords tried to exploit their tenants by charging higher rents or demanding one or more animals each year for the use of fallow land, but at least in the late fifties, the attraction of Baghdad as a labor market had severely reduced the number of available sharecroppers. Many of the more rapacious landlords had been forced to offer better terms to sharecroppers than they had in the past in order to keep even part of their estate in production.

The conditions of tenancy in 1958 varied somewhat from landowner to landowner. A good landlord was one who charged no more than half the crop of the tenant for the use of his land, who made no charges for the tenants' use of non-irrigated land for grazing purposes, and who did not claim any "interest" on the seed which he provided at the outset of cultivation each season. The land was divided between the tenants after the cleaning of irrigation ditches each year and, while the landlord decided what areas of his holdings would be cultivated, the plots were often assigned to the tenants by drawing lots, in order to avoid controversy. As the data presented by Poyck demonstrate, the tenant farmer farms better land and more of it in strict accord with the traditional system of fallowing.

The small landowner forced to farm land which should lie fallow faces another serious *short-term* problem: livestock production is cut down. For as soon as the amount of fallow land in a holding is reduced, the farmer's ability to raise animals is curtailed. Table 4 shows that on the average a tenantholding on a large estate supports twice as many cows, sheep, and goats as the average independent farm owner's, in addition to substantially larger numbers of other animals. The importance of this discrepancy may be understood by examining Table 5, which shows that

47

the small farm owner's gross returns from meat, milk, wool, hair, and eggs are roughly *half* those of the average tenant farmer on a large estate.

Table 5 also reveals how much higher the exploitation costs are for the tenant farmer, who turns over more than 50 percent of his cereal crop to the estate owner as rent for the land. Due principally to this factor in his costs, the tenant farmer's average net income is a much smaller percentage of his gross income than the farm owner's, as may be seen in Table 5. But notice that, at the same time, the exploitation cost for livestock is approximately the same for each group of farmers, if one includes in this calculation only expenses directly attributable to animal husbandry: the relatively small costs of grains fed to the animals, of rent for grazing land, and of cultivating pasture. As can be seen in Table 6, the percentage of gross income devoted to this expense is remarkably similar for all groups. The reason is relatively simple. The greater ability of the tenant farmer on larger holdings to raise animals is the principal reason why his income, on the average, is higher than that of the small farm owner: it is the greater amount of fallow land for grazing which provides the tenant farmer with this opportunity.

One may possibly take exception to Poyck's method of assigning costs in this respect. After all, a tenant farmer is entitled to the use of his fallow land *because* he is cultivating the other half of his holding: it is directly tied to his work as a cereal cultivator and he would not have this land available on which to graze his animals were he not involved in cultivation. Thus, it might be argued, the rent and other exploitation costs of farming should be divided between crops and livestock, as the latter operation is dependent on the former. Only rarely do farmers rent grazing land and only rarely do large landowners try to collect rents for the use of fallow land on the tenant farmers' holdings; the latter is regarded in the Daghara region as the mark of a "bad" landowner and ordinarily no sharecropper works for a man who does not allow free use of fallow land unless compelled to do so because of indebtedness.

Nevertheless, however one may choose to resolve this question of cost accounting, it is clear from Poyck's data that livestock is the key element in the surprising conclusion (summarized in Table 7) that higher income and subsistence levels are enjoyed by sharecroppers on large holdings than by independent farmers, even though the former group is obliged to give up more than 50 percent of their harvest in rental to the landowners. Table 8 provides another statement of this situation.[12]

The ratio of family size to farm size is far less favorable in the case of the small farm owner, whose property, unlike that of the sharecropper, is subject to the fragmentary processes of Islamic inheritance. Even though women here customarily do not receive a share of land and even though some coinheritors among small farm owners continue to farm their land without formal division (as seen in Map 6), there is clearly an inexorable, overall tendency for smallholdings to become smaller. As is shown in Table 9, farmholding size and family size tend to increase together whether in the case of tenant farmer or independent small landowner. However, whether the family includes two persons or twelve, the tenants are seen to have access to more land, on the average, than the freeholders.

The study of a few El Shabana cultivators' household budgets revealed that most cash income was derived from the sale of animals and animal products, while cereal and vegetable production was paid out in kind as rent or largely consumed by the producers. This impression is partly confirmed by the data from Poyck's stratified sample.

As may be seen in Table 7, the small farm owners participate less in the cash economy than do the tenant farmers on large estates.[13] They are able to market only 36 percent of their crop and animal production, and consume a higher percentage of their production than the tenant families: ". . . it appears that in region 1 (tenant families on large estates) the expenses amounting to 83% of the grain production are paid in kind (rent of land, several services, seed and fodder), while 50% of the household expenses are paid in money received mainly from animal production and cash crops. For region 3 (small farm owners) these figures are respectively 46% and 37%." However, despite the higher percentage of the crop paid in kind as rent, Poyck concludes "that the tenants are self-sufficient in grain and sell little of their grain produce. Their welfare is derived from animal production and cash crops. The farmers of region 3 however sell a high proportion of their grain crop, which amounts to about 65% of their net grain production

49

(gross minus payments-in-kind). Besides that, the cash crop production provides for the total cash money they need (26.1 ID per family)." [14]

Despite differences in income levels, however, Table 10 shows not much variation in the overall calorie intake between tenant and farm-owner groups. Tenants spend their greater cash income on larger amounts of sugar and tea, while farm owners consume more dates which, unlike the tenants, they grow themselves. Poyck notes that small farm owners also tend to grow more vegetables than tenants. Certainly the small vegetable gardens tended by women were more in evidence among the palm tree groves of the farm-owner hamlets than in the more transitory treeless settlements of the tenant farmers.

Since I had no contact with communal farm owners nor with the people living on date orchards, Poyck's data for these groups must be presented without comment. He notes that the date orchards are near the city of Hilla, and this proximity seems to encourage relatively greater production of such cash crops for the urban market. Also a significant proportion of the average family income among both small date-orchard owners and the tenants on large orchards is derived from periods of urban labor, as the low market price for dates makes it impossible for most of these farmers to support themselves from agricultural activities. But, says Poyck, non-agricultural work is insignificant among cultivators of the other regions, accounting on the average for less than half an Iraqi dinar a year per holding throughout the region.

However, among the El Shabana cultivators, both small property owners and tenant farmers took part in the seasonal labor migration to Baghdad. In 1957, tribal leaders estimated more than 60 percent of the men went to Baghdad to work during the summer months, largely in the construction industry. A group of kinsmen, accompanied by one older kinswoman who cooked for them, often sleeping on the building site or sharing quarters in a *serifa* hut made of a few palm mats, mud and wattle, could save most of their summer earnings. These earnings made it possible for them and their families to survive during the winter months in their own rural homes, cultivating their own holdings of land which did not provide year-around subsistence income.

Still other families among the El Shabana were able to live in their ancestral tribal homes only because at least one male was gainfully employed elsewhere the year around (usually in Baghdad) in a nonagricultural job. Such land as was not too badly salinated continued to be cultivated but the crop formed only a fraction of the family income.

Poyck identified neither migratory labor pattern in his sample. Yet unquestionably some of his informants were involved in such activities. How else would it have been possible for those farm-owner families to survive whose holdings were significantly smaller than average? It is probable that some information about non-agricultural sources of income was not collected in this predominantly agricultural survey.

While Poyck fully supports his conclusion that, on the average, tenants on large holdings actually have slightly higher income levels than small farm owners, he has little to say about the intermediate category, those tenants on medium holdings. This group is of particular interest here because it includes a large percentage of El Shabana tribesmen.

As may be seen in Table 2, the average amount of land farmed by a tenant farmer on medium-sized estates is less than that of his fellow sharecropper on large estates. Furthermore, the tenant on a medium-size estate is unable to fallow 20 percent of his holding, on the average, while the figure for unfallowed land on the large estate tenant-holding is only 2 percent. Thus, the sharecropper on estates less than 4000 mesharas in size not only must exhaust the soil through violating the fallow system, like the independent small farm owner, but of course must also endure high rental costs like the tenant on the large estates. The result is to provide him with an annual net income lower than that of the farmers in either of the other two categories.

But why, we may ask, should tenant farmers remain on medium-sized estates when large landowners, at least in the Daghara area, universally complained of a shortage of sharecroppers? The land-owners said it was difficult to find good farmers and still harder to keep them on one's property. Thus many large landholders tried to tie their tenants to the land through indebtedness. The owners deliberately sought to become creditors for their share-croppers, taking over accumulated debts from the merchants in the market or advancing money to their tenants on unharvested crops. Yet during the 1950's, and in spite of the cooperation of the police with the landowners, it became comparatively easy for sharecroppers to run away to Baghdad. So great was the need for sharecroppers that estate owners often accepted "runaways" from other areas without asking too many questions.

Another factor which may have made cultivation on medium-sized estates attractive to some farmers was the relatively greater likelihood of having sufficient water available for summer cultivation. Estates under 4000 mesharas in size were officially allotted more water per meshara than estates larger than 4000 mesharas. Perhaps largely for this reason summer cropping is a much more important factor in the income of the tenant on medium-sized estates than it is in the income of sharecroppers on larger estates (see Table 5).

However, the prospect of working year-round for a net income well below that of neighbors on large estates working only part of the year would seem to discourage rather than encourage the average sharecropper. Estate owners use the possibility of summer cultivation as a blandishment to attract new tenants, but it seems obvious that the economic realities of this situation are eventually realized.

Why, then, do tenant farmers remain on less profitable, medium-sized estates rather than move to larger, more fertile farms on the bigger landholdings? Debt alone, even combined with summer cultivation possibilities, is not sufficient reason.

In the Daghara area, the largest estate owners were universally men without interest in their tribal affiliations, who spent as much time in Baghdad or Beirut as they could afford, and who had little contact with the tenants on their estates. These owners were generally of heterogeneous origins, often coming from as far away as the Tigris basin. In contrast, all the active, resident tribal leaders were owners of middle-sized estates.

It might, somewhat cynically, be argued that these less well-propertied landlords could neither afford to spend so much money in urban surroundings, nor to hire truly competent agents to run their estates. On the other hand, men like Shaykh Mujid of the El Shabana apparently have conservative tastes which do not run to the fleshpots of city life. For whatever reasons, such men were deeply involved in tribal affairs, regularly sitting in their mudhifs, arbitrating disputes, holding traditional feasts, and representing the tribe vis-à-vis the local government officials. They were a power in local affairs and it could be both advantageous to remain in good standing with such men and somewhat risky to provoke them. Longstanding ties of obligation and responsibility existed between the shaykh and certain of the tribesmen. The shaykh's land, legally registered in his name, was regarded by the tribesmen as consisting of two parts: his private land and the land set aside for the support of the mudhif. Even though not all tribesmen followed the custom, work on the mudhif land was a traditional obligation, as the mudhif and its activities were the common responsibility of the entire tribe.

By remaining on such medium-sized estates, tribesmen also remain in contact with their own fellow tribesmen and kinsmen rather than living among strangers. This too was frequently spoken of as desirable, especially by the older men. Thus if one is a small landowner and one's own land (which was part of the historic tribal domain) becomes less fertile or one's inherited share of land is inadequate, work on one's landowner-shaykh's estate is a kind of middle ground, a way of remaining physically and socially within the tribal universe. To many tribesmen, this was far preferable to working in the city or on a distant estate, where they would be cut off from native residence and traditional patterns of association.

The weight of tribal tradition plus the hope of maximizing advantages and avoiding difficulties in everyday life are factors helping to explain the rather anomalous position of the tenants on medium-sized holdings. This is true at least in the case of those tenants working on the estates of their own tribal leaders, cultivating what was once tribal property, on land near their own private holdings and homes, and in the company of their kinsmen and fellow tribesmen.

Turning now to the broader aspects of the economic situation, Poyck's data clearly demonstrate that the largest estates in the Middle Euphrates region are more productive than small farms. They are more productive in terms of quantity and value of crops per unit area of farm land, but also, and more surprisingly, appear to provide a higher income for the tenant-cultivator, despite the high rents the sharecropper must pay to the landlord. Why? The

53

answer is clearly that the small, independent landholding tenure system is maladapted to traditional methods of cultivation still followed in this region. Extensive cultivation requires a flexible relationship between land and people, a situation in which land may be used for a time and abandoned, as its fertility declines, to the natural processes of recovery. The niren-niren fallow system is obviously a conventionalization of this process, for some areas may recover in a year of rest while other soils may progressively "weaken" even if this system is rigorously followed.

Unquestionably, under traditional methods of cultivation, the "best" condition of land tenure found at the time of this study, that is, the one most likely to preserve a high level of soil fertility for the longest period of time, was the one concentrating a large area of land under the ownership and direction of one man. On such estates the necessary prerequisite of extensive cultivation could best be met: flexible land use with rigorous adherence to the fallowing pattern.

The traditional tribal system of land tenure and use was also well suited to traditional methods of extensive cultivation; indeed the two aspects of agriculture must have evolved together in this region. What is perhaps most unusual about this eco-agricultural pattern in general is that it is *both* extensive and depends upon irrigation. The economic implications of the situation cannot now be further explored without additional attention to the sociological setting, and it is to this subject that I now turn.

IV

The Town of Daghara

A stranger in Daghara quickly learns that socially the world is divided into three parts and all members of the community fall into one of three classifications: administrators (muwaddafin), market folk (ahl el suq) or tribesmen (el afrad). These are broad categories; an administrator may be anyone employed by the government; an individual may move from one category to another. Yet the terms reflect social and economic distinctions which are fundamental aspects of village social structure, even though a certain amount of ambiguity exists concerning the proper classification of a few marginal individuals.

In village conversation the characteristics of each group are discussed over and over again; the terms are heavy with connotation. The most important aspect of an individual's social identity tends to be how he is classified in this regard. Of the three groupings, each claims moral superiority and each enjoys a system of social relations which excludes other people in the community and extends beyond the social and physical boundaries of the village. Each group has its own criteria for the assignment of ingroup status. At the same time, no one group is sufficient unto itself, and the interdependence of the three groups constitutes a major focus of community life.

Much of the daily life of the community consists of interactions and transactions between administration, market, and tribe, and no one of the groups could survive without the others. But common residence in Daghara remains one of the weakest bases on which the recognition of common interests rests.

The tribesmen, who will be considered in detail in Chapter V, are part of a ramified socio-political system of which the Daghara tribes are only a small fraction. The El Shabana trace historic ties with the Shammar, a superconfederation of tribes with branches in at least three Middle Eastern countries. Tribesmen cite ancient alliances with people of the Nejd, their ancestral home. In recent times the more modern phenomenon of labor migration has taken many tribesmen to the cities, particularly to Baghdad, and much movement takes place between the capital and the countryside. Thus the tribesmen too look outward from Daghara at horizons shaped both by the past and present. For tribesmen the fact that they are tribesmen is far more important than the fact that they happen to live in Daghara.

Among tribesmen, the status and prestige differences which are most widely acknowledged follow closely the differences in land-based wealth. But the economic criterion is not the only basis of status difference, for the individual's position in the kinship system as well as his approximation of traditional standards of conduct strongly affect his position in the tribal group. In the mudhif of the shaykh, patterns of seating and salutation constitute public recognition of a tribesman's status. The tribesman identifies himself by the name of his tribe and the name of the section to which he belongs. Proud of its history and traditions, the tribe considers itself superior to other groups in the community. Any kind of public display of wealth is considered undignified and public labor or concern with money constitute disesteemed conduct.

The administrators also consider themselves separate from and superior to the other groups of the community. As Carleton Coon noted in a larger town in this same region, most of the administrative group come from outside the village in which they work.[1] Thus they usually have no kin ties within the community, though in some cases they may eventually marry local women. This group is set apart by the western-style clothing its members wear, and by generally greater formal education and knowledge of the world at large. The control exercised by this group over various aspects of community life is a result of its relation to the central government. The village does not expect to pay for their services nor does it expect to exercise formal control over them. Because of the administrators' adoption of certain customs such as drinking or gambling, the rest of the community — tribesmen and market folk alike — tend to regard the administrative group as corrupt. Although the teacher's or official's economic position may be admired, the traditionalist tribesman regards himself as morally superior, as does the market man, an attitude strengthened by the fact that administrators are in some cases Sunna in contrast to the local Shiʿa population.

Daghara is the center of administration for the Daghara *nahiya,* the smallest unit in the hierarchy of territorial divisions established and controlled by the central government of Iraq. Thus the responsibilities of the local officials and civil servants are not confined to the town alone but extend outward into the tribal countryside. Preparing reports which are sent out of Daghara and receiving orders through a chain of command over which they have little control, the administrators are part of the bureaucracy which radiates outward from the central government in Baghdad.

In 1957 fewer than a hundred administrators lived in Daghara, the majority working as teachers, medical personnel, clerks, and police. The chief of this group was the mudir nahiya, a member of the Ministry of the Interior. However, the lines of promotion for each administrator did not depend on the mudir nahiya, but were firmly fixed in the hierarchy of each individual ministry in Baghdad. Thus, though the mudir nahiya could order the engineer to make technical investigations and file reports, the engineer's ministerial superior, the chief district irrigation engineer, resided in the provincial capital of Diwaniyya. It was this man, not the mudir nahiya, who most directly determined the professional futures of the local engineers. But frequently rules and regulations governing relations between local representatives of various ministries were far from explicit, and cooperation at the local level often depended more on ad hoc informal arrangements than on official directives.

The Daghara administrators tended to live in the same residential area, to work together, and to spend their leisure time in one another's company. The administrators' clubhouse, *nadi el muwaddafin,* was as essential for their leisure as the government offices were for their work. Built by the government for the exclusive use of government employees, the club consisted of two rooms and garden, with a staff of a caretaker and tea-maker. Tables and chairs, a few decks of cards, a radio, and a pingpong table were the physical components of this modest establishment. Here the civil servants could relax and enjoy themselves. Affairs of common interest were discussed: national politics, advancements and dismissals in Baghdad and elsewhere. A great deal of local business was done in this context too, for it was far easier to solve many troublesome problems through an apparently casual exchange of remarks at the club than to send memoranda back and forth, copies of which had to be sent to the respective ministries in Baghdad.

The club then is the important social locus for the administrative group, serving many of the same purposes as the mudhif in tribal life and the coffee shop in the social life of market. Subtle distinctions of salutation and seating are indicative of the administrative ingroup hierarchy, just as surely as tribal status differences are expressed in the rubrics of guest-house behavior. However great the differences between, for instance, the doctor's position and the clerk's position in the status hierarchy of the administrative group, together the two see themselves as superior to the rest of the community.[2] The administrators admire as modern and progressive many of the same patterns of behavior which are considered immoral by tribal and trading groups.

Also clearly observable are the subgroupings among the administrators which persist irrespective of bureaucratic affiliations. One conspicuous coterie consisted of men who might be called the Old Effendis. Relics of the colonial past, these men generally held minor positions, mostly in the school system. Conservative, both politically and religiously, this small group of Old Effendis had mostly been educated before western-style schools were widely available; they had attained all their formal education in the *kitabs,* religious schools devoted primarily to the memorization of the Quran. Opportunities for the kind of advancement that might have taken the Old Effendis out of Daghara had passed them by; a few such men had actually been exiled here after reaching higher levels of employment at other times and places. Suspicious of outsiders and, in a number of cases, said to be extremely authoritarian in their dealings with students, the Old Effendis were the only members of the administrative group likely to spend the rest of their lives in Daghara, a prospect which did not appear to give them great pleasure.

The top administrators were usually middle-aged men who had begun their careers during the British Mandate period or in the early days of independence and who had advanced in the ranks of their individual bureaucracies partly by avoiding the dangers of political activism. In the purges which followed the 1958 revolution, the worst that could be said of these men was that they had loyally supported the status quo. Many had their jobs back a few months later.

These highest ranking administrators — the mudir nahiya, the police chief, the doctor, and the irrigation engineer — had few social equals in Daghara with whom they could relax during leisure hours. Therefore they tended to spend less time at the local club than others, preferring to socialize with their equals in Diwaniyya's Administrators' Club — a preference which they could indulge partly because these men had access to government cars for transportation. One's life was subject to less scrutiny in Diwaniyya, though of course Baghdad was really the only "safe" place to carry on as one pleased.

The younger effendis were mostly teachers, recently graduated from teacher-training secondary schools, and full of revolutionary zeal (young conservatives being as rare as old radicals before 1958). The younger men in particular chafed at the lack of diversions in Daghara and affected to despise all that they did not identify with the city. Many of these young men looked to a future full of revolution and Arab unity, events which they equated with their own elevation to positions of greater responsibility. At the same time little connection seemed to be made in the minds of these young men between "the people" who would benefit from the New Society and the population around Daghara, for most of the newly educated men were largely indifferent to and ignorant of the tribal cultivators.

Thus substantial differences in point of view and aspiration were found among the administrators in Daghara, differences which corresponded largely with age and background. The one principal exception was the irrigation engineer whose important position and college education placed him near the top of the local hierarchy, but whose age was well under that of comparably placed men. Although he was admired and envied by the young men, and his political views were as radical as theirs, his salary and education placed him beyond their ken. Such was the engineer's position in Daghara that locally he had no choice except to fraternize with the very loyalists whom he professed to despise but who nevertheless were his only equals. This circumstance encouraged him even more to spend as much time as possible in Diwaniyya with like-minded, college-trained friends of his own age.

Most ambitious administrators regarded Daghara as a phase in their careers, a temporary scene of employment which would surely change after some period of time. Clerks, police, and other comparatively low-level civil servants, once settled in a job, were likely to spend much of their life in the same place. But higher-level officials could expect to be transferred fairly regularly; in fact for most men advancement of any kind necessarily involved a move to a larger town or city. Many of the administrators in Daghara had lived in a number of towns during their career as well as in their home town, and so, in addition to connections within their ministry, had friends and acquaintances among administrators in a variety of places. Thus this group was part of both formal and informal networks of officialdom, spread over most of the country and bridging the gulf between country and city.

Since the top ranking administrators were transferred about and lived in homes provided by the government, they had little reason to become deeply involved in the life of the Daghara community. Some even felt that involvement in local affairs, beyond the scope of their assigned tasks, would be a hindrance. As the irrigation engineer stated, "If I become friends with one of the shaykhs, others will think I am favoring him in the distribution of water." In a society where the boundary between personal obligation and official duty is not well defined, this view has considerable validity.

The market folk had a more long-term investment in Daghara than the administrators and frequently owned homes and gardens in and around the town. The shops of the bazaar were also privately owned, though not necessarily by the merchants occupying them.[3]

The people of the market pride themselves on their commercial prowess. In market coffee shops they too observe forms of salutation which mark their differential assessment of one another. Coffee shops are to the ahl el suq a focus of social life just as mudhifs are a physical locus of tribal life. While the ahl el suq are free to visit the mudhif, and may do so on business, in general they confine their activities to the marketplace and visit among

60

themselves in that context. As in the tribe, kinship both unites and divides the market folk, but the origins of market families are diverse: some have only recently ceased to be tribesmen, but most are descendants of generations of tradespeople.

Even when born in Daghara, the shopkeepers and merchants always seemed to be from somewhere else. Daghara (whose precise age as a settlement is not known) was apparently not old enough to have fostered many indigenous merchant families. Furthermore, the collateral kindred of the market folk were often widely dispersed in villages and towns throughout the area, working in shops identical to those in Daghara. A single shop could only support so many sons and, rather than compete with the members of his own family, a young man would strike out elsewhere on his own — with family support. "Brothers must help each other, not compete in business," said one of the shopkeepers. The ethic of familial solidarity drives brothers out in various directions to open shops in different marketplaces.

All the shopkeepers and tradesmen have contacts with people in other markets, if only for purposes of securing supplies. Many of the more prosperous shopowners have investments in other markets in villages and towns near Daghara. A common way of disposing of surplus capital was to invest in outside enterprises: enlarging one's own shop, or adding conspicuously to the variety of goods offered for sale were less common.[4]

Investment in other suqs is apparently regarded more favorably than attempting to expand one's business at the expense of neighboring merchants in the same bazaar. Not infrequently a man spends part of the week at his shop in Daghara and the rest of it with his son (and junior partner) in his shop further down the Daghara canal in Jilla village. Thus branches of the same families are frequently found in suqs from Baghdad to Basra.

Merchants often change residence in response to changes in personal fortunes and in local economic conditions. In 1958, due to the declining fertility of the land around Daghara and the consequent impoverishment of much of the region, nearly a third of the available space in the covered bazaar had been deserted and a number of shopkeepers had left with their families to establish shops in other towns where business was better. In 1966 the empty spaces were again filled with new shops and the total area of the covered market had expanded — a response to the dramatic increase in government activity here and the resulting number of new customers with government salaries who patronized the bazaar.

The Daghara market is largely a retail outlet for wholesale supplies coming from the cities. Larger farm owners sell their grain in Diwaniyya; the small farmers and the sharecroppers consume most of what they grow. Surplus goats and sheep are brought to a corral once a week on the tribal side of the canal, across from the marketplace, where for a few piasters to the corral owner they can be displayed, graded, and bid for by representatives of meat merchants from the cities. Boys on bicycles travel back roads and paths collecting chickens and eggs, many of which also found their way to Diwaniyya.

In 1957, only two merchants were regularly involved with both buying from the farmers and selling to them. Both were cloth merchants; one bought clarified butter (dihin), and the other wool. Although some farmers were paid in cash, most received credit on their debts in exchange for the produce. These products were not locally resold but were transported to Diwaniyya or Hilla to be sold.

The fact that practically nothing other than agricultural goods is produced in Daghara to be sold means that the local suq is dependent on the cities for a supply of all manufactured goods, from bolts of cloth to pots and pans. With the exception of bottled soft drinks, goods were rarely shipped to the community at a wholesaler's initiative and expense. The merchant himself arranged for the transport of supplies to his store, frequently by sending his son or going himself to the cities. Since the 1958 revolution the government has begun to organize and regulate wholesale activities through cooperatives. However, until the last few years, each purchase of supplies involved a search for the best bargain on the best terms. Merchants strove to pay as little cash down on the purchase as possible, for the less capital involved, the more the credit that could be extended to customers and the greater the total volume of business.

Maintaining good relations with the wholesale market and good sources of information about market values in the city was of prime importance to the Daghara merchant. Advantageous deals

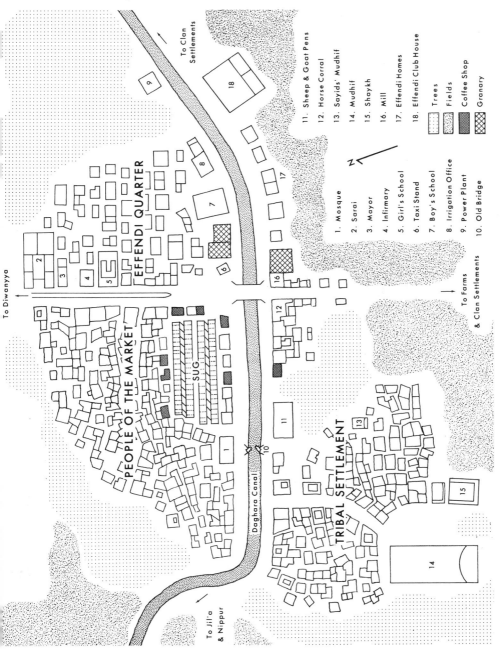

1. Mosque
2. Sarai
3. Mayor
4. Infirmary
5. Girl's School
6. Taxi Stand
7. Boy's School
8. Irrigation Office
9. Power Plant
10. Old Bridge

11. Sheep & Goat Pens
12. Horse Corral
13. Sayids' Mudhif
14. Mudhif
15. Shaykh
16. Mill
17. Effendi Homes
18. Effendi Club House

Trees
Fields
Coffee Shop
Granary

EFFENDI QUARTER

PEOPLE OF THE MARKET

SUG

TRIBAL SETTLEMENT

To Diwanyya

To Clan Settlements

To Jil'a & Nippur

To Farms & Clan Settlements

Daghara Canal

Schematic view of Daghara village.

View of El Nahra canal.

Tribal settlement on a feast day. In the foreground men are performing a *dubki,* or line dance.

ribesmen perform a *dubki* to the music of a small flute.

small *mudhif* under construction in a tribal settlement outside
aghara. The men are placing woven palm mats on reed pillars that
ve been woven together to arch at the top.

Tribesmen loading sacks of barley on their camels.

A tribesman.

in wholesale transactions were widely regarded as being a principal source of profit. For while haggling between merchant and customer in the market does take place, no merchant deliberately sets out to undersell his neighbor. The real source of substantial gain for the merchant lies in his ability to buy a bolt of cloth more cheaply than the merchant in the shop next to him, while selling it at approximately the same retail price.

Compared with the average tourist-bazaar owner in the cities of the Middle East, the Daghara merchant is a modest and unassuming individual, patiently awaiting the arrival of customers as he sits all day in the front of his stall-like shop. The "hard sell" is definitely absent and most merchants conduct their business with the same dignity as their tribal customers. The merchant frequently seems quite indifferent to the progress of a transaction, as if the matter were of little or no importance to him personally. Correspondingly, little overt competition is apparent between the several merchants who sell identical products. One cloth merchant watches another sell his goods without comment and, at least overtly, they pass the time of day with one another in friendly fashion.

The only area of market activity which at all approaches competitive sales activities lies outside the shops, along the street and up and down the corridors of the bazaar where peddlers sell for cash or short-term credit (a week being a common period for payment.) These peddlers were alone among market folk in hustling trade, and sometimes wore pants and shirts, rather than the flowing dishdasha and western-style jacket which were standard garb among both tribesmen and merchants. A man might appear with fresh fruits which he had carried in from Diwaniyya, an old woman might sit on a cloth beside the road and peddle her own eggs and vegetables, or offer a couple of chickens. The price for these items, sold without overhead costs for shop and electricity, was less than in the stores — but the number of people who could take advantage of such bargains was largely limited to the salaried administrators with cash-in-hand.

Artisans were a small minority in this market, including a carpenter, a tinsmith, two ironsmiths, and a man who dyed, black or indigo, skeins of locally produced wool yarn to be used by village women for abbayas. The ironsmiths were rarely paid in cash.

Rather, they took care of farm implements, sharpening the points of the plows and flattening out the ends of spades, in return for a seasonal payment of barley from each client-farmer. The iron-smiths fitted iron parts to the wooden plows which were purchased in Diwaniyya or made by the local carpenter. The carpenter also made wooden cabinets (*dulabs*) and other furniture on commission, as well as window and door frames. Extensive carpentry work, called for by the building of burnt-brick houses or offices, was usually done by specialists called in from Diwaniyya.

Most tribesmen are closely linked to particular merchants in the market by debts which accumulate through the season before each harvest and which, in many cases, are never fully paid. Buying goods on credit means paying as much as twenty percent above the cash price. It also means that one cannot switch from one merchant to another, for no respectable merchant will take another's debtor unless the accounts are fully paid up. The merchants know the economic circumstances of their client-customers and will not let them get in debt beyond a certain point. When that point is reached, cash must be raised — crops mortgaged, or money borrowed or begged, or raised through sale of an animal, or somehow earned. The constant fact of sustained indebtedness helps account for the merchant's relatively cool attitude toward most of his tribal customers.

Only two groups escape the system of indebtedness — the relatively rich and the very poor. The former category, which includes almost all of the administrators, can pay cash or meet bills once a month with little or no surcharge on purchases; the very poor will not be accepted as debtor-customers by any merchant and so must find the cash to pay for any purchase they make.

This system determines that each merchant has a relatively fixed turnover of merchandise. Sales and bargain days have no place here; each shopkeeper can carry just so much indebtedness and no more, as too many customers, on a credit basis, are an invitation to bankruptcy. In such circumstances it is of some advantage for the merchant to be socially distant from the rest of the community. How could a man resist the importunings of his kinsmen or fellow tribesmen and still behave according to the traditional standards of generosity and hospitality?

The only formal political office associated with the market is that of *mukhtar*. While all the adult males living within the borders of Daghara town are eligible to vote for this official, it is largely only the people of the market who take any interest in the matter, and the yearly election, held in the government building (sarai), is usually not attended by either administrators or tribesmen. The government pays the equivalent of about $2.00 per month to the mukhtar in return for which he is called to witness the registration of births and deaths and swear, if necessary, that nothing irregular was involved. He is also expected to accompany the police in the case of house search in the town and may be called upon to shelter with his own womenfolk a woman detained by the police till she can be transferred to the women's quarters in the Diwaniyya jail. Reportedly, the mukhtar may supplement his income by, for instance, testifying to the authorities that drafting so-and-so would work an undue hardship on his family — and otherwise bearing minor witness in return for small tokens of appreciation. For the last ten years there had been no competition for the job in Daghara. The incumbent was a lorry driver and sheep trader of good reputation and modest income. No important merchant would care to be bothered with such work and, in fact, any man of high standing in the market dealt directly with the administration as the situation required.

Among the market folk, certainly, a social hierarchy existed, but one of individual status and prestige rather than of formal rank. The men who owned their own (and in some cases other) shops, and who had a reputation for fair dealing and good temper, were respectfully greeted by their fellow merchants. Perhaps the least prestigious of the market folk were the artisans: the metalworkers, the dyer, the carpenter, and the goldsmith. Yet since everyone stayed in his own shop most of the time and since it was not customary throughout the Daghara community to visit in one another's homes, conspicuous acts which might suggest attitudes or value judgments were rare. One merchant said, "It is necessary to be honest and to avoid speaking about one's neighbors here. Things go [well] for people who do this." Thus the predominant attitude of the market folk seemed to be to live and let live — and to avoid casting stones.

The market folk were reluctant to discuss either their own or others' affairs. "To speak of one's wealth is to lose it." There was no pattern of conspicuous consumption; while everyone knew who prospered and who did not, overt differences in wealth remained hidden behind the brick walls of the homes. Far better to speak of one's last pilgrimage or the next to come than of investments made or contemplated. In a situation where privacy in affairs of public consequence was nearly impossible, everyone struggled to keep money matters to themselves.

The people of the market, like the administrators and tribesmen, tend to be endogamous. To some extent, this is a by-product of a general preference for marriage within the family. Prosperous merchants are particularly anxious that the business should not pass out of family hands through inheritance. Marriage is regarded as a particularly sound way to insure good business relations and such relations are frequently between kinsmen. Little is to be gained in most instances by marrying an outsider, particularly someone unconnected with the market. On the other hand, a tribesman of traditional persuasion would be unlikely to marry a merchant's daughter and would never permit *his* daughter to sully tribal honor by marrying a merchant. Obviously, a poor tribesman, for whom economic advantage might outweigh considerations of honor, would never be offered such a temptation by a merchant-father!

The attitude of the tribal community around Daghara toward the market is much the same as that described by Salim in his study of ech-Chibayish.[5] The tribesman, despite his poverty and loss of political dominance in the rural community, cannot admire the merchant, whose values are antithetical to his own creed of generosity and courage — the two basic sources of honor. The self-display of the merchant, his unabashed desire for personal enrichment at the expense of others, the obvious value placed on material possession — all this makes the market man an inferior order of being in the eyes of the tribesman, and places him outside standards of the tribal community. On the other hand, market people regard tribal customs with indifference and consider the tribesmen as generally lazy and lacking in ambition. The tribesman is regarded as a fit object for such economic exploitation as the tradesman can manage.

Yet in the long-term trade relations between merchant and

tribesman they clearly become partners in an economic bond which cannot be broken without the loss of debts that are due, or of credit that is essential. Tribesmen and tradesmen, dressing alike, observing the same conservative standards of public conduct and, perhaps most important, firmly rooted in the local community, share more in common than they do with the administrators. Thus, while both tribal and market groups express convictions about the general inferiority of their opposite number, relations between individuals from tribe and market often lose their merely economic character in time and may even become institutionalized by intermarriage or expressed in some joint enterprise such as the purchase and operation of a taxi. Nonetheless, one group remains relatively indifferent to status positions in the other group. While a group of tribesmen may suggest that a particular merchant is the best man with whom to deal, their evaluation may have little correspondence with the esteem in which that merchant is held by his market associates.

Relations between the market people of Daghara and the administrators are both economic and political. Merchants and shopkeepers of all types have to conform to largely uniform rules and regulations established throughout the country for markets of every size and complexity. The processes of justice were also in conformity with urban practice. Though the police could, perhaps, be arbitrary with the merchants, their major activity seemed to be to see that everyone who attempted to do business had the proper permits and licenses.

The tribesmen, however, were in approximately the same position vis-à-vis administrators as they had been during the days of English rule. Until 1958 most of rural Iraq was governed according to a Tribal Disputes Regulation, largely a legacy from the British mandate period. The original intent of this practice was to give "official status to tribal custom, so that tribal arbitration and tribal courts (*majlis*) convened by administrative officials take the place of law courts." [6] In effect, however, the provisions of this code also gave to the administrators sweeping powers in their dealings with the tribesmen, and, in many instances, robbed the latter of even nominal access to the guarantees of personal liberty (such as habeas corpus) set forth in the nontribal codes of justice. Even though the tribesman, accused of some crime, theoretically had the right to choose between being tried before the tribal or civilian courts, the issue was frequently settled long before such formalities began. Mass arrest and torture were common responses to criminal acts. In one case (1957) in which a traveling official was beaten and robbed, scores of tribesmen of all ages from the vicinity were taken to the Daghara jail to be held for several days, interrogated and, in a number of cases, beaten. Men were tied by their thumbs to overhanging beams and, in winter weather, had buckets of cold water flung over their naked bodies. In this fashion enough pressure was put on the local tribes so that a man was finally obliged to come forward and confess to the crime.

While this example is perhaps extreme, the fact is that most tribesmen were at the disposal of the administrative officials for detention and questioning; their civil rights being, for all practical purposes, nonexistent. As we shall see, the shaykh played an important role in modifying the relations between tribe and police. Nevertheless, as guardians of law and order the Iraqi administrators' basic attitude toward the tribesmen was just as arbitrary as that of the British and Turks. The tribesman exhibited little sense of identification with this alien force against which his most effective defense was to disappear into the cities or the outlying marshes.

However, as was true for tribal-market relations, individual bonds of obligation and responsibility are established between individual administrators and individuals from the rest of the community in spite of hostile ingroup-outgroup attitudes. The gifts which pass from market people and tribesmen to administrators in exchange for favors granted or promised are tokens of trust, symbolizing the substitution of personal relations for impersonal, bureaucratic contacts. The tribesman expects that the administrator who has accepted his gift will make some effort to see that the tribesman's problem receives attention. The administrator trusts that the tribesman has presented his case honestly and is not dealing behind his back with some other administrator. Any member of the administrative group is considered a good person with whom to develop such a relationship, particularly if he enjoys a reputation for dependability, though one selects the most influential patron one can afford. The salaries of teachers, clerks, doctors, or engineers are not sufficient to support them in the style which they feel is befitting. Many of these people depend on local gifts just as the members of the market and tribal groups depend on them to help deal with government regulations, the education of the community's children, or the mysteries of modern medicine.

Thus we have three vertical divisions in the formal social structure of this community, but at the same time an informal network of interpersonal relations of considerable durability which laces individuals together across group lines. The persons of high status from each group are recognized by the other groups as constituting an elite.

The shaykh is officially recognized by the government, as is the mukhtar (the elected official of the market people). Perhaps as a legacy of British administrative practices, the shaykh and the mukhtar must be consulted in the administration of village affairs. Thus the ranking members of each group participate in the activities of the local government-appointed administrators. The work of the administrators is made easier by cultivating the shaykh as well as the mukhtar and important merchants. On the other hand, the shaykhs, enjoying surplus wealth, invest it in market enterprises. The shaykh of the El Shabana owned a small mill, a granary, and several coffee shops, in addition to his many acres of farm land. Such a man participates with the richer merchants in a futures system, speculating on market prices for coming grain crops. The shaykh is therefore not only nominally leader of his tribe of farmers, but to some extent must also be regarded by market folk as a competitor and fellow entrepreneur. Both the rich merchant and the respected official correspondingly may be invited to the tribal mudhif as *muhakkim,* to arbitrate disputes when a neutral third party is needed.

However, intergroup relations are not based on economic self-interest alone. Although I have not exaggerated the socio-economic differences between tribesmen, effendis and market folk, it must not be forgotten that all the people of Daghara share a background of belief in the traditional culture of Islam. Perhaps the most striking evidence for the existence of this community of belief, despite group differences and individual reservations, is found in the manner in which religious ritual is organized and expressed.

69

The entire community is involved and yet at the same time the independence and the identity of each of the groupings I have described is preserved, and even reinforced.

The Shi'a sect of Islam, to which the majority of southern Iraqis belong, provides its adherents with a richer ceremonial calendar than is found among Sunna Muslims. The deaths of Hussayn and Ali, for example, two of the twelve Shi'a Imams, provide subject matter for passion plays and acts of mourning which are regularly performed throughout southern Iraq. Emrys Peters has given us a good account of such a play in a Lebanese Shi'a community[7] and mention of these plays is found in literature about Persia and the Indian subcontinent. A less technical description of the play presented in the Daghara area in 1957 is given by Elizabeth Fernea.[8] Although the people of Daghara by no means take full advantage of all opportunities for expressive ceremonialism, certain Shi'a ceremonies are observed year after year and are clearly of considerable significance for both religious and other reasons.

One of the most popular of such ceremonies is the *kraya,* or religious reading, held in southern Iraq daily throughout the month of Ramadan and during the first ten days of the month of Muharram. Krayas are generally privately sponsored and can be as elaborate as the host desires and can afford. A wealthy merchant may hire a *mumin* specialized in such readings and turn an entire aisle of the covered market into a meeting hall. Hundreds of men from all sectors of the community may attend to hear the recitation, ritualistically weeping together during the tragic climaxes of the martyr's tale and then enjoying a moment of quiet conversation afterward when the host serves tea and perhaps candies and cigarettes. The shaykh of the El Shabana used to engage the services of a reader for the entire month of Ramadan who would proceed to tell one episode after the other from the lives of the Imams — much as certain Christian groups hold devotions each day during Lent. These readings were attended primarily by tribesmen but every night or so men from the market and effendis from the government offices would stop by, perhaps exchanging a few words of business with the shaykh after the proceedings were over.

While the administrators were not observed sponsoring such

ceremonies, their wives did entertain for the other women of the community by hosting several krayas. These were the only occasions in the year when women from throughout Daghara assembled together, the sacred quality of such gatherings being sufficient to justify letting the women go out after dark and walk through the village streets in their abayas and veils, even though ordinarily a respectable woman tried not to leave her home at all.[9] Of course, the most frequent krayas for women were held by and for neighbors and did not involve such wide participation.

Ashura, the tenth of Muharram, anniversary of the death of the Imam Hussayn, is in Daghara the occasion for the most dramatic public religious ceremony of the year. At this time, several hundred men and boys, largely from the market families, participate in the *ta'aziya* (also called *subayya*), mourning for the death of the religious hero which takes the form of public self-flagellation. Groups of men stripped to the waist or wearing black robes cut open in back, march in procession, rhythmically chanting and beating themselves with lengths of chain and leather whips. Comparably arranged groups of young boys often follow behind the groups of men, learning the chants and imitating the actions.[10]

The individual teams of men who make up the ta'aziya usually come from the same neighborhood or street within the residential area primarily occupied by the market families of Daghara. Membership in the ta'aziya teams is of course voluntary, but many young men join as a result of religious vows. (A woman may pray for the birth of a son, and promise the boy's participation in the ta'aziya in memory of Imam Hussayn.) The ta'aziya's expenses are usually assumed by an older man, *sahib el 'aza*. The sahib el 'aza buys such special clothes and equipment as may be needed and, most importantly, contributes money to send the team to the great ta'aziya in the holy city of Karbala which occurs 40 days after Ashura. The clothes and equipment are stored each year and are not the property of participants but rather of the families making up the street or small neighborhood.

In the Daghara area, the tribesmen were not observed to participate in either the local ta'aziya or in the Daghara 'aza, the delegation of teams participating in the grand ta'aziya in Karbala. Economically, the expense of such an activity could not have been borne by other than the shaykh or members of his lineage who owned substantial amounts of property. However, since he and other members of his family obviously took pride in providing krayas and performing other religious duties, it seems likely they would also have supported tribal ta'aziya teams if this were considered a proper tribal activity. It is more likely that ta'aziya participation was not considered quite in keeping with the public demeanor required of a proper tribesman.

Nevertheless, the Ashura ceremony did involve the tribal community. By long established custom, the route of the ta'aziya procession passed along the main streets in the market and administrative neighborhoods, then crossed the Daghara canal to the tribal settlement, ending at the shaykh's mudhif where the two hundred or more men involved were all served tea as guests of the tribe. The tribal men and women lined the road to the mudhif and the event was the cause of considerable anticipation and excitement. Thus, in this case too, one section of the community became the guest of the other, acknowledging and confirming their mutual obligations in celebration of a religious event of comparable significance for all concerned.

This situation is reversed on the anniversary celebration of the birth of the Prophet Muhammid when the merchants play host to the tribe and administrators. The festival occurs in the evening in the central aisle of the covered bazaar. The mudir nahiya, as well as the local mullah may make a brief speech but the general atmosphere is that of a carnival. Skits are presented in which stock characters are satirized — the Englishman, the Turkish effendi, the country bumpkin farmer. Local administrators are also the subject of mild ridicule, and are expected to laugh at what would on other occasions be a totally unacceptable infringement on their dignity. Candies are provided for the children and shopkeepers will ask particular friends to sit in the fronts of their shops to enjoy the proceedings. Tea-brewers stroll back and forth offering trays of tea which the members of the audience, with some ceremony, purchase for each other. The tribe *and* the administration are definitely guests of the market, but the atmosphere is less formal and much gayer than in the tribal guesthouse — as might be expected in this thoroughly secular setting.

The administrators are not prominent participants in either of the above ceremonial occasions, but on the rather formal occasion of 'Id el Fitr at the end of the Ramadan fast, the shaykh spends the entire first morning receiving the officials, teachers and police who troop to his mudhif to repeat the prayer of the day with those assembled. They then accept a glass of tea and a cup of Arab coffee.

The administrators did not host any comparable inclusive ceremonies, but it was clear that the leading merchants and the shaykhs were always welcome at the administrative clubhouse. The shaykh of the El Shabana and frequently one or more of his brothers and sons (in addition to a retainer or two) made it a habit to stop by the club after naps, around four or five in the afternoon, to pass half an hour over tea with the effendis. While the shaykh's presence noticeably cramped the style of some of the more ribald men, who lowered their voices and put away their glasses of alcoholic arak when he was visiting, the shaykh was treated as an honored guest, whatever the private opinions of the younger administrators. Furthermore, on national holidays all men of standing in the community customarily called on the mudir nahiya as the local representative of the Crown. Merchants and tribesmen were both careful to observe these occasions.

Clearly then, the leaders of the market, tribe, and administration could expect to be treated with respect by all members of the community, though only the officials exercised universal authority. The administrators needed the advice and counsel of the shaykh, who knew his tribe, indeed all the tribes of the area, as no transient official could hope to do. But above and beyond the practical considerations, the merchant who was both honest and successful, the shaykh who demonstrated the traditional virtues of generous hospitality and maintained the loyalties of his tribesmen, and the effendi-administrator who was capable and who did his job honestly — these men commanded the respect (albeit grudging in some instances) of the entire community, no one portion of which was totally independent of the affairs of the others.

Socially and geographically, the type of community represented by Daghara is somewhat distinctive in this region. Such communities constitute an arena in which the three most important segments of Iraqi society face one another on equal ground. This is not the case in smaller villages which may be composed only of tribesmen, and a handful of shopkeepers. Nor is it true in the city where the single tribesman faces the merchant or government employee as an isolated individual, the majority of his tribesmen being far from the city. In Daghara, three extensive systems of social relationships come together as integral units and form enduring contacts across group lines. The tribesman may be a villager but at the same time he, with his tribal group, is part of a confederation of tribes which may finally include hundreds of thousands of persons. The village tradesman is not only part of a worldwide economic system, but also, as he travels from village to town and city purchasing supplies he develops a wide range of personal relationships with other tribesmen outside his own community. And the administrative group, which lives in this village and unavoidably is involved in its affairs, looks toward the city, the center of a ramified administrative system with outposts in all sections of the country.

In communities like Daghara, tribesmen, tradesmen, and white-collar workers can maintain their primary identifications and associations with their own group, while developing relations and learning about people with whom they have neither kinship nor occupational bonds. Each group has its own independent sphere of action; each individual can depend on members of his own group for support. Nonetheless, the differences in origins and activities among the groups result in a considerable range of differing ideas, attitudes, and styles of life. While the tribesman draws strength from his tribal association, he may at the same time see in the teacher's or doctor's example a role of coming importance for his son. The merchant and administrator may exchange and share political convictions. Recognition of common interests as members of a district or state may, in this context, replace more narrow views. Thus is change a product of such communities; not change born of the overwhelming impact of an alien culture, or the imperialism of a great city, but change coming about as individuals of widely varying backgrounds and group loyalties find regional and national interest overriding attitudes stemming from older and more traditional group identities.

Even before the overthrow of the monarchy in 1958 signs of change in traditional social patterns could be seen in Daghara. Perhaps the most important was the increasing attendance in the local

74

schools by children from all sectors of the community. It took several years before the shaykh would agree to send his daughters to the girls' primary school to sit with the children of shopkeepers but this was fully accepted by 1958. Even more significant, the young tribal boys of school age clearly had begun to aspire to administrative jobs; a number were away at secondary school in Diwaniyya, a few were in training institutes or colleges in Baghdad, and one son from an extremely poor tribal family had recently returned from the United States with a degree in irrigation engineering from the University of California at Davis. The presence of young administrators in the community tended to stimulate and encourage the younger men to seek opportunities and experiences undreamed of by their parents.

In 1967, much more than in 1957, the same subjects were being discussed in tribal mudhif, market, coffee shop, and administrators' nadi. News about politics and international affairs is now broadcast with equal effect into all three social centers. The opinions of the teachers are discussed in tribal circles; merchants know about the political views and opinions of the administrators. As has elsewhere been argued, the potential for the growth of common attitudes and concerns at least about problems of national importance may in fact be greater here than in an urban context.

The social structure of Daghara village has been described as if a perfect balance existed between the three sectors of the community. Of course, this may not be the case at any given point in time. Occasionally the government forces may still incarcerate hundreds of tribesmen in attempting to solve some crime or to suppress some political movement. In the past, the tribes were capable of overwhelming and driving out administrators from the central government, just as they may have occasionally sacked the establishments of local merchants. Nevertheless, the relationships between tribesmen, merchants, and muwaddafin which have been described are reasonably enduring and are the basis on which equilibrium is restored in community life when, temporarily, one group overwhelms another. For each sector of the community is ultimately necessary to the other.

In the following chapter I shall concentrate on the social organization of the tribe, primarily the internal differentiations typical of tribal organization in this region. Subsequently I shall return to the relationship between tribal and nontribal sectors of southern Iraqi society, in particular the increasing importance in the lives of tribal cultivators of the local representatives of the national government.

V

The El Shabana Tribal System

Tribesmen in the Daghara area proudly claim descent from the great Bedouin tribes of the Arabian Peninsula and the Syrian Desert. The El Shabana tribesmen assert that they came originally from the Nejd during the eighteenth century, and are ultimately related to the Shammar. If this is correct, the tribal system of the El Shabana is partly the result of transformations that have occurred as the ancestors of the present-day tribesmen switched from the pastoral nomadism of desert life to a more sedentary existence in the Euphrates basin. The importance of this change should not be exaggerated, however. For the borders between Iraq and the rest of the Arabian Near East have never been effectively closed, and the settled tribesmen along the southern Euphrates have had continued opportunity for interaction with nomadic Bedouin. Although the settled tribesman sometimes appears to look down on the Bedu nomad of today, he takes pride in being able to demonstrate certain traditional characteristics of the desert Bedouin.

Pride in ancestry, emphasis on generous hospitality, recognition of the duty to revenge kinsmen wronged in feud, and belief in the values of warriorhood — these and other features are widely shared by both settled and nomadic Arabs from the deserts of Saudi Arabia, Syria, and southern Iraq. Therefore, although it is not the purpose of this discussion to trace the differences and similarities between traditional Bedouin culture and the culture of the Daghara Arabs, it should be remembered that close, persistent relations existed historically between these two groups and continue to exist at the present time.

In the last thirty years the introduction of effective local administration by a national government has brought many changes in the Daghara area, including pacification, taxation, land registration, and control over the large waterways. Formal classroom education and medical facilities have been introduced. Possibly a course has been established which will result in the ultimate dissolution of the tribe as a social system. But the tribe remains an organization of importance in the current affairs of this region and cannot yet be totally regarded as of merely historical interest.

The tribal system of the El Shabana may be defined either as a cultural ideal or as an imperfectly realized sociological reality: there is no absolute correspondence between the two possible statements although they are importantly related. As a cultural ideal, the tribal system is of considerable importance to the tribesman. Utilizing the idiom of kinship in some instances or the proper names of tribal groups in others, a man identifies himself and other tribesmen as if the cultural model absolutely prevailed. By so doing he helps perpetuate a system which originated in other than the present circumstances. Only by understanding the tribal system as part of the felt and conscious cultural equipment of the tribesman can we accept and understand the present apparent contradiction between the tribal cultural model and the equally real atribal economic and political relationships.

The contradictions may be partly explained by assuming that certain values and convictions rather than economic and political "realities" reinforce the cultural ideal. In Islamic culture as a whole, the pervasive and dominating belief is that earthly differences between men which place one above the other in an economic or political hierarchy are absolutely unimportant when compared with the differences between man and God. For men in submission to God are equally His servants and the God of Islam sanctions no status differences between men.[1] This is not to suggest that Daghara tribesmen believe God has ordained the cultural ideal of the tribal social system, but only that considerable congruity exists between a man's view of other men according to the tenets of Islam and a man's conception of himself and other men in the perspective of the cultural vision of the tribal system. The "real world" of superordinate and subordinate human relations and the "ideal world" of equality before God seem nowhere to have achieved better mutual accommodation than in the predominantly Islamic states of the world.

The cultural ideal, derived from information provided by numerous informants, may be explained by utilizing the descriptive category of "segmentary lineage systems," originally specified by Evans-Pritchard and Fortes and others in *African Political Systems*,[2] and later elaborated in such studies as *Tribes Without Rulers,* edited by John Middleton and David Tait.[3] In order to present the cultural ideal, and as a point of departure for the remainder of the discussion, the concept of segmentary lineage systems appears to be useful. After utilizing this concept, however, we shall begin to see how, in terms of interpersonal relations, the social organization of the El Shabana is not a functioning segmentary system.

Middleton and Tait expand the typology suggested by Evans-Pritchard and Fortes, noting two basic features of segmentary systems:

The term "segmentary" has been used in reference to several types of social systems, but the essential features are the "nesting" attribute of segmentary series and the characteristic of being in a state of segmentation and complementary opposition. The series may be one of lineages, smaller ones nesting inside and composing larger ones, which in turn compose still larger ones, and so on; or it may be one of the territorial groups (hamlets, villages, sections, tribes, nations) or of others. Subtraction or change in size of segments leads to a re-organization, although not necessarily a re-structuring, of the total system. Analysis of the process involved in this re-organization within an unchanging total structure has led to the use of the term to refer to the second characteristic. This is the process of continual segmentation of the structure.[4]

By "continual segmentation of the structure" the authors refer to the process whereby new segments of the same order within the structure separate (or merge) in response to factors such as population pressure or subsistence requirements. The process of merging or uniting is such that the parts of the segmentary system remain formally equal, whether or not the population or wealth of the segments remains equal. The cultural model may prevail whether or not the society's resources are sufficient to fill all the parts of the theoretical structure.

When, however, factors in the natural or social environment are such as to result in an inequitable distribution of economic wealth or political power between the ideally equal segments of the social systems, the latter clearly may cease to function as described above. Once a subsection within such a system has a monopoly of power, the checks and balances of complementary opposition are clearly at an end and the tribal system becomes centrally rather than segmentarily ordered for most political and economic purposes. This is very close to being the case among the Arabs of Daghara.

The Arab Bureau in 1918 estimated that the El Shabana had a population of 900 adult men.[5] Modern government censuses include El Shabana tribesmen, but population figures are no longer broken down into tribal groups. The El Shabana population also varies with the seasons; sometimes tribesmen return to the settlements only during important festivals; in other instances they may work in cities during the summer and return to live with their fellow tribesmen during the cold months. Conditions made it impossible for me to carry out a formal census; however, the informal guess of local residents is that the present population of the El Shabana is from 450 to 600 adult males. Tables 13 and 14 are based on a household survey conducted in 1958 among the El Shabana tribesmen living close to Daghara village.

The El Shabana are only one of 12 tribes or ashiras belonging to the El Aqra, a loose tribal confederation or *sillif*. In 1919 the El Aqra was estimated to include 5050 adult males. Using the same kind of informed guesses, I conclude that the El Aqra today numbers between 2500 and 3000 men. In any case, the twelve ashiras of the El Aqra sillif constitute only a part of the tribal population of this region of southern Iraq.[6]

Ideally and traditionally, the sillif should control a single dira or domain of contiguous land in one region. Before 1918 this was the case. The El Shabana, living on approximately thirteen square miles of land with hamlets of tribesmen scattered over the area, formed part of a larger territorial unit controlled by the El Aqra sillif.

The Agrah group lies along the Daghghara from its mouth to about five miles below Daghghara village, from the Shatt el Hillah. It continues along the left bank of the Shatt el Hillah from the mouth of the Daghghara up to and including the Dahayah Canal, some 10 miles below Diwaniyah, and on the right bank of the Shatt el Hillah from below the Bazil canal to opposite the Dahaya, with the Albu Muhammid (Khazᶜayl) scattered among them.[7]

Today, as Map 4 (drawn by the local irrigation engineer) shows, El Aqra tribesmen continue to occupy lands near the mouth of the

Daghara canal. However, other individuals and small groups have now moved in, presumably after purchasing land in the area. Gertrude Bell, writing in 1918 as secretary of the Arab Bureau, noted that the El Aqra seemed to be split into two factions. The movement of several ashiras out of the Daghara area is associated with this split.[8] Today some ashiras of the El Aqra live some forty miles away from the El Shabana in Shamiyya, the rice-growing district of Diwaniyya province. The ashiras of the El Aqra sillif still living in the vicinity of the El Shabana may be noted on Map 3. Thus this tribal organization no longer controls, according to traditional ideals, one dira or contiguous area of land.

The gradual break-up of land control is also evident at the ashira level. Presently tribesmen from eleven subsections or *shabbas* are identified as occupying El Shabana territory, while members of two or perhaps three others have scattered. Among the shabbas, great inequality in population size is found, partly because the land belonging to some groups is productive while in other instances it is so poor that tribesmen have been forced to find employment elsewhere.

The regional terms for the lineage-based segments among the tribal people of Daghara are as follows, beginning with the smaller groupings and ending with the most inclusive grouping. Segments are listed in order of their "nesting."

primary section[9]	*fakhd*
secondary section	*shabba*
tertiary section	*ashira*
quaternary section	*sillif*

Among the El Shabana, a shabba may contain two or three fakhds. Structurally, each of the segments "opposes" the other segments of the same level which share its "nest." Informants stress equality of status among comparable tribal subsections; no segment is superior to other segments at the same structural level. Smaller segments may cooperate as part of the same ashira for limited purposes. On other occasions shabbas may even resort to physical violence against each other.

The lineage system is based on aggregates of agnatic kinsmen defined according to descent from a common paternal ancestor. Patrilineality is of overwhelming importance in this society; the

81

tribesman's position within the formal organization of the tribe as well as his more general reputation and social standing in the community at large depend on his paternal ancestry. The fact that marriages are preferentially contracted within the descent group in no way modifies the unilineality of the kinship system upon which tribal organization is based.[10]

The following chart of the tribal system outlines the actual kinship groupings within each segment:

Tribal Segment	Approx. no. of adult males	Kinship
1. sillif (El Aqra)	5000	1. No traceable kinship except by recent marriages. The belief exists of common descent from the Shammar, a great tribal division with both sedentary and nomadic sections.
2. ashira (including El Shabana, El Amaysh, El Zillazla, Elbu Zayyat, El Amr, El Nayil, El Hillalat, El Murad, etc.)	500–900	2. Descent from a common ancestor or from the ancestor who first became associated with the given ashira. Only experts can provide a complete line of patrilineal descent.
3. shabba (within the El Shabana, these include the Elbu Ubayd, El Jamiʿyyin, Elbu Khazʿal, El Shidayda, El Mujarilin, El Hakam, El Khalat, Elbu Salih, Elbu Jurayd, El Ghrush, El Shawahin, etc.)	20–50	3. Descent from a common ancestor. Usually a complete patra-genealogy can be provided but with a sharp decline in knowledge of collaterals above the fifth generation.
4. fakhd (within Elbu Ubayd shabba: Elbu Najim, Elbu Muhammad.)	10–30	4. A group of not more than five nor less than three generations depth. Collaterality usually completely known except for cognates resulting from occasional "foreign" or exogamous marriages.
5. hamula	See discussion below	
6. bayt		

The two additional segmentary divisions, the *hamula* and the *bayt,* are of a still lower, less inclusive order than the fakhd. The hamula was given as a division of the fakhd. Yet persistent questioning revealed only one instance of the hamula among the

82

fakhds of the El Shabana: this term was used to distinguish the shaykh's father, his sons, and the shaykh's sons from the rest of their lineage group. This lineage, to be discussed further, is one instance in which the realities of this system depart from the characteristics of a model segmentary system.

The term bayt ideally refers to a living man and his descendants. Normally this would include a father and his sons (including married sons and their young siblings) who live together. However, married sons frequently do *not* live with their fathers. In such cases, the individual households were also called bayts. Any fakhd is composed of numerous bayts, but the use of the term varied between reference to the "ideal" father-sons grouping and to actual households (see Table 13).

In the idiom of kinship, ego refers to the members of his shabba as *awlad ammi,* that is, "my father's brother's sons." The usage is classificatory as the group may include men whose agnatic tie is a common ancestor four or five generations distant. Several collateral lines of descent are thus often joined in a shabba. Of course, affines usually also enjoy bonds of cognatic relationship because of the preferred practice of endogamous marriage.

Where segmentation into fakhds has occurred within a given shabba, a man may also refer to the members of his fakhd as awlad ammi. The agnatic ties between the men of any one fakhd obviously will be closer than the ties they share with the members of the other fakhds of the shabba, but the terms of reference do not commonly take the distinction into account.

The residence pattern of these parallel lineal and tribal systems may be expressed in the following diagram:

bayt	same house	same area within hamlet	same hamlet	same or nearby hamlets	contiguous land and neighboring hamlets	the same area but not perfectly contiguous land-holdings — may have been one dira historically
hamula						
fakhd						
shabba						
ashira						
sillif						

Residence is patrilocal; men state that it is good for brothers to live together in the same household with their father.[11] However, men frequently establish independent households when their father dies, and for various reasons (specific quarrels were frequently cited) may leave the parental home before the father's death. It is said that brothers are more likely to continue to live together if they are uterine siblings; this deserves fuller investigation, for there is some indication that uterine brothers may also most frequently register land jointly or avoid formally dividing their patrimony.

A single residence may include a courtyard, sleeping and reception rooms, as well as animal shelters and other detached structures; all buildings are contained within a single area surrounded by a wall. The local definition of a single "household" is not based upon simply living in a single compound. Rather, several men may live in a single compound but a man is considered to have a separate household if he manages his financial affairs independently of his kinsmen. In collecting the census data (see Table 13) the local social definition of a single household was adopted, so that if two brothers and their wives and children lived in the same compound but the brothers did not pool their resources, the men, with their dependents, were listed as individual households. Evidence indicated that separating finances was the first step toward the establishment of individual residence, and that the separation of joint families was frequently desired but impossible because of the high cost involved in building new dwellings.

The shabba is the tribal segment most frequently identified with a hamlet. When one asks to whom a cluster of houses belongs, the proper shabba name is the most common response. In some instances shabbas have not divided into fakhds, but where such segmentation has occurred, lack of suitable land may make physical separation impossible and the members of the fakhds are often obliged to continue to reside in the same hamlets. If the fakhds separate as a result of some serious quarrel and a desirable location for a new hamlet is available within the landholdings of the shabba, then it is probable that a new hamlet will be established.

Thus residence is also patterned, generally in accord with the kinship and tribal systems. Traditionally, the closer the kinship between two men through a common ancestor, the greater the likelihood that they will be living in the same vicinity. If men lack any traceable kin ties it is unlikely they will be living in the same tribal hamlet. The shabba which is unsegmented or which may include as many as three fakhds is the largest (most inclusive) tribal grouping in which men are likely to live in the same hamlet, cultivating adjacent plots of land and in some cases owning land jointly (this will be discussed further below, but see Map 5). However, all segments of the El Shabana ashira hold land in a common territory.

Let us compare this system for a moment with that of the Nuer of the Sudan, the classic example of the model segmentary system. Evans-Pritchard states that "Nuer lineages are not corporate localized communities," though certain lineages have special associations with certain localities. Local communities become a network of kinship ties, in spite of the fact that different lineages reside together within them, because of rules of exogamy applying to the lineage groups.[12] Such is obviously not the case with the El Shabana where the lineage-based hamlet tends to be endogamous and contiguous with a tribal division.

Quite obviously the closer the kinship tie and the closer men live to each other, the more interests they have in common, and the more frequent the contacts between them. The range of common interests shared by the members of tribal groupings is most inclusive within the fakhd, and common interests are fewest between individuals who are related only by sillif membership. Structurally the reasons for this are clear: the interests which men have in common through kinship are of the same order as the common interests of members of the same tribal segments. Furthermore, the lineage-based tribal segments follow a pattern of territorial localization exactly paralleling social segmentation; each segment literally, as well as figuratively, "nests" within the other. Finally, the preference for and percentage of endogamous marriages is most intense at the "center" of the parallel systems of tribe and kinship, as may be seen in Tables 11 and 12.

Conflicts occur between fakhds of the same shabba, between shabbas of the same ashira, and between ashiras of the same sillif. The "higher" the segmental level at which conflict occurs, the less intense the social sanctions which can resolve the dispute or prevent its developing into a long-lasting feud.

I will show how differences in landholding (in particular) may make segmental equality at each level less than a social reality. Finally, I will turn to the ties which bind this somewhat segmental organization together. The evidence to support the contentions thus far presented must emerge slowly as I proceed with the discussion. The next paragraphs will provide an outline of some of the functions and activities at each level of segmentation in this tribal organization.

TRIBAL SECTIONS

The Sillif. Members of the El Aqra sillif claim historic relationship with the Shammar. Yet for all practical purposes the sillif itself is the most inclusive tribal grouping with which individual tribesmen identify themselves. The sillif includes groups of members living far apart, and while it is concentrated in one general area, it does not hold land as a unit. Under such conditions, it is not surprising that the nature of the intrasillif relationship varies considerably from group to group.

The only institution which is identified with the entire sillif as well as with some section of it is the mudhif or guest-house of the sillif leader or ra'is. Such a mudhif is also an ashira center, just as the sillif leader (the ra'is) is also shaykh of an ashira. The building takes on an inter-ashira character on those occasions when a sillif-wide feast is held or an inter-ashira dispute is arbitrated.

Traditionally, the mudhif of the ra'is or sillif leader is built with the help of the entire sillif; in practice, this help is by no means universal and whether or not such help is forthcoming depends on the warmth of the relationship between the ra'is and wealthy and influential men in the other ashiras.[13] It is in the mudhif that ashiras, on specific occasions, publicly acknowledge sillif membership. Tribesmen claim that when the ra'is of the El Aqra, Haji Atiyah, died in 1950, all adult males of the El Aqra visited the Haji's mudhif during the thirty days of mourning (*fatiha*) following his death. In general, when the shaykh of any ashira dies, or when an important marriage takes place, the shaykhs of the other ashiras of the sillif customarily travel to the mudhif of the leader involved. During the days of feasting associated with the 'Id el

Fitr and the ʿId el Adha, leaders of some of the component ashiras usually visit the mudhif of their sillif leader. Such visits imply a formal declaration of membership in the sillif and an avowal of loyalty to the sillif leader.

The expense of a sillif-wide feast is borne first of all by the host ashira, but privately contributions are offered by and accepted from other wealthy men in the sillif. Unless other members of the sillif shared the cost, such feasts would be a real financial burden to the host ashira, for a large meal is served to all those present on the day of a marriage, on each day of the religious feast, and on each of the thirty days of mourning following the death of a shaykh.

In 1957 Haji Mujid Atiyah El Shaʿlan, the present shaykh of the El Shabana tribe who is also leader of the El Aqra sillif, traveled five hours by car and by boat to attend the fatiha for one of the shaykhs of an El Aqra ashira. The fatiha was held in the mudhif of the deceased. Over a thousand men were present, not only from El Aqra but from tribes of neighboring sillifs. Thirty sheep had been killed to feed the guests, and 400 kilos of rice and 500 of barley were consumed on this one day. Attendance was not, of course, so heavy on each of the thirty days; this was a special day, for Haji Mujid, the rais of the sillif, had come. But feasts on ʿIds and at marriages may involve at least ten sheep and a proportionate amount of rice.

The institution of the *hosa,* a kind of group rally, is a tangible expression of group membership within the sillif. The hosa is performed as part of any general gathering, and when more than one ashira participated in the celebration of a feast, hosas were always a conspicuous part of the day's activities.

In the past, the hosa was an expression of group solidarity before going to war or setting out on raiding parties, and today continues to be somewhat like a pep rally. Although it involves rhythmic group movement, the hosa is not principally a dance. Before or after the meal on the feast-day, tribesmen from the same ashira gather together outside the mudhif (if it is only an ashira-wide feast, the men from the same shabba gather together). A tribesman known for his talent in the hosa begins by chanting a verse to which the other tribesmen add a refrain or chorus. At the end of the chorus, the versifier chants another stanza which is again followed by the chorus. Other tribesmen in the meantime have composed verses and will break in with their own offerings. The verse leader stands slightly in front of the crowd of men who circle during the chorus, moving together, holding rifles high above their heads, and firing them into the air from time to time. The sound and sight of dozens, sometimes hundreds of men chanting and moving together in the hot sun and firing rifles is a spectacle not soon forgotten. Hosa chants are usually rhymed couplets praising the courage, the wisdom, the honor of the rais or shaykh, or describing past glories and feats of arms of the tribal group. Tribal leaders did not take part in the hosas themselves but stood watching in modesty, inside the mudhif.

The common interests of sillif membership rest in the traditions of peaceful relations between member ashiras and of mutual aid in common defense. Within the sillif, an alternative to self-help is always present in the opportunity to negotiate peacefully, abetted by other parties in the sillif who are not directly involved. For the sillif constitutes the maximal indigenous jural community in the system. This is its major formal function at the present time. The shared belief is that members of the same sillif should be at peace, and within the sillif precedents have been set and social customs exist by means of which feuds may be settled and fighting ended. The general agreement that unresolved conflicts within the sillif are improper does not suffice to end such disputes in a short period of time; in fact it is possible that some quarrels within a sillif may never be fully resolved. Such consensus does, however, create an atmosphere of expectation, places subtle pressure on contestants to negotiate settlement, and provides a large number of interested third parties who are willing to contribute their time and energy toward the resolution of enmities.

Arab tribesmen have been justly recognized for their prodigious ability to remember lengthy genealogies. They deserve equal attention for their development of an elaborate and detailed oral customary law. For example, within the sillif an unwritten traditional rate of compensation has been established for all recognized offenses occurring between ashiras. In the case of homicide, one ashira is required to give three women as *fasl* (blood-payment) to the ashira of the murdered man (ultimately such compensation usually goes to the kinsmen of the deceased). If, for various reasons, women are not provided, equivalent payments in guns or money must be made.

To understand something of the mechanisms and procedures of sillif adjudication, let us examine one case:

A man from the Elbu Nahud fakhd of the Elbu Nayil ashira met a friend of his from the Elbu Zayyat ashira on the road near Daghara village. (Both ashiras are from the El Agra sillif.) The man from the Elbu Nayil had a gun. Somehow an argument developed centering around the gun. The man from Elbu Zayyat grabbed the gun and killed the man from the Elbu Nayil. Two months later the man who did the killing had been caught and jailed by the government. However, the dead man's gun had not been returned to Elbu Nayil, nor had there been any fasl settlement. The Elbu Nayil shaykh insisted his group would not consider beginning negotiations until the gun was returned. He said the return of the gun was an entirely different issue from the fasl. Haji Kadim, from the family of the man now in jail, claims the gun cannot be found and that it was probably thrown into the canal.

This interchange took place in 1958 in the mudhif of Haji Mujid, rais of the El Aqra sillif. Discussions normally take place on neutral ground, and the mudhif of the sillif leader is commonly selected as the site, if the leader is not a partner to the dispute. Intermediaries — friends of one or both of the groups involved — prepare the way for face-to-face meetings between those most directly involved in the dispute.

I asked Kamal afterward why the groups had come here to the mudhif of the leader of the El Shabana ashira and Kamal replied it was because the shaykh of the El Shabana is also the rais of the entire sillif. When I asked why so many people were participating in the discussion who were apparently not from either contesting group, Kamal replied that they were asked to come by both sides as "witnesses" (shahud, sing. shahid). These witnesses appeared to do most of the talking, insisting on certain procedures necessary for the settlement of the problem. Kamal said that those witnesses who are not from the two ashiras directly involved, are from other ashiras who in the past stood with one or the other of the contesting ashiras in fights with other groups.

After the preliminary condition of the return of the gun was met, discussions began about the fasl which would be paid to the murdered man's group. This case had not been settled by March, 1958, and it would have been surprising if the murdered man's group had been willing to discuss fasl so soon. Yet the pressure is there from the rest of the sillif, and particularly from the leaders, at least to begin discussions. Until fasl is accepted, however, the way is open for a feud to develop; if no settlement has been reached nothing within tribal custom forbids the murdered man's family from taking the life of a member of the offending group. Usually a revenge killing has as its victim a son or brother of the murderer, although in one case a killer's father's brother's son was slain in revenge. In the past like incidents apparently grew to such proportions that two whole ashiras became mortal enemies. Once the *qadma,* or down payment of the fasl, is accepted, however, blood revenge becomes socially censurable.[14]

Besides constituting a jural community within which shared expectations and customs exist concerning the arbitration of inter-ashira disputes, the sillif also has a range of standing agreements with neighboring but unrelated tribal groups. If a killing takes place between the El Aqra sillif and sillif X, past agreements are remembered and used as a basis for settlement of the new problem. In contrast to intra-sillif disputes, disputes between two sillifs cannot be brought to the point of arbitration unless the parties involved wish to arbitrate, to avoid further trouble. Since 1918, however, the local representatives of the central government have frequently put considerable pressure on responsible tribesmen to see that discussion gets under way.

The entire sillif of El Aqra, with its twelve ashiras and total membership of more than 5000 men, appears rarely to have fought as a single group. Instead, certain ashiras traditionally came to each other's aid. In the last quarter of the nineteenth century, those ashiras located around the mouth of the Daghara Canal joined forces to protect their water supply and their relatively contiguous holdings of land from the tribes of Afaq, further down the Daghara waterway. The common bond of sillif membership is permissive, but not compulsive, with respect to mutual aid. Gertrude Bell in 1919 noted that there was a long-standing division in the El Aqra sillif between certain ashiras.[15] In 1930, Haji Atiyah El Sha'lan, leader of the El Aqra sillif and shaykh of the El Shabana (father of the present shaykh), led the tribes of the Middle Euphrates in revolt against the authority of the central government. But even on this occasion only certain ashiras of the sillif joined in the fighting with the El Shabana. Thus it appears that in intra-sillif relationships the cultural ideal of equality between the structurally equal tribal segments is most nearly realized. While, in the case of the El Aqra sillif, the ashira of the sillif leader, the El Shabana, is stronger than any other ashira in the sillif, any several ashiras combined are equally as strong. Thus persuasion rather than coercion appears to have been the most important factor in determining the course of intra-sillif relationships.

The Ashira. Interaction between members of the same ashira is much more frequent than among men sharing only affiliation with the same sillif. Traditionally tribesmen of the same ashira gather at the mudhif of their shaykh on each of the major religious feasts of the Islamic year. Since the mudhif of Haji Mujid Sha'lan, the present shaykh, is located near Daghara village, tribesmen frequently stop there en route to or from their homes. Tribesmen may eat a meal at the mudhif, spend the night, or simply pause to visit for a few minutes with whomever may be present. The mudhif is in this sense a common social center shared by all members of the same ashira. A man who is the guest of the shaykh in the tribal mudhif is also considered a guest of all tribesmen in the given ashira.

The cost of building a mudhif is borne primarily by the shaykh, but contributions of labor, food to feed the specialists who direct its construction, and money, are made by members of the ashira.[16] Similarly, the various segments of the ashira contribute sheep, chickens, and grain to the ashira-wide feasts which occur several times a year. A large section of land is set aside to supply the mudhif with food. While this land is now registered in the name of the shaykh, and while it is doubtful that all the produce from that land is necessary to supply food consumed by guests and tribesmen in the mudhif, this tradition of "mudhif land" is sometimes mentioned to justify (in part) the much larger holdings of the shaykh.

The mudhif is, then, the most important focus of ashira activities. Until the area was pacified, the mudhif was the center where members of the same ashira gathered before going into battle, where, in fact, political issues important to the whole ashira were discussed. As Shakir M. Salim notes, the mudhif serves as a "social center, political conference chamber, and a court of justice"[17] for the group associated with it. A man's reputation with his fellow tribesmen is witnessed in the mudhif by the behavior of those present when he enters. If it may be said of a man "They rise for him in the mudhif," *yqumun ila bil mudhif,* this is indicative of relatively high prestige.

Less than ten years ago no El Shabana tribesman would sit in the village coffee shops; his coffee-drinking was limited entirely to the mudhif of the shaykh or to other smaller tribal mudhifs. Today the mudhif is less used than before as a meeting place by members of the ashira. Nevertheless, on the great feasts 'Id el Fitr and 'Id el Adha) the mudhif of Haji Mujid, shaykh of the El Shabana, may still be visited by nearly a thousand tribesmen in one day. As a common meeting ground for members of the ashira, its importance cannot be underestimated and the reported decline in mudhif attendance might well be considered indicative of the waning importance of ashira membership to the tribesmen.

When hosas are performed at ashira-wide feasts, performing groups again express segmental solidarity within the unifying larger group. Hosas begin with the participation of the largest exclusive groups present; in the sillif feast all present members of a given ashira act as a single group. In an ashira-wide gathering, individuals participate in hosas with the other members of their shabba who are present. One group opens the hosa and other groups begin performances of their own. Then the hosa assumes a new variation: the groups of men, chanting and firing guns into the air, run toward each other, stopping when they meet, circling back and coming forward again to repeat the pattern. An element of competition and mock combat may be seen in such activity, as each group vies to produce the finest and most moving verses and generally to make the best showing. Tempers run high and occasionally scuffles occur. In the past, all of this took place on horseback, perhaps providing an even greater similitude to battle and an opportunity for demonstration of skill.

The occasions when the hosa is performed appear charged with emotion and conviction. Whether they occur on the level of sillif organization, in ashira, or even shabba groupings, they constitute an activity which is organized on the basis of the tribal sections present at a given gathering. In a sense, these occasions are an expression of the latent opposition between segments at the same level of tribal organization, and indicate some depth of emotional commitment to membership in the particular tribal groupings involved.

The ashira is also a jural community; but different from the jural community of the sillif, for it is one within which the shaykh (whose authority will be a subject for discussion in the following chapter) could force disputing parties to come to terms. If necessary, informants say, the shaykh could send armed men to bring disputants to the mudhif to discuss the problem and arrange for a customary settlement. Individual crimes which conspicuously violated the moral code of all tribesmen — such as rape or thievery — might result in physical punishment as decreed by the shaykh and the *ajawid* (or elders) of the tribe, or in banishment of the defendant and the kinsmen who supported him. In one such case, a whole fakhd is reported to have moved elsewhere after one of the men of that group had been accused of stealing.

The mudhif of the shaykh of an ashira is the center of jural activities. Disputes which arise between members of two shabbas are argued before the shaykh and the ajawid. No matter how strong the feelings between contesting parties, they must, in the mudhif, sit quietly and behave with dignity. The mudhif of the shaykh even has some sacred character in that it is a place for swearing strong oaths of vengeance or of peace.

The Shabba and the Fakhd. Among members of the same shabba, interaction is much more frequent than among men sharing membership only in the sillif or the ashira at a structurally "higher" level of tribal organization. The small mudhifs typically found in shabba hamlets are meeting places where the men gather informally in the evenings, or for most of the day when no work needs to be done. Several mudhifs may be found in the same hamlet, depending on the wealth of the members. These mudhifs are commonly supported and built by a minimal lineage group: in one instance three brothers and two grown sons of a deceased fourth brother took turns in supplying coffee and food for any guest, the responsibility returning to the same man every fifth week.

The fact that notably less formality is observed in behavior within the small shabba mudhifs may be related to the relative absence of differential rank between members of the same shabba (or fakhd). Except for the respect paid by young men to their elders (typical of all sectors of Arab society), in the shabba mudhifs no special deference is shown to any particular man, as it is in the shaykh's mudhif, reflecting the lack of institutionalized leadership at this level of tribal organization. While for each shabba a man is recognized as *surkal,* members of given shabbas consistently stated that surkals never settled conflicts themselves—in fact, questions about the surkal were met with humorous remarks, and it was clear that the title carried little prestige.[18]

On the jural level, shabbas, which were sometimes subdivided into fakhds and at other times in other cases undivided, were said to be responsible for a standard contribution to fasl or blood payment when one was required from the whole ashira. One shabba, larger than the others, was said to pay one and one-half times more than the others because of its greater size. When a member of one shabba committed an offense against a man from another shabba, the latter group was spoken of as requiring compensation from the former, regardless of whether either or both groups were internally divided into fakhds. Informants reported that one fakhd could require compensation from or exact vengeance against a second fakhd within the same shabba.

The shabba, as a named segment of the ashira, may have originated through the landholding function of a lineage group. All other terms designating parts of the tribal organization (sillif, ashira, fakhd, and hamula) have Arabic roots relating to parts of the body or blood relationship.[19] But the term *shabba* stems from a root from which words like "area" or "district" may be derived. Although "shabba" is not used by nomadic tribesmen in the area, the term has become so accepted among settled tribesmen that a man from the El Shabana was obviously surprised when speaking with a Bedu (at my instigation) to find that the Bedu had no such grouping. Among the settled tribesmen, the use of the term to designate a social grouping is so firmly established that tribesmen refer to men as belonging to such-and-such a shabba even when the men no longer own land among the El Shabana and the membership of that shabba is scattered. At the same time, the less abstract application of the term is still found in situations where, for example, the sons of male siblings of Abdullah have a serious disagreement with the sons of the male siblings of Hassan. One group becomes then the Elbu Abdullah and the other, the Elbu Hassan: neither retains the original name of their common ancestor, Jawad. Regardless of the difficulty which caused the split, both groups continue to occupy the same section of land and neither can move without losing its land rights. Thus the term Elbu Jawad, the name of a fakhd which occupied a "shabba of land and water," becomes a term which also names a larger-than-fakhd grouping; the original term is retained and Elbu Jawad thus refers to the two fakhds, the Elbu Abdullah and the Elbu Hassan, as well as to the section of land they jointly occupy.

The shabbas of the El Shabana were not all established at the same time. Informants report that groups of men would agree to fight beside the El Shabana and share fasl with them and would be assigned land to cultivate after the fighting had ended. Thus a shabba may, in a sense, have been the unit of tribal adoption, so linked was land use to this process.[20]

The Sada: Blessed are the peacemakers, for they shall be called the sons of God. The Sada, though small in numbers, are an important part of the El Shabana. Strictly speaking, they are an independent group who live with the tribe and constitute perhaps 20 percent of the tribal population. Sada are men and women who claim descent from the Prophet Muhammid, and carry the honorific title "Sayid" before their proper names. Some religious specialists come from their ranks, but the majority of Sada take part in the same subsistence activities as the ordinary farmer-tribesmen.

The Sada associated with the El Shabana are members of two "tribes," that is, they classify themselves into two named groups. However, the named segments of these two groups do not occupy contiguous areas of land, as is true of the secular tribe. Rather, small numbers of Sada live on land within the shabba areas; this land has been given to the Sada by each shabba of the El Shabana. Thus one Sayid and his sons may live with one shabba and another minimal lineage group with another shabba. Sometimes the Sada live in the hamlet of the shabba whose land they have been given; at other times, groups of Sada live in small hamlets of their own. Direct questioning about why a Sayid was given land reveals only that it is considered a religious duty. In some areas of southern

95

Iraq (which is almost entirely occupied by members of the Shi'a sect of Islam), a few large landholders today provide land which Sada may cultivate without paying rent. By providing land for Sada, a Moslem upholds charity, one of the five pillars of Islam. Most tribal families have Sada neighbors to whom they traditionally give gifts of food on the great Islamic feasts, and many pious Moslems donate their services to the Sada occasionally or provide goods at specially low prices for them.[21]

In return for being an object of good works among the tribesmen, a man claiming the descent and privileges of a Sayid is expected to lead an exemplary life, which incidentally may contribute to the unity of the whole ashira and minimize the conflicts between ashira segments. All good Moslems ought to be at peace with all but non-Moslems; Sada are never supposed to participate actively in fighting. Thus in the days of feuding between shabbas, the Sada associated with each shabba theoretically remained free of active fighting and did not become involved in blood feuds. In view of this, it is not surprising that both by tradition and practice, Sada take an active part in peacemaking.[22]

Sada do not appear to be particularly prominent as *muhakkim* (judges) between disputing factions. Rather they are prominent as emissaries between alienated groups. Since a Sayid living with shabba X frequently has a brother or cousin living with shabba Y, when these two groups become embroiled in controversy no more convenient channel of communication is available than the Sada, who may formally or informally find out what is the feeling in the opposing group, and provide information necessary for negotiation between the feuding groups before formal face-to-face adjudication ever begins.[23]

When the shaykh wants the support of the entire ashira, for fighting or for some other corporate enterprise such as building a mudhif or giving a large feast, his first action is to call in Sada with whom he has had close relations (for example those to whom he has given land or goods in the past) and insure their support for his project. The Sada then accompany a son of the shaykh or some other *wakil* (representative) to the hamlets of the various segments, assuring the tribal groups of the justice and goodness of the shaykh's cause, and reminding them of the advantages of being part of the El Shabana.

Sada, then, by virtue of their quasi-sacred position, their abstention from fighting, plus their residence with all the segments of the ashira, contribute importantly to the restoration of unity among subtribal groups and help in the formation of a general consensus of opinion on issues involving the entire tribe.

Land Holding. Historically the tribe in southern Iraq has been a landholding unit, the proprietary interests of its members presumably becoming ever more localized as their subsistence pattern became increasingly agricultural. Contiguous and common landholding has played an important, even fundamental, part in maintaining the institutions of tribal life in this region.

As may be seen on Map 4, the El Shabana today occupy a continuous area of land. No clear evidence suggests that land was ever considered the corporate property of an ashira. Rather, informants say, segments of the ashira always claimed certain sections of land, and within the segments individual men and their sons claimed the right to farm certain fields. Dowson reports that in general shaykhs assigned landholdings to their tribesmen.[24] However, El Shabana informants insisted that when the El Shabana took over their land from the El Khaza'il they had enough land so that there was no controversy about who was to take what holding. Clearly, the shaykh did not, in such circumstances, have to assign a piece of land to each warrior but rather may have been called upon to resolve disputes over choice locations. But during the eighty years the El Shabana has occupied this land the relative amounts held by each shabba have changed through fighting between shabbas within the ashira, and later, through purchases of land.

Today certain members of the same shabbas and, in greater degree, of the same fakhds, are frequently joint owners of small plots of land, and, insofar as this is true, land ownership is one of the common interests and ties between kinsmen. Joint ownership also helps retard the division of land into plots too small to be farmed or without access to irrigation water. On the other hand, a tribesman always stated that if it were possible, he would *prefer* to own land individually, even though owning land with one's brothers and cousins was spoken of positively. If land could be acquired easily, lawfully or otherwise, it is likely that more men

97

would own land individually. Under present conditions, however, additional land cannot be acquired except through the expenditure of money which the average tribesman does not have. Some tribesmen have sold land to the shaykh or his relatives (the only tribesmen with investment capital), but many individual tribesmen also have retained some property, for owning even a very small amount of land confers considerable prestige whereas to be landless is to forever join the lowly ranks of the fallahin.

Map 6 illustrates the type and amount of joint land registration in the Elbu Blaw district of El Shabana land holdings. Within the total of 505 registered plots of land, a single man may be registered several times as an individual or joint owner. The land belonging to the shaykh's shabba is for the most part owned jointly by him and his close agnatic relatives, the largest amount being held by the shaykh and his two uterine brothers. Excepting them, approximately equal amounts of land appear to be registered as (a) owned by individual men; (b) owned jointly by brothers; and (c) held by brothers and patri-cousins together. Proportionately the smallest amount of land is registered in the names of *all* the men belonging to a fakhd or shabba. What accounts for the different types of registration?

One answer is suggested by comparing genealogies with registrations. At least three generations of men have worked the land in the eighty years of its occupation by the El Shabana. When the land registration took place in the nineteen-forties, some members of the second generation still survived, but in most cases these survivors had outlived their siblings and many of their collateral relatives. Generally these surviving men appear to have registered their holdings as individuals; thus old men or men without male siblings are most likely to have landholdings independent of others.

While second-generation men could have jointly registered land with third-generation men, out of the 505 registrations only ten were shared between father's son and father's brothers. The only other instances in which such a group of kinsmen were registered together was when land was registered in the name of an entire fakhd or shabba (see Map 6). Sons take considerable care to see that uncles do not usurp their inheritance, a classic source of bad feeling and disputation. Third-generation men (brothers and cous-

98

ins), faced with registering land which brothers had jointly farmed, may have discovered that division of these holdings into individual pieces was out of the question if water access was to be preserved. If a piece of land is to be farmed in the Daghara area, it must connect with a distributary canal, and while in theory one can always dig another feeder canal, in practice there are limitations. First of all permission to pass a canal through someone else's already small acreage is very difficult to obtain. And in a majority of cases division of already small plots into still smaller ones would have made the returns from grain farming on each piece so small as hardly to warrant the trouble of planting.

Rather than being registered individually, these small plots were registered jointly. One or two men farm these small pieces of land and then divide the crop with other co-owners who may have been working elsewhere as tenant farmers. While the share each receives may be miniscule, each can still claim ownership of land. Individuals who derive only the smallest fraction of their livelihood from land which they own, and who live and work most of the year far from the El Shabana holdings, still maintain a dwelling in their hamlet and regard it as home.[25]

Thus many pieces of land have been kept cultivated under joint ownership even though they could not possibly support all those to whom the land belonged. Since the El Shabana holdings have, in the past twenty years, progressively deteriorated through salination and waterlogging, income has accordingly decreased. An estimated third to a half of El Shabana land is now useless for cultivation,[26] and only a small percentage of El Shabana tribesmen earn their entire living from farming their land. But joint holdings are not often abandoned until the land has deteriorated to the point where not even one farmer can support himself and his immediate family.

Land owned by groups extending beyond the circle of cousins and brothers is usually either land on which a date palm garden exists, claimed by all members of a shabba, or land on which the shabba hamlet is located. Date palms demand little care and their produce is practically infinitely divisible.

Joint ownership of land undoubtedly has been encouraged by a cultural tradition which places high value on the solidarity of lineal kinsmen. But what is the effect of registering land ownership upon the process of segmentation within the shabba? If land is owned individually in the first generation, registered between brothers in the second, between patri-cousins in the third, and so on, by the time distance between living adults and their common ancestor is so great that the group splits into two fakhds, rather distant collaterals may be registered as joint owners of plots of land. Also the territorial distribution of the registered land can hardly follow the descent pattern; individuals may inherit jointly registered pieces of land scattered from one end to the other of a common ancestor's original holding.

LANDHOLDINGS AND COMPLEMENTARY OPPOSITION

Land and water rights are both permissive and restrictive factors in the internal organization of the ashira, and affect the relative position of the segments. To understand the relationship between landholdings and a segmentary social system, let me propose a hypothetical history:

Several fakhds together establish control over an area of land. Each fakhd begins to cultivate its own section of land. In the beginning there is enough land so that the initial fakhds "adopt" other small lineage groups in order to bolster their strength. This, of course, increases the ability of the ashira membership to enlarge its total land area, should there be resistance from nearby groups. Eventually the other tribal groups in the area surrounding the ashira in question may finally succeed in firmly establishing their own land rights and successfully prevent further encroachment. When, by chance, the number of men in one fakhd becomes greater than another, the larger fakhd may attempt to expand its landholdings at the expense of neighboring fakhds.[27]

However, neighboring fakhds, now constituting another shabba or shabbas, might combine to prevent this encroachment on their territory; structurally, we might say this illustrates the process of complementary opposition between segments at equal levels of organization.

This hypothetical history cannot be proved to *exactly* fit the course of events among any group of tribal cultivators near Daghara. But it is true that in the past frequent "revolutions" took place within the ashira; "revolutions" in which one shabba would rise up and take land from others. El Shabana tribesmen recall that three different shabbas have held the largest section of land at various times in the eighty years of control of El Shabana's present land area. The shaykh of the El Shabana in each case came from the lineage group which controlled the largest area of land. (Today, of course, landholding is fixed through registration.)

The end product of the process we have been describing is graphically illustrated in Maps 4, 5 and 6, which show one of the five contiguous sections of land owned by men of the El Shabana. The Elbu Blaw section was selected for illustrative purposes not because it was necessarily representative, but because it contained the largest number of landholding divisions (505 separate registrations.)

Map 5 first of all provides an illustration of the correspondence already mentioned between tribal groupings and land: the complete holdings of the Elbu Khazal shabba are seen to lie within a common boundary. The Elbu Ubayd lands similarly lie within a common boundary. Only part of the land belonging to the Elbu Salih is shown on this map — the rest of their holdings fall in the adjacent district, to the west. The fragmentary holdings of the El Naqish shabba represent the remaining land belonging to a group which left the area after 1900 during failure of water on the Daghara canal. The Elbu Qlawa similarly have lost most of their land; what is left is badly situated in relation to the canal system, and nearly all members of this group live and work away from the El Shabana area. It is thus apparent that some shabbas of the El Shabana are in a far superior position to others.

Today one shabba, El Jami'yyin, that of the shaykh, owns the greatest percentage of tribal lands, five to six times more land than any other shabba within the ashira. This is far more land than is necessary to support the ashira mudhif or to fulfill the responsibilities attached to the position of the shaykh. He and his close agnatic kinsmen are economically in a position far superior to any other tribesmen. In the past shaykhs of sedentary ashiras may have customarily held more land than their fellow tribesmen; today men loyal to the shaykh continue to justify his disproportionately large holding by saying that it is necessary to support the mudhif — in other words, to permit him to extend the customary lavish hospitality characteristic of such establishments. Yet it is obvious that, at least under present conditions, being a shaykh offers the possibility of securing more land, and owning more land is characteristic of men who are shaykhs. Upon the death of Shaykh Haji Atiyah, his son Mujid, the present shaykh, was able to successfully claim much more land than his brothers because Mujid was recognized as shaykh by the government. However, that land was already in the possession of Mujid's group, and under present conditions it is unlikely that the land would have been given to some other man whom the tribesmen might have wanted to be shaykh.

Shaykh Mujid's father and kinsmen claimed lands belonging to other lineage groups within the El Shabana who deserted their fields at the time of drought around 1900. These other groups did return but were never able to regain full occupancy of their previously held lands. The interference of outside powers since the advent of British control has prevented segments of the El Shabana from combining to strip the shaykh and his kinsmen of their holdings, if, indeed, such a course of events would have occurred.

The relationship between landholding and tribal segments within the ashira may be further understood by looking at the El Shatti group's holding on Map 5. This single holding is as large as the contemporary landholdings of several other shabbas combined. Tribal informants mentioned the El Shatti as a shabba. Other informants (including men from the shaykh's family) never mentioned a shabba called El Shatti, but said that El Shatti was part of the shaykh's shabba, the El Jami'yyin. In terms of descent, the group of men called El Shatti are as closely related to the shaykh and his brothers as are many kinsmen witin the same fakhd.

Shatti (the man for whom the group is named) was the only son of the present shaykh's father's father's only brother. Shatti had five sons who, in the 1940's, registered their land jointly. Of these five sons, three are now dead, but their sons, the two living original sons, and *their* sons, now constitute a group of eleven men, the El Shatti. The eldest sons of the shaykh persistently referred to the El Shatti as a fakhd of the shaykh's shabba: other tribesmen did not mention the El Shatti's agnatic tie with the shaykh, but said that the El Shatti constituted a shabba with one fakhd. Further, in outlining the named sections of the El

Shabana, many tribesmen list the El Shatti, a shallow descent group, as equal to other shabbas, or groups of much deeper descent.

Thus it appears that the acquisition of an exceptionally large amount of property by one kin group is of primary importance in establishing its equivalence to groups of a very different structural order. This is yet another example of the confounding of the segmentary system and at the same time the tribesmen's persistent efforts to fit unequal tribal groups into their idealized conceptions of the tribal system.

The shaykh's segment provides other clues to the nature of the relationship between landholdings and tribal organization, for the El Shatti example is not the only way in which the shaykh's group constitutes an exception to the model segmentary system. The El Jami'yyin, the named group to which the shaykh and his agnates belong, was sometimes referred to by tribesmen as a shabba and at other times was called a fakhd. When tribesmen included the El Jami'yyin in listing shabbas of the El Shabana, they would be asked, "then to what fakhd of the shabba El Jami'yyin do the shaykh and his brothers belong?" Frequently, after a pause, the tribesmen would say, "he and his brothers belong to the hamula el Sha'lan." This is the instance in which the hamula was mentioned — a group ideally at a lower "nesting" level of organization than the fakhd. What is the explanation of its presence within the shaykh's lineage group? The father of the present shaykh and the father's brothers constituted a faction which fought other men within the tribe and within the shaykh's own lineage group to secure the shaykhship. The father and his brothers became known by the name of their father, Sha'lan. The success of this struggle and the permanence of the resulting split within the shaykh's descent group presumably led to social recognition of the faction as a single unit. As the maps of landholdings illustrate, it is this group, the shaykh and his paternal uncles, which holds by far the largest amount of land in the Elbu Blaw section. No hamula division was mentioned for other fakhds; it may be that no issue leading to a development of factions was sufficiently strong to overcome the several ties between members of such groups.

Both the example of the El Shatti "shabba" [28] and the two-generation "hamula" distinction within the El Jami'yyin, constitute phenomena not consistent with the model segmentary system. In both instances shallow lineage groups have been made conspicuous through acquisition of large amounts of land. By their large landholdings the El Shatti are economically much better off than the average tribesman and the shaykh's uncles and brothers are the wealthiest group of agnates in the El Shabana ashira. This is not lineage segmentation according to the classic model, but rather economic stratification according to land-based wealth. The land reform act, passed after the July, 1958 revolution in Iraq, required that the shaykh dispose of all but a thousand mesharas of his land. This meant that over half of his holdings must be redistributed. It was conceivable, but not likely, that redistribution might have a salutary effect on tribal organization by permitting other El Shabana segments to recover lost land, and thus permit more than the present fifteen percent of tribesmen to make a living exclusively from farming their own holdings.[29]

The segmentary model, which still seems to be part of the tribesmen's conception of their organization, may possibly have "fitted" the presedentary social system of the Daghara Arab, presumably in the sense that inequities would have been more readily adjusted under the more flexible conditions of nomadic life. Even after the El Shabana settled, a somewhat more segmentary system might have prevailed before the area was pacified, the shaykh recognized by the government, and landholdings within the tribal dira fixed by registration. For convenience, the divisions within the El Shabana ashira will continue to be referred to as "segments," but it is obvious that since the lineage system does not altogether correspond with the named groupings within the ashira, the segments which tribesmen may name as similar to one another are structurally not always at the same level. In reality, then, the structurally "equal" segments of this system have, under contemporary conditions, been deprived of the capacity to stand in balanced complementary opposition to one another.

VI

The Shaykhship and the Dominant Lineage

The existence of a dominant lineage group, a group having proportionally greater control of resources and ultimately greater power within a tribal group than any other segment, runs counter to the cultural model of the tribal system present in the Daghara region as well as to the classic model of the segmentary system. Yet the development of a dominant lineage is understandable within the framework of a segmentary mode, for it is, in a sense, the end result of conditions undermining those checks and balances which keep structurally equivalent segments equal in politico-economic terms. It is difficult to see how *any* segmentary system can persist under conditions which permit a single segment or alliance of segments to achieve a monopoly over sources of wealth. Observers note the practice of central governments in southern Iraq to register disproportionately large amounts of land in the names of shaykhs. This, they state, has been responsible for transforming the tribe from a "democratic" institution where wealth was widely shared and decisions consensually based, into a "feudal dictatorship" in which the shaykh is absolute ruler and the tribesmen mere tenant serfs.[1] Yet it is possible that under the conditions of an agricultural subsistence adjustment, where wealth may be accumulated, socio-economic equality may be lost between structurally equal segments *without* outside interference. This suggestion should be kept in mind during the following history of the rise of the lineage of the present shaykh of the El Shabana.

Earlier the temporary loss of water in the Daghara canal was explained as due to upstream changes in the Euphrates river regime at the turn of the century. At this time some sections of the El Shabana deserted the land they had occupied and turned to sheepherding or sought land elsewhere. Other tribal segments lost membership through desertion of individual families. The El

Naqish, which can be found on Map 5, is a good example. This group left the area at the time of water loss so that the El Naqish members now own only the fragmentary few acres of land shown on the map. Atiyah and Sha'lan, the father and grandfather of the present shaykh, were both apparently men of considerable foresight and personal charisma. Counting on the eventual return of water to the Daghara, first Sha'lan and later Atiyah gathered members of their lineage about them and proceeded to occupy abandoned lands. To do this, Atiyah first captured the shaykhship, which had resided with the Elbu Ubayd shabba. This action provoked serious fighting among the shabbas of the El Shabana, but Atiyah was aided by great personal popularity, by twelve sons, and by the fact that many otherwise opposing lineage groups were weakened by loss of men. Furthermore, it seems likely that much land was acquired without opposition, since many men must have been convinced that farming by irrigation was doomed on the Daghara canal. Shortly after water had returned in substantial quantities to the Daghara, following the construction of the Hindiyya Barrage (1908–1913), the British occupation and pacification of the area began. This outside occupying force suppressed any attempt on the part of other segments of the El Shabana to redress the imbalance of landholdings.

Whether or not the other shabbas of the El Shabana would have been able to correct the balance of landholdings within the ashira if the British had not arrived, is a matter of speculation. However, some of the actions taken by Atiyah and later by his son Mujid to reinforce their hard-won superiority are interesting. First of all, Atiyah and later his sons took wives from the shabbas they had alienated in their successful struggle for tribal control. Today, of all the shabbas who suffered considerable loss of land and position during that period, only two, El Ghrush and El Shawahin, remain somewhat aloof from the shaykh and his lineage. The El Ghrush and El Shawahin prefer to be counted as a separate ashira. Only during 1956–1958 did members of this group begin once again to visit regularly the mudhif of the shaykh. Significantly these two shabbas are the only major groups with whom neither Atiyah nor the present shaykh Mujid succeeded in establishing an affinal bond. Secondly, Atiyah and Mujid, plus their brothers, have married women from large estate-holding

106

families bordering the El Shabana lands, thus helping to insure good relations with powerful neighbors. Finally, members of the shaykh's lineage group have married women from the shaykh's lineages in different ashiras in the sillif El Aqra.

Thus through marriage the dominant lineage has succeeded in establishing a series of affinal bonds throughout its own ashira, as well as with powerful families outside the ashira. The complete genealogies of the Elbu Ubayd and El Mujarilin shabbas show that during Atiyah's time three men from these two groups married women from the El Jami'yyin, so exogamous marriages included women leaving the shaykh's lineage. Women from the shaykh's family traditionally do not marry "foreigners." However, the Elbu Ubayd and the El Mujarilin are original, not adopted, members of the El Shabana and thus consanguineously related to the shaykh's lineage, and not "foreigners" in the true sense. In practice a few other exceptions to the rule have been noted, especially a sister of the present shaykh, who is married to a shaykh who is not a member of the El Shabana, but a powerful neighbor, who owns lands bordering on the El Shabana holdings.

Any shaykh, in reinforcing his own position, gathers a loyal retinue about himself. The retinue includes not only loyal kinsmen, and slaves or descendants of slaves, but also tribesmen from lineages other than his own. These men, including *wakils* (representatives) and *haras* (guards), are supported, along with their dependents, by the shaykh. They not only guard his person, but look after his interests, particularly by protecting his crops and giving orders to his tenant farmers. Presumably in the past, when violence was a real possibility, the shaykh gathered as many such men about him as he could afford to retain, as well as slaves and servants. The size of the personal retinue of the present shaykh is modest compared with the reported size of those of his forefathers, undoubtedly a reflection of the security insured by government forces. Nevertheless, it is instructive to look at the sources of the shaykh's present retinue.

First of all, the shaykh depends heavily on two uterine brothers with whom he owns much land in common (see Map 6); one of these men, or the shaykh's eldest son, takes the shaykh's place in the guest-house in the latter's absence. The shaykh does not depend so much on his other brothers, and relations with some of

107

them have for some time been strained over a dispute involving their common inheritance of land.

The shaykh is also very close to the descendants of El Shatti, having twice married women from this group. Two men from this group help manage the shaykh's landholdings and are presumably compensated in some fashion for their work, though the financial details of such arrangements are not discussed.

The shaykh's guards change from time to time but usually are drawn from the settlement of El Shabana tribesmen living near Daghara. As armed hostilities are a thing of the past, the position is not as important as it was only two decades ago. However, there are always armed men sleeping near the door of the shaykh's quarters at night, and these accompany him when he visits distant settlements. Some of the guards cultivate land of their own, living at the shaykh's expense only when they are with him. Again, however, such arrangements are privately made. Only one guard appeared to be totally dependent on the shaykh for support, as were a handful of household servants. In sum, however, the group of men closest to the shaykh and involved in his personal affairs is recruited from close kinsmen other than his uterine brothers and his eldest sons.

No rule of primogeniture operates in relation to the shaykhship; the position may pass to anyone of good standing within the tribe, but usually goes to a son or brother of the last incumbent shaykh.[2] We have seen that struggles over succession within the family of the present shaykh have led to radical factionalism within his minimal lineage. The incumbent in fact came to power before the death of his father, partly to appease the government, against which Sha'lan Atiyah had led armed uprisings in 1935,[3] and partly to insure that the position would not be captured by one of Sha'lan's ambitious paternal uncles. To this day, the shaykh remains on bad terms with some of these uncles and their descendants.

Thus it is clear that in the struggle for the shaykhship whoever emerges as shaykh may well have alienated many of his closest kinsmen. At the same time throughout his life all of his close male relatives remain heirs apparent. Therefore the numerous exogamous marriages contracted by the shaykhs and the drawing into the shaykhly retinue of men from all sections of the tribe serve two ends. Such alliances strengthen the position of the shaykh vis-à-vis the entire tribe, helping him, in a sense, to rise above the structural limitations of lineage segmentation. They also strengthen his hand against his own brothers and paternal uncles, the most likely source of conspiracy and coup. Strained relations between the present shaykh and certain of his father's brothers and their sons may well constitute the basis for the emergence of another named grouping as these men, their sons, and their son's sons grow older.[4]

The general question of authority, including the authority of the shaykh, will be discussed in the next chapter within the context of irrigation problems. However, one general observation about the authority of the shaykhship may be made at this point. The mere existence of a situation in which one man and his kinsmen have proportionally greater wealth than their fellow tribesmen may be a basis for power, but it is not necessarily a factor in the development of socially recognized authority. Whatever authority may be enjoyed by the present shaykh, its source and exercise are different from those of the authority enjoyed by his father and grandfather. Both his father and grandfather enjoyed the relatively great wealth of the present shaykh, but these men also fulfilled the traditional role of tribal leader in that they were fighting men; the last major battle was fought by the El Shabana about thirty years ago.

The conditions of central government control in Iraq may constitute another explanation, in addition to the presence of small landholders, for the comparatively strong expression of tribal tradition among the El Shabana. In the uneven pattern of government control of southern Iraq, Daghara emerges as one region in which the government was not able completely to prevail until this decade.[5] Thus tribal leaders in the Daghara area have been able to fulfill more of the role requirements associated with the shaykh's status than was the case in many other regions of southern Iraq. For while a good shaykh must have been a reservoir of tribal law and an astute judge, he must first of all have been an activist, leading his group and opposing others. The change in the shaykhship in only one generation was summarized by a tribesman, who said: "The last shaykh was a fighter; this one is a politician."

Under present conditions, the institution of the shaykhship

109

still further limits the applicability of the segmentary model to the tribal organization herewith described. But more political justification may have existed for the still-current idea that the lineages of the tribe are equal, under historic conditions, when the shaykhship was held by various lineages of the El Shabana, and when one shaykh perhaps had to cultivate support for his actions and remain responsive to consensual processes among the tribesmen. The shaykh could utilize available opportunities to develop support among tribesmen and increase his personal strength. But he was never entirely free of the consequences of complementary opposition: other lineages within the tribe could always combine to overthrow him and his lineage. Yet however fragile the power of the shaykh, however much of it rested on consensus, the institution of the shaykhship definitely did not in the past accord with the idea model of the acephalous segmentary social system. And in the more recent past, of course, the "guaranteed" shaykhship makes the tribal organization of the El Shabana resemble the segmentary model even less.

THE TIES BINDING THE SYSTEM

Thus far the interests of the individual segments within the ashira have been stressed, particularly in terms of kinship and landholdings. But the ashira also acts as a single body in defense of its land or in expansion of its holdings. Members of the ashira also were, and are, able to act as a coordinated faction to maintain and establish the irrigation works upon which their agriculture depends. Certain institutionalized relationships link men across shabba boundaries. Furthermore, the character of a shaykh's lineage is such that certain statuses and associated roles transcend the self-interest of individual ashira segments and form the basis for centralized authority within the ashira itself.

What customary practices serve to bridge segmented lineages so that when concerted action is necessary, the ashira can and does act as a single group? Unless traditional social relations have been established between the members of these territorially localized, preferentially endogamous, lineage-based segments within the ashira, cooperative action would be unlikely to be found on an ashira-wide level of participation except, perhaps, under such extreme duress as outside attack. The shabbas of the El Shabana, while not perfectly equal in terms of the lineage system, nevertheless constitute a strong basis of ingroup interest and are a potential source of intra-ashira conflict. To explain why shabbas join in common action on occasions other than the ashira's self-defense, we must explore inter-segmental links other than the formal, culturally defined bond of belonging to one ashira.

One important tie which may exist between members of ashira subsections is exemplified in that of horse ownership. Horses are important in the Daghara region not so much for transportation (actually few men ride horses) but as the only source of power for plowing. All farming tribesmen must have access to a plow and horse during every fall planting season. Yet a horse is costly and expensive to maintain, and not more than one horse is found for every ten adult men among the El Shabana. Only a few wealthy men, principally of the shaykh's family, own whole horses; in the majority of cases a man may own only an eighth of an animal. One might assume that a horse would be jointly owned by members of the same fakhd or shabba. However, this is usually not the case. The owners of a horse may live miles apart and commonly are members only of the same ashira. Horses are offered for sale at public markets in Daghara village, as are sheep, cows, and occasionally donkeys. Agreements are struck on the spot between tribesmen who happen to be interested in investing in a horse. The man who feeds the horse has use of it as a riding animal, whereas a man who owns only an eighth of a horse and cannot afford to maintain it may only use the horse a few days each year and receives only a small proportion of profits realized from the sale of colts. A man who owns a fourth of a horse may, during his period of use, also plow his non-horse-owning brother's land in return for cash or, more commonly, for a substantial meal. Thus use of the horse extends even beyond its multiple owners.

One effect of this practice is to minimize the risks of horse ownership, and ease the problem of raising capital for investment. The death of an expensive horse would be a tragedy if the horse were owned exclusively by one group of brothers and cousins.

111

As it is, the loss of a horse is spread over a wide number of people, and no one fakhd or shabba is unduly deprived. Similarly a man, when he wishes to invest in a horse, might well have to raise the money through loans from his nearer kinsmen; it would be generally impossible for the same group to raise enough cash to purchase an entire horse. The horse is the most familiar object of non-lineage partnership, but other less general examples exist, founded on the same principle of extensive partnership.

Intermarriage constitutes another very important source of institutional relations between ashira segments. Such marriages of course violate the preference for lineage endogamy and run counter to the explicit preference for parallel-cousin unions. What are the reasons for these exogamous marriages? They appear to stem from three quite unrelated cultural patterns: (1) the settlement of blood feuds, (2) the demonstration of personal wealth, and (3) the institutionalization of friendly relations between other than kin groups.

While cash payments have been permitted as a substitute for the giving of women in the settlement of a feud, a fasl which is based on cash payments alone is regarded as "black" and unlikely to end the bad feeling between the two groups involved. If the payment of a woman is part of a fasl, the fasl is considered to be "white," and likely to herald real peace between the disputing segments. According to informants, mixed fasls, involving both women and cash payments, are most common; the cash standing for one or two of the three women who traditionally must be turned over to the fakhd of a murdered man's group — ideally to any of his close relatives needing a wife. Offspring of these marriages are tangible evidence that a feud has truly been settled. Neither the offspring nor the "foreign" wife are second-class citizens of the father's group, but the mother's origins are well remembered (for five generations, in one genealogy), and her group of origin is referred to as "sons of our mother's brother" (*awlad khalna*).

If such an exogamous marriage is fruitful and the offspring prosper and increase, the number of men within a shabba who refer to another shabba's men as *awlad khalna* may be large enough so that a special relationship of mutual aid and attendance at each other's festival celebrations may be established. Under such conditions future marriages often occur between the two groups; it is frequently said that "if you have no relative to marry on your father's side the next best thing is to marry your mother's relatives." [6]

Intermarriage between lineage groups is also an expression of economic abundance. Parallel-cousin marriage is the least expensive source of a wife. Prosperous older men, who may have married a cousin in their youth, may decide to take another wife and this second (or third) wife will often be a "foreigner," that is to say someone from outside the man's fakhd. Similarly, a prosperous man with a marriageable son may encourage a "foreign" marriage, particularly if he is in any way estranged from his brothers. Generalizations about the bases of such marriages are difficult to make; some cement long-standing friendships between fathers, others are the culmination of "falling in love," and others seem to be purely prestigious acts of men who are wealthy and wish to enjoy the fact. However, taking a "foreign wife" is expensive, for her family must be well compensated for her loss to another group. If a woman has a cousin who claims her, his permission must be secured and often he too must be compensated. One way of avoiding the higher bride price of a foreign marriage is to arrange a sister-brother exchange. Such exchanges are usually the outcome of long-standing good relations between the two families; kinship, based on earlier marriages, often exists between the two groups. Exchanges of this kind between brothers with children of a marriageable age are also not uncommon.

In addition to horse ownership and intermarriage, several other institutions cut across shabba lines and tend to unite the ashira. Most of these ties have already been described, but it is perhaps worth summarizing them once more. All members of the El Shabana belong to the same sect of Islam, the Shi'a, and participate together in the rituals of the sect, especially during Muharram. The Sada, or descendants of the Prophet, who reside with the various shabbas of the ashira, act as intermediaries between the shabbas when conflicts arise. Celebrations upon the major Islamic feasts bring together all segments of the tribe, as do funerals and weddings. The hosa dramatizes the solidarity of the ashira as a unit. And, of course, the mudhif of the shaykh, site of the celebrations, the hosas, the gatherings at the time of funerals and weddings, is another bond. The mudhif is built with help donated by various shabbas and supported by tribal or mudhif

113

land set aside for this purpose. Guest-house, assembly, jural court: the mudhif is tangible evidence of the existence of the ashira as an institution.

But actually how "tribal" are the El Shabana and similar tribes? I have shown the several ways in which the tribal system departs from the segmentary model. Yet many social systems, not segmentary in structure, are commonly regarded as tribes: the segmentary model is, after all, only a construct, a tool utilized by the investigator. Of what concern is it that the El Shabana do not now exhibit all those characteristics typical of segmentary organized tribes?

The cultural model of the tribal system still held by tribesmen is of a segmentary system insofar as the lineage-based subsections of the tribe are stated to be equal at each "nesting level" of organization within the system, with respect both to composition, and to political and economic power. What I have attempted to demonstrate is how far the "realities" of the contemporary social order department from the "ideal" order which still seems to be fresh in the minds of the local tribesmen. More than this, lacking an adequate description of tribal organization prior to the introduction of state controls, it is tempting to use the cultural model provided by informants as a base line against which to measure change. Yet it is also clear that, at least in this part of the Arab world, the tribal system has traditionally incorporated two apparently contradictory tendencies. Certain political and economic processes have tended to favor lineage stratification, or the development of dominant lineages. This has led Dickson, for instance, to speak of "royal clans" among the Arab nomadic pastoralists of Kuwait,[7] and Salim to talk of Ahl Khayun as the "noble clan of Beni Isad"[8] — a tribal group from the marshes of the southern Euphrates. Obviously whoever happens to be shaykh has a number of opportunities to reinforce his position. He is not merely a benign figure-head, unable to make a move without seeking consensus, but rather is in a position to actively command support through combinations of alliances and patronage. However internecine the conflicts among members of the shaykh's minimal lineage may be, the coalescence of this group in the face of efforts to remove the shaykhship from its control is entirely consistent

114

with a point of view, found throughout the Arab world, placing the interests of the family above those of the individual.

On the other hand, in contrast to the tendency toward lineage stratification, the formation and organization of the units of tribal organization *do* depend on the continuous process of lineal segmentation, and the ideology of the tribal unity rests, by and large, on the shared belief in common descent.[9] Both the social process and the ideology favor lineage equalitarianism — as do other traditional beliefs and values. Islam itself does not sanction social distinctions within the community of believers. Nothing could be further from the traditional conception of leadership among tribal Arabs than the notion of Divine Right to rule. As all students of traditional Arab societies have noted, qualities such as personal courage, generosity, and luck make a man a leader, rather than any God-given birthright. Salim's description of social stratification among the Beni Isad, while revealing a great deal about the relationship between ascription and achievement in determining social status in this rapidly changing society, nevertheless does not convince one that the traditional position of the noble clan was in fact sanctioned by universal belief in their innate superiority so much as it was a product of well-managed political and economic opportunity.[10]

Within the El Shabana, fixed and unequal landholdings plus official governmental support have been primarily responsible for the near monopoly of power and wealth enjoyed by the shaykh and his lineage today. While the Sada and certain forms of economic partnerships are still important and effective links between members of differing tribal sections, the loss of land under present conditions, and the general decline in productivity of the land still held by the "average" tribesmen, has obliged more and more men to seek their livelihood outside the tribal domain. The fact that here and elsewhere in southern Iraq more men are constantly being forced to spend most of their lives away from their tribal setting and their fellow tribesmen, returning only part of each year, constitutes perhaps the single most important factor in the declining importance of the tribe. Men simply do not interact as frequently as they did in the past in terms of their position within the tribal organization.

Yet, with all of these qualifications, the El Shabana are not now mere sedentary agriculturalists using terms reminiscent of a tribal past. A world of difference exists between the attitudes and behavior of the men of the El Shabana and those of the landless farmers who for several generations have been separated from any large grouping of fellow tribesmen. Obviously the majority of the men from the El Shabana, assembling for feasts, visiting at weddings and funerals, or merely gathering for coffee in the various mudhifs, still regarded themselves as set apart because of their tribal affiliations and drew satisfaction from that identification — even as many of them recognized some of the inequities now characteristic of their organization.

How can this organization continue to function and have some vitality in the face of evidence that sociologically it has "decayed" or at least is not what it was as an indigenous system? Perhaps the best answer is to recall that the "decay" began relatively recently. The period of radical change began only in 1922 with the establishment of British administration in the southern Euphrates valley. From 1922 to 1958 is sufficient time for many social, political, and economic changes to take place but it is, perhaps, a short time for the dissolution of the basic cultural attitudes and ideals of the tribal system.

Three decades ago, in the nineteen-thirties, the El Shabana rose in arms against the central government; tribal leaders were sentenced to be hanged but were finally released after imprisonment. This revolt, in providing an opportunity for joint action in the traditional activist sense, helped to strengthen the tribe against the weakening changes already well under way.

Shaykh Mujid, the present shaykh, is after all the first shaykh to come to power under the present conditions. Furthermore, as we shall see in the following chapter, certain of the central government's administrative policies, rather than dividing the tribes further, have actually acted to encourage the people of the Daghara area to continue to think of themselves as "tribal." So also it is conceivable that the more recent struggles in republican Iraq to achieve a new integration of political and social forces may strengthen tribal loyalties as individual politicians reach out for all possible sources of support.

The basic question for the future is whether relations will be between tribe and state, or citizen and administration. In a number of African countries the tribe seems to have gained new importance in the politics of the post-colonial New Nations. But in Iraq it is unlikely that tribes will again assume overt importance on the national scene.[11] However, so far as the individual tribesman is concerned, the continuing significance of the tribe appears to hinge on the nature of authority as he experiences it in his daily life. The manifestation of local authority can be clearly seen in the operation of the area's irrigation systems, past and present, for the equitable division of water is a basic concern of the entire community. Not only is irrigation a matter of traditional and tribal concern in Iraq but one of national interest and survival.

VII

Changing Patterns of Local Authority: Irrigation

In the discussion which follows I shall examine some of the ways in which gravity-flow irrigation has been carried out by the tribal cultivators around Daghara over the last several decades. Underlying this discussion is the assumption that understanding how the problems of irrigation have been managed will provide basic insight as to local patterns of authority. Irrigation is essential to agriculture in this region and cultivation is a basic means of subsistence for this population. The nature of irrigation here, involving as it does the digging of canals and the damming of artificial waterways, imposes at least minimum levels of cooperation between those sharing canal systems, while the potential for conflicts of interests between individuals or groups of individuals sharing a limited supply of water is relatively high. On logical grounds alone, then, the operation of an irrigation system would seem to require some degree of both executive and jural authority.[1]

Although observers have noted that it was first the shaykh, then the British administration, and today the Iraqi government irrigation official who runs the irrigation system, we shall see that the matter is not so simple or clear-cut as this. Around these figures lies a complex web of interrelationships woven over the years which have passed since the origin of tribal cultivation in this region; the warp of physical circumstance and the woof of socio-political systems have become inextricably intertwined.

The tribal organization constitutes the framework for such aspects of contemporary irrigation as are the responsibility of tribesmen. As already observed, conditions in recent years — particularly fixed landholdings and outside support for the shaykh — have apparently robbed the tribal system of much of its indige-

118

nous character. The government's assumption of important responsibilities for the local irrigation system has proceeded side by side
with changes in the sociological character of the tribe. But tribesmen do still successfully operate parts of the irrigation works.
The irrigation problems which remain the responsibility of tribesmen generally arise within shabba and fakhd segments — which
are composed of kinsmen; however decayed the system may be, the
bonds of kinship still form an important basis for social action
within these smaller social units.

To explain the reciprocities between the social and the natural
order in the Daghara region, I shall begin by examining customary
practices of the tribe associated with both historic and contemporary irrigation. These irrigation practices are related to the
question of both traditional and contemporary patterns of authority, and to the changes in the patterns of authority with the
advent of outside interference in water supply problems, changes
which began with the period of British administration. As we
move to questions of power and authority in recent times, an
analysis of recorded irrigation disputes which have arisen in the
last several years will provide evidence for what seems to be a
newly emerging authority.

CUSTOMARY TRIBAL IRRIGATION

In the middle of the nineteenth century, when the El Shabana
first settled in the Daghara region, the area from the mouth of the
Daghara canal to the town of Afaq was covered with intermittent
areas of marshland.

The El Shabana farmers irrigated by utilizing the waters of the
Daghara branch of the Euphrates, their efforts resulting in the
canal called the Harunniyya shown in Map 2. While no longer in
use owing to government-instigated changes in the canal system,
this canal is still in evidence as a dry bed. The following account
of its origin is related by informants. Each of the original four
shabbas of El Shabana El Qadimin (the old El Shabana) owned
land which lay either next to the Daghara branch or in marsh
areas, and thus was suitable for cultivation. When water was
needed for irrigation, temporary dams (badkha)[2] were built on the
Daghara and water was flooded over the land and partly directed

119

with ditches. The Harunniyya canal was not dug all at one time, but gradually developed. Each year more earth was added to the banks of an originally modest ditch, and the canal's length was extended by members of the El Shabana who were interested in increasing the area of land which could be cultivated. The underlying reasons for bringing more land under cultivation through canal irrigation are not known, but possibly these efforts stemmed from some combination of (a) a gradual decrease in marsh area; (b) additions to the El Shabana by "adoption"; and (c) population increases among the original settled group.

The fact that the Harunniyya canal grew from year to year rather than being dug all at once was strongly emphasized by informants; this canal was *not* the product of a single concentrated effort. The Harunniyya canal was shared by several shabbas of the El Shabana; if the present residence pattern of the shabbas prevailed at the time the canal was used, it appears that the newer adopted groups acquired land toward the tail of the canal while the original four shabbas of the El Shabana were closer to the mouth of the canal or were situated on the Daghara branch of the Euphrates itself.

Informants state that no problem of water division existed among the El Shabana (except from natural drought) until 1922 when the government began supervising water use on the Daghara. Since the El Shabana land lies near the mouth of the Daghara, until 1922 members of the tribe were able to block the stream and take water as they wished as long as they were strong enough to prevent downstream tribal groups from breaking up their dams.[3] Other ashiras of the El Aqra, such as the Elbu Sultan and Elbu Nayil, living upstream or across the Daghara from the El Shabana, may sometimes have fought with the El Shabana over water rights in occasional periods of shortage. But as members of the same sillif, the largest inclusive tribal grouping, the upstream users were linked with the El Shabana by a common desire to prevent tribal groups of the downstream Afaq area from breaking the dams. Thus a sufficient water supply apparently had a generally positive effect on tribal unity, encouraging the El Shabana to increase their number through adoption of other shabbas, and providing numerous occasions on which the sections of the tribe joined together for mutual defense.

120

Changing Patterns of Local Authority: Irrigation

Shortage of water, on the other hand, seems to have had an opposite effect. I have already noted in reviewing the history of the El Shabana that one water shortage disrupted the tribe: several sections left the land to return to sheepherding or to farm elsewhere. And during the same period of drought, a political revolution occurred in which the present dominant lineage was established and another lineage reduced to a secondary position.[4]

In the past, fighting to expand landholdings, or to better a group's position with respect to water, was often undertaken by single segments within the ashira or even by an entire ashira, with the shaykh as leader.[5] As long as segments of the same ashira were not pitted against one another, no strong social sanctions existed to prevent such fighting. The *niza,* or dispute which arose, would be arbitrated by the shaykh, if it had taken place between members of the ashira, or by members of a third ashira, if the dispute were between two different ashiras. Intermediaries from the Sada would usually help in the settlement of such disputes.

But as the Harunniyya canal developed and several sections of the El Shabana, as well as the shaykh, became more dependent on it, the canal became a constant source of friction between the shaykh and other sections of the tribe. "In those days," the present shaykh's eldest son recalls, "it was dangerous for the shaykh to have large numbers of tribesmen angry with him, so my great-great-grandfather persuaded the tribesmen to dig another canal, aided by his fallahin." [6] The digging of the second canal, the Lafaliyya, apparently served to reduce tensions between the shaykh and some sections of the tribe by eliminating the source of constant disputation.

Such tensions are less likely today as the national government, in the person of the irrigation engineer, now controls outlets from government-owned canals. But before examining in detail the role of the modern Iraqi government in irrigation, let us look for a moment at the canal system and its operation from the perspective of the tribal cultivators themselves.

THE IRRIGATION SYSTEM

The major parts of the irrigation system in the Daghara area are summarized in Map 7. Water comes from the Euphrates via government-controlled canals, including the Daghara canal and the Hurriyya canal, with its north and south branches. The Daghara canal is a natural waterway which has been brought under technical control by the construction of sluice gates and various abutments. It has also been dredged and straightened since the advent of the national irrigation authority in this region. But the Hurriyya canal, completed only in the 1940's, is a totally new addition to the local scene. Water flows from the government-controlled canals into a series of smaller canals. The *bada* (first off-take from the *jadwal,* or main canal) distributes water into *naharan*[7] (secondary off-takes) and from them the water may flow into *umuds* (smaller canals). Umuds frequently run through the center of the low earth walls *(fariq)* which enclose the small plots of land (lowh)[8] under cultivation. From umuds, *mirriyan* (still smaller canals) carry water down the length of a lowh. *Sharughs,* irrigation furrows, carry water from the mirriyan into the lowh, within which the water may be more conveniently controlled. Map 7 illustrates this system.

No single order of canals universally carries water to the fields. As the diagram shows, a variety of arrangements of canals is possible, depending on the position of a given piece of land relative to the source of water supply. A man whose land is located adjacent to a major canal might take his water directly from the bada. In that case, the sequence of canals would begin with the jadwal and continue with the bada, and the mirriyan would carry the water down the edge of the subdivided field into the irrigation furrows. More frequently, water must travel further from the main canal, so the naharan and other intermediate waterways are necessary.

Along the government-controlled canals, the irrigation engineer runs concrete pipes through the banks, pipes large enough to permit specified amounts of water to escape. The size of the pipe is determined by the area of land which must be supplied relative to the total amount of water available from the main canal. Large areas of land under the ownership of a single man will generally be supplied by one or more pipes. However, as we have seen, there are many owners of small farms in the El Shabana area. For obvious practical reasons, each of the small plots cannot be

122

provided with a separate water outlet from the government canals; therefore it is often necessary to provide a single pipe for several farmers who cultivate in one area.

Responsibility for the upkeep of the system rests both with the Directorate of Irrigation and with the individual users. The irrigation engineer has the legal right to requisition labor from the users of government canals and to raise funds for their cleaning through special levies. But while local irrigators may be required to contribute their money and efforts to the upkeep of these major canals, all the decision-making responsibility is reserved to the Directorate of Irrigation. After the water leaves the government canal the responsibility for construction and maintenance of canals rests with the cultivator or cultivators. The small canals or umuds are the joint responsibility of all the farmers taking water from them. While technically umuds are owned length by length by each of the farmers whose land they edge, in practice they are treated as the common property of all who depend on them for water.

Irrigation engineers in Iraq differentiate between *kharajiya* or external distribution of the water supply from the government canals, and *dakhiliya* or internal distribution of the water. Kharajiya distribution is the direct responsibility of the engineer; he must decide on the basis of his maps, records, and observations what is the correct amount of water for each section of land. The internal distribution of water among a group of small landowners who are provided with one pipe is not, technically, the irrigation engineer's responsibility, for it cannot be accomplished directly by an adjustment of outlets from the government canal. The cultivators themselves must allot this supply.

Disputes arising over external distribution must be taken to the irrigation engineer, who may request the chief government administrator in the area to exercise his police powers in case someone refuses to abide by the engineer's decision concerning water from the main canal.

Internal distribution problems are more complex. In theory, in the case of multiple cultivators using a single pipe, if a mutually satisfactory system of distribution of water and maintenance of joint supply canals cannot be achieved, any man or group of men has the legal right to carry his (or their) grievances in a petition to

123

the mudir nahiya. But in practice, this solution is seldom resorted to; cultivators may first appeal to kinsmen, to the shaykh, or even to the irrigation engineer.

IRRIGATION AT THE ASHIRA LEVEL

Members of the subsections of the El Shabana share several social and economic bonds: kinship, identification with named groups, contiguous and sometimes joint landownership, intermarriage, and often residence within the same hamlets. Intermarriage is more likely and kinship closer between members of the same fakhd than between members of the same shabba (see Table 11). But whether a shabba is unsegmented or whether it is composed of two or three fakhds, the members of the same shabba farm and live in the same area of land and frequently reside in the same or proximate hamlets.[9]

Another important bond linking members of the shabba is a common system of field canals, which begins at the off-take from the government-controlled waterway. In some cases a single farmer or brothers may share a pipe; usually more cultivators share a single pipe and in most cases they include users who enjoy membership in the same shabba.

The case of the El Mujarilin, one shabba of the El Shabana, is a good example of the shabba-canal system relationship. The water supply for all El Mujarilin cultivators comes principally from one bada off-take of the Hurriyya canal, which has been named El Khurays. The El Khurays off-take is shared by the entire shabba. From the bada El Khurays, the water is distributed through six naharan canals. Each naharan supplies water, through field canals, to a part of the landholding of the subsection. It would be an exaggeration to say that the group sharing a single naharan canal perfectly corresponds to one subdivision of the shabba — a fakhd or a bayt. Yet each naharan is usually found to be shared by close kinsmen. This happens because of the large number of land areas which are registered between brothers, or between brothers and paternal cousins.

Each of the six naharans has been given a name and is allowed to draw water from the El Khurays canal for a specified number

124

of *waqts* or periods of time during each agricultural season. One waqt equals the time from sunrise to sunset, or from sunset to sunrise. The number of waqts allotted to each naharan does not change from year to year, but was established in the 1940's when the El Khurays complex was dug, after the completion of the Hurriyya canal.

1. Alwiyya naharan receives 4 waqts of water each season
2. Burrimal naharan   4 waqts
3. Ruffiyya naharan   3 waqts
4. Jawba naharan   3 waqts
5. Elbu Sultan naharan   4 waqts
6. Atiyya naharan   2 waqts.

This is a rotating system. For example, the group of farmers on the Burrimal canal is allowed two days, that is four waqts, to accumulate its total water supply. Then they must close their off-take and the next group, the Ruffiyya, has use of the El Khurays water for its appointed time. The sequence in which the naharan will be opened and closed is decided by lot at the beginning of each agricultural season. Some third party is given six sticks, each stick standing for one of the six canals. The sequence in which the sticks fall determines the order of rotation.

The El Mujarilin clean their naharan canals twice each year, usually in October, before the winter growing season, and in April, before summer cultivation.[10] The period of canal cleaning by shabbas may extend over a period of twenty days, each of the men working as it suits him for perhaps two or three hours per day. El Mujarilin informants claim that the ownership of land is so split up that most men work on several naharans; one man usually farms a few acres of land in several different places and each few acres may be watered by a different sub-canal. However, the approximate amount of work required of each man is generally known among the reported thirty-eight men in the shabba. If a man is feeble or ill or must be away, he can ask his friends and relatives to do his share of the work for him. If, however, he neglects his responsibility, he will not be allowed to take water in the forthcoming growing season.[11]

The system of irrigation canals is slightly different in the case of the shabba Elbu Ubayd, whose landholdings are shown in part on Map 5. The two fakhds of the Elbu Ubayd have land which is more perfectly contiguous for each group. That is, members of one fakhd farm one area of land and members of the other fakhd farm a second though contiguous section. Their principal source canal is the Daghara itself and water from it passes first through one fakhd's land area and from there into the second. The entire shabba is responsible for maintaining the bada off-take, but as we shall shortly see, this arrangement has been a source of dispute within the shabba. The men say, *"ihna thlathin; nakhud mayy minn jadwal wahid"* (we are thirty men taking water from a single canal). They are obviously not pleased with the situation.

The El Shawahin and the El Ghrush shabbas of the El Shabana demonstrate still another arrangement of social groupings vis-à-vis water supply. In this case, both shabbas share a single outlet with a small hamlet of Sada. The Sada were given their land, not by the El Shawahin or the El Ghrush, but by the shaykh of the ashira some two generations ago. When informants were asked to name the shabbas of the El Shabana, beginning with those having the best water supply, and proceeding to the group with the least favorable water supply, the El Shawahin and the El Ghrush shabbas were consistently listed as being in the least favorable position. The ground cultivated by these two groups is high and other sections of their area are salted, so that the farming situation is also unfavorable for reasons other than water supply. From these two groups combined, only about twenty to thirty-five men attempt to cultivate the land. Each shabba section is responsible for digging its own section of the bada off-take canal, but again, this arrangement is the source of much disputation in contemporary times.

Informants from the Elbu Khaz'al, the largest shabba of the El Shabana still living in one place, tell an interesting history of their canal system. This shabba section includes three fakhd subsections. One fakhd has a pipe and bada to itself, while the two others share a canal. The names of the two canals are Qatb and Abu Dahab.[12] A discussion which took place in the Elbu Khaz'al mudhif revealed that originally the entire shabba worked together on a single canal. Then a serious fight over water occurred and a group of brothers, sons of a man named Zarzur, insisted on

126

establishing their own canal. El Zarzur is now the proper name of one of the fakhds. This dispute and the subsequent separation of the water supply into two canals took place at the same time that the sons of Zarzur set themselves apart from the parent organization and thus created a third fakhd in this shabba. The connection between the creation of a new canal and a new fakhd was considered obvious by the tribesmen.

The positions of several shabbas with respect to the canal system have been cited. Table 15 summarizes the available information on shabba ownership of canals. Shabbas are listed in order of the excellence of their position in relation to water supply: the order was unanimously agreed upon by informants.

Table 15 shows that most shabbas of the El Shabana have at least one major off-take canal from the government-controlled waterways. The cultivators themselves are responsible for dividing water from these off-takes between the members of shabbas, and for digging and maintaining the smaller field canals. It must be emphasized, however, that these cultivators do not each year establish a new canal system and redistribute their water. Once a system of field canals has been dug it commonly remains unaltered season after season and the allocations of water to the various sections of the system, once established, are largely taken for granted. Tribesmen regard problems of water distribution between themselves as unimportant compared with their joint concern with having an adequate allocation of water from the government.

As may be seen from the above description, the system of small canals and walled fields maintained and managed by tribesmen is complex and requires experienced attention to remain adequate for the needs of crop irrigation. Under these conditions, the members of each shabba *must* cooperate in this basic subsistence activity. Sharing the same canal system — as well as occupying the same area of land — must surely be a condition of life which tends to limit any possible active hostility between fakhds. From a structuralistic point of view, the common canal system within a shabba may be another factor which contributes to the confounding of principles of segmentary organization. While the fakhd segmentations within certain shabbas have apparently occurred since the El Shabana settled near Daghara, concern with and dependence

127

upon the same canal system — as well as occupation of the same area of land — may have limited the consequences of these divisions.

"What do you do if someone refuses to clean his section of the canal?" "What happens if someone takes more water than that to which he is entitled?" The initial response of almost all informants to such questions was, "Such problems do not arise for we are all brothers." As we shall see, this is not true; disputes over water are a common occurrence. What is important about the reply is that it points to values which define as culturally good the unity of the tribal subsections. A visitor to the mudhif of a fakhd (or to that of a shabba if there is a mudhif which shabba members share) will find it very difficult to elicit an admission that *any* issue divides or ever has divided the members of that group. Members of a fakhd or shabba find it important to keep their quarrels to themselves; there is a suggestion of shame in the idea of bringing intra-sectional differences to the attention of outsiders for it constitutes a public admission of weakness. Thus undoubtedly a very great percentage of disputes over water is resolved within the context of the primary tribal sections.

In the subsections (groups of from 20 to 50 men) the differentiation of status is not based upon an institutionalized hierarchy of authority but primarily upon position in the kinship system. No status within the kinship structure carries more than very limited authority and this falls off rapidly as social distance increases; traditionally, a father exercises unquestioned authority over his wife and children, but any authority which he may have over his sons' collaterals is a function of the content of his relationship to his own sibling group and collateral kinsmen. It is, in a sense, only with their permission that he may give orders to their offspring. While at every point in the kinship structure respect is characteristic of the attitudes of younger toward older men (except between the very young and the very old), being treated with respect in this society is by no means equivalent to being able to command, except in limited areas of public social etiquette. Within the fakhds and even the shabbas of the tribe, most disputes are solved, not by the word of any one man, but through the processes of consensus — including conversation and group discussion among men who are, after all, linked to each other on so many grounds as frequently to make "self-interest" almost synonymous with "group-interest." To be sure, observation of group discussions revealed some men being listened to more than others and some men scarcely speaking at all. Yet the greater influence of a given man is, I believe, mainly a result of historical accident which may, for instance, have resulted in his owning a comparatively greater amount of land, or such accidents of temperament as permit one man rather than another to express more fully and eloquently a culturally-valued personal behavior. In short, within subsections of a tribe men do not appear to command but rather to influence one another. Such patterns of authority as may exist are not part of an ongoing system of institutionalized statuses, but rather the result of economic differences and of group interaction within the framework of the kinship system.

But what of conflicts which, in spite of cultural norms, cannot be resolved within a subsection; and what of conflict over water between subsections? The nature of these conflicts and their disputation today is most revealing, not only of the dynamics of the social system I have described, but also of pervasive and important changes in both the internal structure of this system and its relation to its social environment. In order to provide additional perspective for this analysis, it will be useful to focus attention briefly on ashira-wide authority, on the years spent under British rule, and then on the period of growing involvement by the national government in the Daghara area. It was during the latter years that the tribesmen began to see choices rather than imperatives in deciding how to solve problems related to irrigation. At the same time, it was during the period from the beginning of British control to the present day that, because of outside control over supply canals, natural drought, and limitations on self-help, the irrigation problems of the cultivator-tribesmen increased rapidly in both quantity and complexity.

IRRIGATION WITHIN THE TRIBAL SECTIONS

Although today no common cultivation is undertaken by the ashira as a whole, ashira-wide cooperation to insure a sufficient water supply for irrigation still takes place. When it is necessary to clean one of the large canals used principally by the shaykh and secondarily by other tribesmen owning small sections of land, the shaykh calls for *awna* or *musaʿada*. Both terms may be translated as "aid" or "help." Canals, depending on their size and use, must be cleaned before both winter cultivation and summer farming. To rally forces for the awna, the shaykh sends forth a wakil or representative (in one instance, his eldest son together with a respected Sayid). The wakil and the Sayid travel to the various hamlets of El Shabana shabbas, announcing the day on which the canal will be cleaned and asking that the shabba send all available men to help the shaykhs's fallahin dig the silt from the canal. In mudhifs of the shabbas the Sayid reminds the men of the past glories of the El Shabana under the leadership of the shaykh's lineage and urges that it is the duty of the shabba members to help the shaykh.

On the appointed day, representatives of the shaykh meet each shabba of the tribe as they arrive for the awna, and assign to them particular portions of the canal. Each man is given a section of canal, measured off by lengths of a *mesha* (shovel handle), from which to dig out the accumulated silt. The general expectation is that in one day each tribesman will be able to clean a section of canal about fifteen feet long, three feet wide, and a foot and a half deep. This is arduous work as the silt must be tossed to the top of banks which are already piled high with formerly accumulated silt.

The cleaning of the canal may last several days, depending on its size and the number of men who appear for work. Customarily a tribesman will contribute his labor only one or two days. The work which remains unfinished — and this will vary depending on the number of tribesmen who have turned out for the musaʿada — is completed by the fallahin of the shaykh and his brothers who are, of course, forced to work.

The shaykh rides out to the canal during the cleaning, exchanging salutations and passing out cigarettes to those at work. He checks with his representatives who superintend the project and who must carefully record the name of everyone who has come to help. The shaykh then speaks with men from each of the tribal sections who are represented to find out why more men have not come; he often inquires after certain individuals by name. He

130

exchanges banter and small talk with the tribesmen, and provides a lunch of bread and cucumbers.

On what basis can the shaykh claim the labor of small land-holding tribesmen for his canal cleaning? Several factors are in operation here. By tradition, the income from some part of the shaykh's large holding supports the tribal mudhif. Part of the shaykh's land produces food which is served daily in the mudhif to guests and tribesmen. Therefore, some informants argued, it follows that the tribesmen should help clean the canals which provide water to irrigate mudhif land. However, it is doubtful if many tribesmen take this argument seriously. The simplest explanation lies in the fact that it is potentially dangerous or at least disadvantageous for any tribesman to be out of favor with the shaykh. The shaykh is still in a position to grant or refuse many sorts of favors, due to his unique relationship to the non-tribal world. As his younger brother stated, "If you visited a man or sat down next to him in a coffee shop and he didn't provide you with tea, would you serve him tea when he came to visit you?"

But the pattern of behavior associated with the appearance of men from the same shabba at the site of the musaʿada for cleaning the shaykh's canal, suggests something else, something of traditional attitude and precedent underlying this ashira-wide effort. Tribal sections arrive on horseback in full regalia — guns held aloft, knives roped on. Flags of different colors bearing religious inscriptions are carried by men in each section. Enthusiastic hosas are often performed before the men, somewhat anticlimactically it seems, tie up their long garments and jump into the silt-clogged canals to begin work. The arrival, the dress, the hosa performance, are much the same sort of behavior as occurs on the occasion of ashira feasting. Informants agreed that in "the old days" similar activity took place when the ashira gathered for attack or defense in warfare.

Furthermore, in the past when the shaykh requested the support of the tribal sections for purposes of war or raid, this "asking for aid" was also called musaʿada. The shaykh's sending out of wakils and Sada to the other sections of the tribe was similarly part of the pre-warfare pattern of behavior. Gathering of the ashira for purposes of canal cleaning appears then to be reasonably closely

131

related to cultural patterns associated with past cooperation by ashira members for purposes of armed combat. The accommodation of this precedented behavior (the roots of which must tap a far longer history than the eighty or so years of sedentary existence which this group has known) to the demands of irrigation is an interesting adaptation for a segmentary organization. It suggests that inclusive segmentary groupings may be capable of a more constructive social action than mere "opposition" to groupings of similar size and composition.

The oral history of the tribesmen records two major tribal canals; Map 2 shows one of these. There is no evidence to indicate that the El Shabana ever depended solely on these two canals, nor that these canals were completed in one season by a massive expression of tribal labor. However, local traditions do record that the ashira semi-annually participated in canal cleaning projects under the leadership of the shaykh. The fact that contemporary musaʿadas for canal cleaning have certain ritual characteristics suggests that the institution is not a contemporary innovation.

Contrary to expectations, the total amount of time devoted to the cleaning of canals is remarkably small. In response to the frequently asked question "How many days do you spend cleaning irrigation canals?" most informants said seven or eight days, some mentioned longer periods of time but said they worked only two or three hours a day over a twenty-day period. Men of the area do not attach very much importance to the work, nor does the work appear to be a burden. The shaykh's canal, which was fed by a 342-cubic-meter-of-water-per-second capacity pipe, accumulated from a foot and a half of silt a year near its head to six or seven inches of silt near the tail, but the total amount varied per winter season depending on the amount of rainfall and the amount of mud which had washed back into the canal from its silt-piled banks. A large number of men can quickly clean this canal, which is perhaps half a mile to one mile long. But it would be impossible for only a few men to clean a canal of such size in the interim between agricultural seasons. To this day, though the traditional position of the shaykh has changed considerably through the interference of the government, the shaykh is forced to depend upon ashira-wide aid to successfully complete his canal cleaning.

Changing Patterns of Local Authority: Irrigation

Just as the shaykh depends on the tribe, the tribesmen also depend on the shaykh to resolve certain problems associated with irrigation. As I have noted, decision-making within any section of the tribe is not a prerogative exclusively associated with institutionalized statuses, but is more generally the outcome of consensual processes among individuals sharing not only presumably common values but also ties of consanguinity, conjugality, and locality, as well as common interests in land and water. In this tribal system, the specialized authority-bearing status exists at a more inclusive segmentary grouping, the ashira, in the status of shaykh, and at the most inclusive segmentary level, the sillif, in the position of ra'is. What are the characteristics of the status-role "shaykh"?

The shaykh of an ashira has no religious functions and no sacred quality is attached to the position: the status is not validated by religious sanctions, and individuals occupying the position are not protected any more than any other tribesman by injunctions based on religious norms. The shaykhship is not limited to any one descent group, nor is the status occupied by any particular sequence of individuals within a descent group. Informants reiterate that the shaykhship passes to the eldest son "only if the tribe wants him": in practice, cases may be found where it has passed to siblings, uncles, cousins, or any one of a series of sons of a given shaykh. The position of shaykh must be achieved, although the eldest son of the current shaykh is traditionally regarded as a candidate for the position by the tribe and has an advantage in that he may build on the usually superior economic position of his father. However, before the days when government recognition constituted the de facto achievement of shaykh status, tradition records that bitter struggles frequently occurred when a tribal shaykh died, struggles which often resulted in the permanent division of a segmentary grouping. The history of the El Shabana demonstrates that several sections of the ashira have at different times been the "dominant lineage" carrying the shaykhship. The present shaykh of the El Shabana and several members of his lineage remain totally unreconciled because of events which led to the present shaykh's acquisition of this position.

Today it is obvious from observation that the status of the shaykh carries considerable symbolic importance. The guest of

133

the shaykh is the guest of the ashira; the protection granted by the shaykh secures the stranger from tribal hostility; the feast offered by the shaykh is considered an ashira feast; the grand display of the shaykh demonstrates the wealth and position of the tribe. As the representative of the tribe, the shaykh must perform no demeaning tasks. On the contrary, he is supposed to be an incarnation of manly virtue; proud, brave, virile, generous, wise, and a defender and faithful practitioner of the faith. It is his symbolic importance, the status characteristic of being a kind of ideal Everyman in the eyes of the tribesmen, which makes possible the great contrast, often noted by students of Bedouin culture, between the lavish display and style of life of the shaykh and the apparently impoverished condition of the ordinary tribesman.

The traditional standards of behavior required of a shaykh cannot be fully realized, however, if the opportunity for him to exhibit customary virtues is lacking. Unquestionably a major opportunity for the tribal shaykh to exhibit socially important qualities such as bravery and political acumen lay in leading his tribesmen in raids and warfare. Raids and warfare were, as already noted, the major activities shared by the segments of an ashira, whether in protection of land and water or in the acquisition of new territory. The son of the present shaykh wrote, in answer to a question about raiding, that raids were often made for purposes of acquiring more land, *either because it was needed or because a tribe was strong and simply wanted to exercise its power.* His voluntary mention of this deliberate quality of tribal warfare seems significant in this context. Particularly for the shaykh, but also for all tribesmen, fighting offered a unique opportunity to behave according to standards of conduct characteristic of a *man*. If this hypothesis is correct, it may explain why, in a time when shaykhs are notably unpopular, the shaykh of the El Shabana is still the object of pride, respect, and loyalty among *some* tribesmen. For this shaykh, his brothers, his father, and his grandfather, have all led or been involved in revolts, first against the Turks, then the British, and finally against the government of an independent Iraq. The dictum, "a leader must lead," appears to fit this situation perfectly once we have considered what the cultural requisites of leadership may be.

On deductive grounds, if it is accepted that we are dealing with

134

a segmentary organization, and a status of shaykh which is achieved, not ascribed, the shaykh must remain vulnerable if he is to exercise authority among his tribesmen. As Middleton and Tait note, political authority may not be vested in status attached to lineages or the fundamental principle of segmentary opposition is contravened.[13] In the case of the El Shabana, the process of becoming shaykh appears to have resulted in placing some members of the shaykh's lineage group in a comparatively privileged position (which led me to refer to his lineage as "dominant"), but it also resulted in the alienation and ostracism of other members of his group. The tribe's oral history records three changes in the shaykhship; at each change, the shaykhship was filled by men from entirely different shabbas and fakhds of the ashira.

If a status must be achieved, it may also be lost. Ultimately, the test of whether a man should be shaykh is whether he can be shaykh, whether he is capable of gaining and holding the position. Thus the present shaykh was able to usurp the position from his father before his death without incurring negative social sanction, for apparently the father had grown incapable of exercising the duties of the role and could not prevent his son from gaining the tribesmen's support. Today no tribesman is willing to state who might become shaykh in the future. The attitude is generally expressed as, "it will work itself out, who knows now?"

In contrast to the Sada, whose religious qualifications bulwark their traditional peacemaking functions, the shaykh's activities as a warrior-leader lent strength to his decisions in times of peace. Pax Britannica put a stop to the exercise of leadership in warfare, one of the major ways in which the shaykh or would-be shaykh had demonstrated his ability to ideally fulfill culturally valued norms of conduct. At the same time, the policy of indirect rule meant that the shaykh was expected to exercise other aspects of the behavior associated with his role — principally the jural functions which were earlier mentioned. Recognizing that the shaykh had traditionally sat in judgment over individuals guilty of socially proscribed behavior and had arbitrated disputes between tribal sections, the British utilized cooperative shaykhs in this capacity to carry out their own policies and enforce regulations. In return, the British supported the shaykh both directly and indirectly by enforcing peace and suppressing tribal "rebellions." But, whereas past judgments of the shaykh had enforced culturally defined and traditional norms, and whereas the course of arbitration had carefully included the development of support within the tribe for his decisions, the shaykh, as an arm of the administration, was placed in the position of enforcing regulations which often totally lacked any basis in tradition. Being required to carry out jural duties without having opportunities to demonstrate those qualities which traditionally permitted him to assume jural responsibilities in the first place, gradually undermined rather than strengthened the shaykh's authority among the tribesmen.[14]

THE BRITISH ADMINISTRATION AND THE IRRIGATION SYSTEM

The British began their occupation of the Daghara region in 1918 and British officers first visited the area in September of that year. No time was lost in creating an irrigation district; this was accomplished in November 1918. About the Daghara waterway, Gertrude L. Bell wrote:

This important canal, taking off from the Euphrates between Hillah and Samawah, feeds what was and is one of the most fertile areas in Mesopotamia — the Babylonian city of Nippur lies in its basin. For years the Turks have had no authority in this region; the canal was lined with the mud forts of the shaykhs and for some months after we took over, tribal feuds continued to menace the British peace . . .[15]

What was the nature of the "British peace" in southern Iraq?

In point of fact, over the greater part of Mesopotamia it was not the Turkish judicial authorities who had regulated the relations between man and men or assigned the penalties for breaches in their observances. Behind all legal paraphernalia lay the old sanctions, understood and respected because they were the natural outcome of social needs. The shaykh in his tent heard the plaint of petitioners seated around his coffee hearth and gave his verdict with what acumen he might possess, guided by a due regard for tribal custom; the local sayid, strong in his reputation for a greater familiarity than that of other men with the revealed ordinances of the Almighty, and yet stronger in the wisdom brought by long experience in arbitration, delivered his awards on disputes grave or trivial and the decisions thus reached were generally consonant with natural justice and always comfortable with the habits of thought of the contending parties.

This system of local justice was recognized by us to be a strong weapon on the side of order and good conduct. Just as it was the habit of the British military governors, when hearing cases, to call in the Mukhtars, headmen of the town quarters, and ask them to take part in the proceedings, so the Political Officers turned to the shaykhs of tribe and village and obtained their opinion. This practice was extended by an enactment called the "Tribal Disputes Regulation," issued with the approval of the Army Commander in February 1916.[16]

Thus by the time British military authorities entered the Daghara area in an administrative capacity, the pattern of "indirect rule," long familiar to students of British colonialism elsewhere in the world, had already been set up as the policy to be utilized in Mesopotamia.

When the irrigation district which included the Daghara canal area was formed, the irrigation officer could act independently of the chief political officer. As Miss Bell writes:

Local irrigation officers possessed the power of inflicting small punishments, without reference to the local Political Officers, for breach of irrigation regulations or a failure to fulfil orders with regard to embankments, etc.; yet the delinquent might be a man whom it was advisable from a political point of view to handle with caution, and in any case the existence of separate organizations issuing orders was confusing to the native mind.[17]

However, Miss Bell reports, this situation continued "smoothly" until 1919 when peaceful conditions allowed handing over irrigation and agriculture to civil authorities.

The irrigation authorities were no less anxious to strengthen the hand of tribal shaykhs than were other officers of the British administrative staff. Observing from practice what others have suggested in theory, Miss Bell notes:

The provision of an irrigation staff and the offer of advances of seed were not in themselves sufficient to secure cultivation. Irrigation demands cooperation, and combined effort is possible only where there is control. Three years of war [the Anglo-Turkish war in Mesopotamia] had left tribal cultivators more independent than ever. There were tribes, such as the Hubur, on the Hillah canal below Hillah, split into sections, the sarkals of which were disinclined to recognize any shaykh. There were others, such as the Albu Sultan, who recognized their shaykh, but were openly disobedient. *It was, therefore, a point of policy to restore the power of sarkals and shaykhs,* and the Agricultural Development Scheme was most successful in areas where this control was most firmly established.[18] (Italics mine.)

Shaykh and Effendi

Captain C. K. Daly, Chief Political Officer for the Diwaniyya district, which includes the Daghara region, speaks directly about the El Shabana:

> The Shabana, numbering about 1,500 fighting men, cultivate on the Shatt id-Daghara left bank, opposite Daghara town. Shaykh Sha'lan al Atiyah has the tribe well in hand, is popular, and has a high reputation for straightforwardness. He has been consistently well-behaved and helpful since the occupation.[19]

This report lists the other ashiras in the region and is consistently critical of their leadership. Sha'lan was the only shaykh who was fully approved.

Another administrator (unidentified, but perhaps Daly) in writing from the Diwaniyya district, says:

> I am very strongly of the opinion that it is sounder to leave the distribution [of water] from all except the main canals almost entirely to the Arabs themselves, even at the cost of a certain amount of waste to start with, rather than entrust it to subordinates who will certainly involve our administration in a great deal of odium.[20]

The utilization of what was presumed to be the traditional system of political controls in the cause of peace (and irrigation) was apparently born not only of practicality but also of pious hopes. The same writer remarks:

> With the establishment of the Pax Brittannica through the length and breadth of Iraq, the tribe will cease to be a necessity to the individual — he will live in peace and security and reap the fruit of his toil, not because he is a Bani Hasan or an Albu Sultan, but because he is a civis Brittanicus. Given a continuance of British government in Iraq, this process of disintegration of the tribal system cannot be long delayed; but meantime the tribe is as essential to the Government as it formerly was to the individual, and before the tribal system disappears it is to be hoped that the present Effendi class will have been replaced by officials selected from the best that both tribe and town has to give, and the "best" of the tribe should be very promising material.[21]

The tribal system never ceased to be "essential" to the British administration, and as of 1958, had not ceased to be useful to the administration of the Iraq government. Tribal codes persisted which included the shaykh in the official administrative policy; the surkals in the Daghara region were largely "appointed" by the shaykh at the insistence of the Government in order to have some-

138

one who could be held responsible from groups smaller than an ashira. As late as 1958, these men were called in by the mudir nahiya, when an investigation of some offense was under way or to cast a "fixed" ballot in the bogus elections held in the country.

How, then, did British officials exercise their duties in the light of their policy of "indirect rule"; how did practice compare with theory? Evidence suggests that some British administrators behaved in such a way as to acquire locally validated authority by taking an active part in local affairs in spite of the avowed policy of "indirect rule." The diary and letters of one British administrator in the mid-Euphrates area is at least suggestive of what *might* have occurred in the Daghara instance.

The record left by James Saumarez Mann (1893–1920) and edited by his father, is that of a young Oxford-trained Englishman, wounded in Europe during World War I and subsequently sent as a political officer to a remote area of Iraq (Shamiyya) in the service of the British Mesopotamian Forces. Shamiyya lies in the same province as Daghara, and is occupied by tribal farmers dependent on irrigation, principally for rice cultivation.

Mann's records, consisting of letters to his family and friends, are not the accounts of a deliberate, objective observer, nor is there any reason why they should be. Rather, they describe the frustration and prejudices of an outsider, isolated from his own countrymen and attempting to carry out duties foreign to himself and foreign to those with whom he was dealing. Principally, he was expected to keep the peace, and at the same time raise food production in order to avoid famine and provide a source of taxation. A great many of his problems were related to irrigation.

I have been having a terrific time lately, and on two or three occasions longed to be able to run away and hide. At times one really dreads to go into the office, and for four hours or so on end to have a stream of plaintiffs and defendants, one saying, "If this canal remains open, all my crops will be ruined, *but* I will obey your orders"; and the other, "If this canal be closed, I shan't get any crops at all, *but* I await your orders and will obey them" — and then one has to give one's orders! [22]

Another time, he records:

During my hearing of a quarrel the other day between a shaykh and one of his relatives, the latter said to him, "Well you are the father of

139

the tribe, and you ought to . . ." etc., "No, no," saith the shaykh, "the A.P.O. is our father, he is the father of the whole; and we are all his obedient children." Today I was hearing another similar dispute in which both sides were trying to make a very favourable impression.
A: "Let the A.P.O. decide; his intellect is more powerful than ours;"
B: "More powerful than ours! Why, he has to govern all the people from Kifl to Shymiiya (forty miles) it must be that his intellect is more powerful than the intellects of all his subjects put together." To such remarks I duly ejaculate "Astaghfir Ullah," which means literally "I ask pardon of God," and is the polite way of acknowledging a compliment, and wish I had someone with whom to laugh over these humours.[23]

Not all of the disputes which came to his attention could be resolved in his office. In many instances he was required to ride out to inspect irrigation works and settle tribal disputes on the spot. On one such trip he noted that the dispute he was required to settle had, in 1913, resulted in an inter-tribal fight between the Fatla and the Humaydat ashiras, during which thirty-five men had been killed. The nexus of the dispute lay in whether a certain local canal should or should not be opened for irrigation by the Humaydat. In a letter describing a typical day's work, Mann notes a less dramatic but typical irrigation problem:

I rode to see a place where one tribe wanted to dig a new head to an irrigation channel in someone else's land. He of course protested loudly that he would be ruined, and talked very loudly and very stupidly; and after a fruitless argument and a fairly close inspection, I turned him down and gave them leave to carry on, subject to some fairly strict guarantees in the interest of the owner of the land. There is a day's work for you.[24]

Because of the nature of the writings, it is only possible, through quotations, to suggest the character of Mann's work and the way he went about it. What is obvious is that he did not by any means leave all local decisions up to the shaykhs, but was both available as a source of appeal from shaykhly judgments and made many decisions entirely on his own account. Of his relationship to the shaykh and surkal, he says:

Of the 30 per cent that we take [from agricultural produce] we repay to all shaykhs and surkals three per cent on the whole (leaving our net takings only 27%), as a kind of reward for punctual payment and general good behaviour, and in return we bind them over to arrest criminals and do the public works that we from time to time require of them. This latter arrangement, while in principle very bad for a lot of reasons too complicated to explain, is exceedingly useful at times, and certainly strengthens our hold on the head men.[25]

In speaking of a visit to a tribal gathering upon the death of their shaykh:

His sons are quite the nastiest people in Shamiyah, and are quarrelling bitterly about the inheritance . . . besides which there is great rivalry as to who will be the next shaykh, an appointment which lies in my hands.[26]

The entire account of Mann's experience in the Shamiyya district shows that a great percentage of his time was taken up in the settlement of tribal disputes, stemming not only from his own program of public works but also from the traditional segmentary opposition of tribal groups. This is a state of affairs which might have been hypothesized from what has already been stated. To the degree that the traditional basis of shaykhly authority, and in fact the basis for achieving the status of shaykh, had been eliminated, the judgments of the shaykh began to have increasingly less force. Now it was the political officer (who was given the Arabic name *Hakim,* which means the "giver of decisions") to whom individuals and groups turned for the settlement of disputes, and not in all cases because they were forced to do so. Mann cites one apparently common situation:

As an example of a silly piece of trouble of a kind aroused daily by our double position as supporters of the tribal system and at the same time lovers of justice, here is a case which has given me some annoyance. I have one tract of land occupied by pieces of several tribes, who before my time were invited and compelled to elect a shaykh to themselves. This they did, and the choice fell on a respectable harmless little man called Ali al Hasan Agha, a loyal subject but not a strong character, and of no special family or warlike claims. However, there he is, and as shaykh has to be supported.[27]

When no individual from any tribal section was permitted by circumstances to garner support of tribesmen through behavior which exhibited traditional virtues, it appears that tribesmen chose the most innocuous and least offensive individual. Such individuals exercised no real authority and essentially left the tribe without leadership. It was then the task of the British to support such men in the smallest details of daily life; the remainder of the story cited above tells how this shaykh came in to Mann for help in collecting a trifling debt from some fellow tribesman.[28]

Mann states in a letter to the *London Nation* "the force with which I govern my somewhat unruly subjects consists of thirty-six thoroughly unreliable native police; yet my orders are always carried out." [29] Mann goes on to say that this is probably because of the presence of the British armed forces in Baghdad. This could explain why his orders were obeyed; it does not explain why problems in increasing numbers were voluntarily brought to him for solution. It is possible that this latter development can be explained by the fact that, because of the active role he took in community life, Mann's power began to have the cast of socially validated authority. Certainly this development was limited; it would be unlikely that Mann was able or cared to meet local normative standards in all respects. Yet in his travels through his district he behaved with considerable courage, so far as can be judged from his account, and was quite scrupulous to avoid locally objectionable behavior. The account as a whole indicates that he developed a close personal following among some of the tribal groups, a following which supported him in a revolt in 1920 in which he was killed.

As a final observation concerning the role of the British administrator in southern Iraq, it is surprising to find as late as 1957 the reputation of men like Captain Daly (who was in the Daghara area) still bright among local tribesmen. Many stories were told about the courage and wisdom of Daly, and while he was ultimately recognized as an enemy, he was well respected as a man.

THE PRESENT GOVERNMENT AND THE IRRIGATION SYSTEM

The line of petitioners which formed outside the office of the British administrator requesting that he solve water disputes did not cease to form after the foreigners were replaced by Iraqi officials. Today the local irrigation engineer meets a group of tribesmen as he steps outside his door in the morning to go to his nearby office, and he must turn still other tribesmen out as he closes his door at the end of a day's work. After visits not only to the district irrigation office in Daghara, but also to many others throughout the Middle Euphrates area in the Hilla and Diwaniyya provinces, the impression is inescapable that the bulk of the irrigation engineer's work lies in attempting to adjust relations between his fellow men.

Most of the irrigation engineer's clients want more water. But the way in which they want the water varies considerably. In some cases men want their water supply increased directly from the government canal; in such common instances they see the granting or denial of their requests as a feature of their relationship to the Government, not to their neighbors or distant users of the canal who in each case would be affected only very slightly by a single increase. In other situations, men want more water at the expense of their neighbors through a redistribution of the water they may share. Whatever the nature and ultimate disposition of the problem, the irrigation engineer is involved in a constant round of interpersonal relations in which, by persuasion and force, he must exercise his duty by equitably dividing the water available from government canals.

A fair picture of the range and content of irrigation problems which may face the engineer may be seen in the case histories presented in Appendix III. The case histories in Appendix III as well as the numerical analysis in Tables 16 and 17 are based almost entirely on the written records of the irrigation engineer and the mudir nahiya from 1953 to 1957. However, these petitions represent only the smallest fraction of the problems brought to both these men. To file a petition is both expensive and dangerous; it exposes those involved in the dispute to the possibility of fine or imprisonment. Probably 80 percent of the irrigation problems brought to the government are not formally presented by petition but rather are less formally recited to the engineer or administrator.

Many disputes still remain a matter of internal tribal politics and are not taken to the engineer. The tendency of men within a lineage to deny that a dispute exists or ever existed between themselves over irrigation or anything else has already been noted. When pressed, tribesmen reported that problems which could not be solved among themselves were taken to the shaykh; definitely

143

this was the socially preferable thing to do. However, such problems as were brought to the shaykh or to one of his wakils from men of the same fakhd or shabba were not loudly aired before the tribesmen and nontribesmen who might have been in the mudhif, but were privately discussed with the person chosen as muhakkim. Public discussion of a problem took place only when it involved a dispute between two different shabbas who shared the same pipe and the same non-governmental canal system; but, as has been seen, relatively few groups are in this position and the problems between them have been built into the situation for so long that more formal discussion hardly seemed worthwhile.[30]

The basic design of the irrigation system and the relation of tribal groupings generally precludes inter-ashira water disputes from occurring. The majority of those which do occur are between the individual larger landowners, mostly relatives of the shaykh. But, given the presumed decline in the authority of the shaykh, one might assume that more irrigation problems would have been taken voluntarily to the engineer in recent years than to the shaykh. Curiously enough, this was not demonstrably the case.

The shaykh is now prohibited from exhibiting the "personal charisma" with which shaykhly status is achieved; and tribesmen's attitudes toward the shaykh do not indicate that anything like a "routinization of charisma" has taken place, but tribesmen cultivators still do not decisively turn to a second power source, the government officials, with their problems.

Loyalty to the shaykh and belief in his authority does not constitute a feature of primary importance in the viability of the tribal organization. Rather, belief in customary practices which can only be exercised, in some cases, by going to the shaykh seems to be more important. The tribesmen conceive of themselves as set apart from and superior to the other members of the community. To make a public exhibition of disputes within the tribe over a trifling matter like water is definitely not socially sanctioned. This is not to say that disputes are *not* carried outside the tribe for arbitration; they *are* frequently taken to the government. But among the El Shabana, this is still definitely not approved behavior. Furthermore, traditional methods of settling traditional problems are in many cases preferred to the technical solutions of irrigation problems which the engineer might offer. There is some basis for saying that the shaykh today exercises the "traditionalist authority" of which Max Weber speaks, based on the "attitude-set for the habitual work-day and . . . the belief in the every-day routine as an inviolable norm of conduct." [31] "Inviolable" is, of course, too strong a term for this situation, but something of traditionalist authority still does appear today to attach to the role of the shaykh.

Despite the fact that airing water disputes is not yet socially sanctioned behavior among the El Shabana, and statistical evidence does not show a turn toward the engineer and away from the shaykh, other evidence suggests that this trend may in fact exist. The strongest indication stems from a conversation with the irrigation engineer, who volunteered the following observation:

When I first came here in 1953 I had to be careful to establish that I would not give more water to large owners in return for money. It was very difficult at first but fortunately the Chief Engineer in Diwaniyya agreed with me. However, in the last years many people have come to me with problems of "inside distribution" which are not my responsibility. They want me to look at "inside" canal systems and decide how the water should be divided. [Question: "Do you agree to do such work?"] Sometimes I agree; it depends on how I feel. However, if I do it too often I am afraid more and more will come and I already have too much work with the "outside" problems. [32]

Interestingly, the irrigation engineer was well respected in the Daghara area among all but the large landowners. It was with this man, of all the members of the local administration, that tribesmen had the closest contact. Tribesmen considered him *sharif* (honest) and gave him credit for being free from the influence of any of the local wealthy men. [33] But from the conversation quoted above, as well as later discussions, it became apparent that the engineer was not interested in regularly accepting more than his official responsibilities. He was overwhelmed by the number of tribesmen coming to him with requests and problems involving the distribution of water from government canals, and there was little to encourage him to increase the area of his responsibility by assuming new tasks of "internal distribution" which were not part of his official responsibility.

The mudir nahiya's official duties in Daghara also required him to hear complaints between users of water. When such complaints

145

came to him, he would frequently request the advice of the engineer, which the engineer would give if he were able to take time to look into the situation. It was, however, common practice for the mudir nahiya to ask the tribesmen to choose someone from the tribe to judge the dispute. Unless some clear infraction of the civil code had taken place and there was proof of the theft of water, for instance, it was much more convenient for the mudir nahiya to refer the problem back to the shaykh or another tribesman whom the petitioners might choose, than attempt to acquaint himself with the intricacies of some question of water distribution.

Thus both the engineer and the chief administrator resist making decisions which have previously been settled on a tribal level. There is no real reason why they should not do so. Their reference group is not tribal, but is constituted by other effendis like themselves. Since they are not subject to removal except by the action of the central government, small profit lies in developing a local following. Popularity among the local tribesmen is apparently not scorned, but since administrators tend to believe that they are the product of a social evolution which has placed them at a higher stage of development than the tribesmen, and since popularity among small landowners is without economic profit, any willingness to take on responsibilities beyond the duties of the office stems from something which, for lack of a more accurate explanation, might be termed altruism. That such altruism is not entirely lacking is apparent from such case histories as vii and xii in Appendix III. Case x, however, appears to illustrate a more common course of action.

The bulk of problems which come to the irrigation office stem from the simple desire for more water. The irrigation engineer reports a clear pattern: first, men want individual pipes into the government canal; then, after a year or so, they discover that they received more water when they were dividing with their neighbor the supply from a larger pipe,[34] and come to have the situation redressed.

Most "internal" canal systems are shared by a lineage or some section thereof; no amount of analysis of disputes will reveal whether this sharing is preferred or merely recognized as a practical necessity. Answers to questions about this situation always reflect ingroup solidarity, in the tribesmen's responses that it is

146

preferred to share a pipe "among one's brothers." Yet Table 16 indicates that requests for separate pipes do come from the members of the same shabba or fakhd. Any course of action which would bring the individuals and the group more water would undoubtedly be preferred, and without direct experience tribesmen might conclude that two pipes must be better than one. And there is some evidence testifying to the solidarity of the shabba with respect to irrigation disputes. The Elbu Ubayd shabba has suffered the problem described in Case XIV for several years, with one fakhd in effect denying a fair share of water to the other. Yet the answer to this problem was to petition the irrigation engineer for additional water; there was no indication that the deprived fakhd had ever considered making a civil issue out of the situation by asking the mudir nahiya to force the second fakhd to give them their share of water. When this course of action was suggested as a possibility, informants replied that living on good terms with their neighbors and relatives exceeded the value of the water.

With the advent of government control over major canals, the ashira or even larger inclusive groupings can no longer simply take water from the natural waterway according to their strength of arms. Recourse to self-help is denied and the government becomes the source of water. In a sense, it is the government which must be opposed, the irrigation engineer who by persistent effort may be persuaded to provide more water. This in itself is an almost revolutionary social change; instead of bold assertion by force of arms, the tribesmen have to seek the same ends by meekly petitioning and pleading with government officials. Coupling this fact with the attitudes of the effendis and their tendency to turn responsibility back on traditional tribal leaders, it is perhaps not surprising that considerable ambiguity appears in the patterns of local authority. The successful pacification and relative stability established in the Daghara area since 1922 have undermined the authority of the shaykh by eliminating the activities which he customarily led and in which he excelled. For several reasons, many tribesmen no longer pay allegiance to a shaykh. Yet the policy of the government has continued to encourage the shaykhs and force them to assume unaccustomed responsibilities. This, combined with the reluctance of local government officials to participate in tribal disputes, has certainly not encouraged tribesmen to look to the officials for leadership; nor, as we have seen, is the typical pattern of intercourse between effendis and tribesmen likely to result in such a development.[35]

On the other hand, it was clear that of all the effendis with whom the tribesmen had contact, the engineer was the most respected. He himself often remarked that the tribesmen came to him for advice about many things other than irrigation — particularly problems about dealing with other sections of the government. The development of socially validated authority for the engineer among the cultivators of the Daghara district may still have been too nebulous a phenomenon to pinpoint with a chosen set of statistically based indexes during the 1956–58 period. But the conviction remains that indeed such a process was occurring. From listening to scores of interviews in the engineer's office I concluded that many cultivators realized his decisions to provide or not to provide additional water did not stem from personal willfulness. The rational technical grounds upon which the engineer made his decision were coming to be recognized and respected.

The question of the national government's role in relation to irrigation and social organization cannot be closed without mentioning an ecological result. Adding the government-controlled Hurriyya canal with its north and south branches to the main Daghara canal in effect decentralized the irrigation system of the El Shabana. The addition of the Hurriyya system to the Daghara, the one natural waterway from which tribesmen took water directly or ran canals, means that a larger area now has direct access to water. Furthermore, improvement in the headworks of the Daghara canal has increased the supply of summer water. One might presume that this would have an altogether salutary effect on local agriculture. Yet this has not been the case. In the past, the canals constructed by the tribesmen did not hold water all year. They were filled by the use of temporary dams in the Daghara, and when the cultivation cycle did not require water the canals were allowed to drain, a vital process for this low-lying soil as it permitted excess water to drain from the land. Today, the improvements in the irrigation system have resulted in keeping the Daghara at high supply (in other words, filled with water to its full capacity) for a longer period of the year than ever before, as well as maintaining a supply of water in the Huriyya system. No period of drainage takes place. While the potential for greater summer cultivation has been increased, the side effects of the increased water supply have been disastrous. This appears to be the major reason for the salting and waterlogging of El Shabana land over the past twenty years. Tribesmen report they had not noticed the accumulation of salt until the later 1930's and early 1940's. The decentralization of the canal system and maintenance of water at high level has meant that the Daghara canal can no longer act both as a supplier of water in high water season, and a drainage canal in low season. Local irrigation engineers and Baghdad officials agree that under a regime of yearly cultivation, the Daghara area would eventually have developed areas of salination whether or not the decentralization of the permanent water supply had taken place. However, the fact is that the introduction of large-scale coordinated irrigation works, more massive and technically complex than local tribal organizations might have achieved, has been a mixed blessing.

The agricultural future of the Daghara area is now problematic. Attempts to increase the intensity of cultivation through the persistent application of water to the land in both summer and winter will only increase the rate of salination, a condition which, according to local estimates, has already taken half the land within reach of water out of production. Increasing numbers of local tribesmen-cultivators have been forced to abandon their smallholdings and seek employment elsewhere. Thus the most significant result of government-controlled irrigation may, in a sense, stem from this unforeseen ecological consequence. Unless the deleterious by-products of these improvements are counteracted by further improvements, particularly investment in a large-scale drainage system, the social effects of government control will be to help undermine the agricultural economy of the region. Unfortunately, reports of preliminary engineering studies suggest the expense of installing an adequate drainage system could hardly be justified on economic grounds. Thus, the greater technical efficiency of modern irrigation functionaries like Mann or the Iraqi engineer, though effective in increasing their authority at the expense of traditional leadership, in the end may prove self-defeating.

VIII

Shaykh and Effendi

In the preceding chapters I have tried to provide an ethnographic description of the El Shabana and the town of Daghara. I have also tried to analyze certain problems associated with (1) the increasing involvement of the central government in local affairs, and (2) the subsequent loss of tribal autonomy. The construction and operation of the irrigation system has been used as a case in point. Comparing the roles of the tribal shaykh and the government irrigation engineer reveals the increasing importance of the effendi and the dwindling significance of the shaykh in local affairs. Through control of the irrigation system, the effendi engineer has established himself as a local authority in tribal disputes. On the other hand, the shaykh remains a figure of importance, in part because of his distinguished personal history, but also because of his prestige and influence as an intermediary between tribesman and government.

Decline of tribal authority with respect to irrigation is the end product of changes in tribal organization and authority structure which began during the last quarter century of Ottoman rule in Iraq. Traditional tribal political processes were gradually undermined; first by the registration, in the name of the shaykhs, of land which had customarily been regarded as the domain of the entire tribe; and second by the British authorities' subsequent recognition of and support for particular tribal leaders. In the past, limited centralized authority within the tribe had been reconciled with the decentralizing tendencies inherent in segmentally structured tribal organizations by the ever-present possibility of revolution, replacing a shaykh from one lineage with a man from another section of the tribe. Both this "instability" and the opportunity and need for the shaykh to develop and exhibit the charismatic qualities upon which his authority was based, ceased to

150

exist with the pacification of the countryside and the recognition and wealth which the central government provided for the incumbent shaykhs.

As a case study of these developments, the El Shabana and the Daghara region are somewhat exceptional. Prior to the 1958 revolution, many individual tribesmen continued to own sections of the tribal lands in their own right. The shaykh did not enjoy the near-monopoly of land ownership characteristic of such men in other regions of southern Iraq. Furthermore, the pattern of continued rebellion against the authority of the central government was expressed as recently as the 1930's by the tribes of this region; this provided an opportunity for the shaykh of the El Shabana, as a young man, to exhibit the traditional virtues of courage and skill in battle.

Perhaps it is because of the thoroughly legitimate basis of the incumbent shaykh's authority among the tribesmen that the contradiction is so sharp between the local cultural model of the tribal organization and the socio-economic reality: the cultural model is described by the tribesmen themselves as an equalitarian tribal organization, with the shaykh an equal among equals; the reality is a stratified tribal organization with the shaykh and his family in a clearly superior position vis-à-vis the remainder of the tribe.

While tribal organization and authority have been of major interest, the context in which I have described this situation provides evidence with which to consider other, related, problems of equal or greater consequence. I have tried, for instance, to stress the vitality and adaptability of the traditional tribal organization within the ecological context of this region. The Arab tribe has customarily been regarded as an acephalous social organization, almost by definition incapable of more than sporadic cooperative effort for common defense and offense. Yet both the direct evidence of observers and the indirect evidence of trade records suggest that the tribes both could and did make considerable fixed capital investment in their lands in the form of dikes and canals, transforming their domains into areas of sustained agricultural production. True, the authority by which the shaykhs were able to sustain and control such peaceful endeavors seems to have required opportunities for demonstrating traditional qualities of leadership in wars and raids. However, the extensive, centrally organized

151

irrigation efforts of large tribal confederations like the Muntafiq, suggest considerable administrative potential within the changing patterns of tribal organization.

Furthermore, I have tried to emphasize that there was a congruence or fit between traditional tribal methods of cultivation and land tenure, and the nature of the land, water, and climate in southern Iraq. The tendency of this land to become saline under conditions of intensive use was avoided under tribal control when fluctuating supplies of water limited cultivation to a single harvest each year and tribesmen were encouraged to shift about the areas under cultivation, leaving sections fallow for a year or more at a time. Even under contemporary conditions, the agronomical study cited in Chapter III clearly suggests there are two situations which result both in the highest income levels for individual cultivators and sustained yields from the land: large units of land under cultivation, permitting strict fallowing and family economics based on a combination of cultivation and animal husbandry. This calls into serious question both the desirability of year-round high water supplies, made possible through the techniques and capital utilized by the central government, and the long-term wisdom of conventional agrarian reform as a solution to the political and social ills of this region. Without drainage systems to match irrigation works, and without management of land ownership in such a way as to permit fallowing and the local cooperation necessary among sharers of an irrigation system, the reforms and technical improvements at the disposal of the national government may well prove more a curse than a blessing to the individual cultivator and to the economy of the country as a whole. Indeed, the contemporary situation in southern Iraq provides little cause for optimism in this regard.[1]

Yet, to return to my first point, it is clear that the dependence of southern Iraq on canal irrigation and the existence of experts to represent the central government in managing irrigation do provide a basis for the transition of authority from traditional leaders to a national entity. Civil servant effendis like the irrigation engineer, who have technical knowledge, and who carry out their tasks with honesty and with regard for local standards of justice, provide, in effect, the growing edge of a positive involvement and interest in orderly national government on a very fundamental local level. Perhaps the experience of tribesmen in dealing with local officials who exercise responsibilities in accord with universally recognized standards of performance may encourage expectations of comparable behavior at higher levels of government. For a country like Iraq, where for centuries the central government has been associated with exploitation, this would represent an important change in grass roots expectations.

At the same time, if the government has at its service the means to legitimatize its position among the tribal people of Iraq, and thereby to transcend some of the parochial loyalties which have been so divisive a feature of national life, it must also examine the organizational and managerial aspects of tribalism in the light of its desire for economic growth. Scholars and statesmen have been quick to identify tribalism with reaction and to proclaim the necessity of western-style reforms. Yet as a substitute for tribalism, nationalism has not proved an unqualified success. The possibility of redirecting old loyalties and energies toward new nationally defined goals has yet to be explored.

In the Daghara region, patterns of authority seem to have developed gradually in response to ecological conditions which remain the same, even though social conditions may change. The old tribal politico-economic system, outmoded and inefficient as it may appear to have been, had within it checks and balances between the natural and social orders which developed through many centuries and which helped sustain the productivity of the region. In the rush of change for change's sake which often accompanies the emergence of a new nation, the old lessons, learned by bitter experience, are often brushed aside or ignored as remnants of a painful past. Surely central authority in the Middle Euphrates valley, if it is to insure healthy agricultural growth and to improve the individual farmer's standard of living, could profit from an imaginative examination of the indigenous solutions to the area's problems.

Appendixes   Notes   Bibliography   Glossary   Index

A Technical Description of Gravity-Flow Irrigation

Wherever men irrigate they conform to the limitations of ecological circumstance. Some of the problems of irrigation are universal: for example, a way must be found to divert water from its source to the field when it is needed, providing neither too much nor too little moisture. In assessing the systematic requirements which irrigation makes upon all populations, however, statements which fit all irrigation situations are so general as to be of little use in discussing a particular situation. Consider, for instance, the wide range of differences between irrigation dependent on springs, wells, mountain streams, rivers, marshes, or converted ocean waters. The basic requirement that water must be diverted to the crop-growing area would be met, in each case, by a widely differing technology with varying social implications. It is more to our purpose to examine the particular conditions underlying irrigation in the Mesopotamian basin, and especially that portion of the basin watered by the Euphrates river.

There are several areas with differing methods of water use in southern Mesopotamia, including regions now irrigated by pumps and by tidal flow, as well as sections irrigated through gravitational-flow canals. It is the latter method which was predominant in most of historic southern Mesopotamia, and my discussion will concentrate on that method. The flow canal is presently the most general method of irrigation in the Daghara area.

The Daghara canal has been transformed from a bifurcation of a river, dependable within wide limits as a supply of water, subject to seasonal variation. For it alone to be utilized as a source of irrigation water, what is necessary? The water must flow from the river and onto the land. If the river had flood seasons and, as in the case with the Nile, the seasons complemented the growing periods, the farmer would have no more to do than plant his crops and let the river water them.

However, in the Middle Euphrates basin, water is in short supply just at the peak of the growing seasons for both winter and summer

157

crops. As Hassan M. Ali notes: "Much of the flow of the twin rivers occurs in the spring too late to benefit winter crops and too early for summer crops."[1]

The winter crop of barley is planted in September or early October and harvested in January; wheat is planted in November and harvested in February.[2] Summer crops, which grow better than winter plantings when water is available, are seeded from early April till the end of May and harvested in early fall.[3] However, the water supply in the Euphrates river begins to increase in November and swells throughout the winter; the maximum supply tends to occur during the last two weeks of April and the first two weeks of May.

Since the flood season does not coincide beneficially with the growing season, what alternatives are available to the farming population? (1) They can be content to farm in other than optimal irrigation periods. (2) They can utilize marsh areas and other depressions where water collects in flood season, farming in and around the edges of such regions, manipulating the water through simple ditches and dams. (3) They can attempt to control the flooding, using bunds and dams, sustaining the water supply over a period of time to facilitate flow irrigation from the river.

What conditions are imposed on a farming population who would choose one or another of the above possibilities? Farming at non-optimal times or around the edges of catch basins or marshes involves perhaps the most minimal of special efforts to utilize available water. The amount of land which can be cultivated under such conditions, however, is relatively limited; nor does planting a speculative crop and counting on late rains or a longer-than-average high river water supply encourage extensive agricultural development.

The third choice noted above poses additional problems which are closely related to the nature of the Euphrates river system. The twin rivers of Mesopotamia, after they enter the alluvial plain above Baghdad, are in an unstable regime. Simply stated, the scouring action and the silting action of the rivers are not in equilibrium. The heavy silt content of the rivers, due in large part to the erosion in the headwaters area of the rivers and the consequent muddy run-off of snow and rain water, tends to raise the level of the river beds as it settles in the courses of the rivers. Characteristically in an alluvial basin, the rivers tend to be above the level of the surrounding countryside. The processes of scouring in one place and depositing a relatively greater amount of silt in another are in large part responsible for the fact that the river may alter its course from time to time either as a whole body of water or in terms of several bifurcations. Also, the annual supply of water in the rivers varies widely from year to year. Ahmed Sousa notes that in 1939 the combined river supply of the Tigris and Euphrates was "as low as 22,000 million cubic meters while that of 1941 rose to about 80,000 million." [4] A riverine farming population must face certain facts: their section of the river system may eventually rise to overflow its banks, or change course as a result of the gradual local accumulation of silt; and their river may supply flood waters one year and a dearth of water the next. Local measures can do little about drought, but local farmers can exert a simple measure against floods which will have the desirable secondary effect of helping to maintain a longer supply of irrigation water in an average supply year, after the flood peak has passed.

The "simple measure" involves the following steps, undertaken by the local population: from year to year the cultivators build up the banks of the river (or its natural bifurcation), perhaps motivated by a desire to protect their homes and fields from the full force of the flood season. The effect of this is to control the supply of water for free-flow or gravity canal irrigation. For, with higher banks, the annual deposit of silt may eventually raise the river level. Even a slight difference in the height of the river — which is naturally higher than the basin through which it passes — will mean that for a longer period in the seasonal rise of river water, the surrounding land may be deliberately flooded. Thus water will be available for irrigation sooner in the onset of the flood season and longer after the peak has passed. Irrigating from the waterway may be accomplished by merely breaking the river bank at some point, and allowing the water to flow over into adjacent fields. The use of temporary dams and levees will also help to force water over river banks and onto surrounding fields. Given a gradual slope of land away from the riverway, water will flood for considerable distance without the use of canals. Furthermore, water can be passed from field to field without ditches or canals. This is accomplished by surrounding the field with low mud walls and opening and closing temporary breaches in these walls to permit water to flow from one field to the next. In the middle Euphrates region this method is commonly used both with and without canals; water may irrigate several small enclosed plots of land and finally pass into an adjacent plot which is fallow for the year. (The fallow system in this area does not involve the setting aside of great sections of land; rather, small fallow plots frequently alternate with planted plots. In this way, fallow land serves as an outlet for water after it has been used for irrigation.)

Ditching may be necessary for one or more of several reasons. General flooding of the countryside by damming may damage households situated along the waterway. Also, in flooding, the land lying closest to the canal always is watered when water is supplied to more outlying fields; this excess water often waterlogs and salinates the soil, rendering the land closest to the waterway unfit for cultivation. Ditching or canalization not only avoids these pitfalls but increases the total area of land which may be cultivated and allows greater control of the distribution of water during irrigation.

The most obvious and most important feature of canal usage is that the canal is man-made. Unlike the mere use of the river-way, considerable labor must underlie canal utilization, and the maintenance of the canal will be a constant problem. The activities of the farmer occupying land at the head of the canal will affect the farmers at the tail of the canal much more than was the case on the natural waterway. The physical effect of canalization is to decentralize the water system. If the purpose of the canal is to transport water through uncultivable lands, then presumably its users will be equally interested in keeping the head of the canal free from silt. If, however, the canal is fully utilized from its head to tail regions, the canal users near the head will be less interested in cleaning the canal than those near the tail. What is the reason for this? Paradoxically, the reason lies in the fact that more silt is deposited near the head of the canal than at its tail.

The amount of silt carried by a stream is a function of the velocity of the current as well as the size of the waterway. As water enters a canal from a river, there is an immediate drop in velocity. That percentage of silt which was supported by the differential of size and speed of the parent stream — as compared with the canal — immediately begins to settle to the bottom of the canal where the water enters. If this silt is not regularly cleared away, the total amount of water entering the canal gradually declines. The water level at the head of the canal will remain at the same level as the parent stream. However, if silt is blocking the head area of the canal, the total amount of water entering the canal becomes less and the water level falls at the tail of the canal. In flow irrigation the water level is crucial; it is of little consequence that water remains in the bottom of the canal if it is not high enough to flow out into furrows or distributory canals by force of gravitation. This is the main reason why, in contemporary irrigation, water is often made to flow out of a canal through a pipe sunk in the canal wall below the normal water level; water pressure is thus increased and the water level can sink further (without failing to flow onto the fields) than would be the case if water were taken from the top of the canal bank.

If we imagine independent farmers up and down the length of a canal, each responsible for the cleaning of an equal section, it is clear that those near the canal head will have more silt to remove, with less consequent personal advantage, than those near the tail. The men who irrigate land in the head area of the canal will regularly have a larger amount of silt to clean from their section, silt which is responsible for decreasing their downstream neighbor's water supply, but which causes no personal hardship to the men in whose territory it has settled.

Thus farmers near the head of a canal may have a plentiful water supply, while, because such farmers have neglected to clean the canal, farmers nearer the tail may be without irrigation water. Even if downstream farmers are willing to come up to the head section of the canal and clean it, upstream irrigators must agree to the temporary closure of the canal so that the cleaning may take place.

A further condition of canal usage gives yet another advantage to those cultivators utilizing the canal nearest its head. If a canal is fully used, that is, if it irrigates land along its entire length, the combined outlets of the canal may exceed the capacity of the canal inlet. Thus various outlets must be used alternately or the water level of the canal will fall and only those near the head will be able to use it. If a water shortage exists, those irrigators near the head have the option of blocking the canal so that the water level near their land is maintained at the expense of the down-stream cultivators.

These technical considerations define the conditions under which an irrigation system can be utilized if it includes artificial as well as natural waterways. Sufficient agreement must exist between the farmers at both the head and tail of the canal to insure that enough work is done at the head of the canal to provide water for the tail-region cultivators. This will, of course, necessitate more work than is necessary to utilize the canal at its head. There must also be accommodations between upper and lower canal populations concerning the times of water withdrawal. If a canal is to provide the same amount of water to all its users, the nature of canal hydraulics requires that most of the concessions come from the population in the head region of the canal. And finally, any power absolutely controlling the head of a canal has the rest of the canal users at an ultimate disadvantage. Thus when artificial waterways develop, relationships of accommodation must also develop between their users.

We see, then, that farmers who do not have clearly indicated social relations among themselves could take water directly from a natural waterway and carry on successful cultivation. But as the number of canals which feed from a *natural* waterway increases, some problems of accommodation or conflict may develop between groups sharing the

161

same natural stream. Even temporary damming of the waterway in low flood season in order to increase the flow of water into the canal maintained by group X may seriously reduce the water supply for the canal belonging to group Y downstream. While it is not likely that this would be a great problem on the main branch of the Euphrates, the water consumption of one group has serious consequences for another on any of the smaller bifurcations of the river. A waterway supplying five or six cubic meters of water per second at its head and flowing several miles might provide an irrigation source for thousands of persons. These smaller natural waterways are more attractive to cultivators than the main branches of the Euphrates, since they provide a manageable source of water, even with a limited technology. Most of the larger canals in the central Euphrates area today now under the control of the national government (which has stabilized them by the use of dams, sluice gates, concrete embankments, and the like) were historically natural waterways to which improvements have been added.

The conditions of gravity-flow irrigation described have prevailed for thousands of years on water sources like the Daghara canal and in all similar areas of the Euphrates (and Tigris) rivers. Solutions to the problems posed by irrigation in these regions have emanated both from state-wide centralized authority systems and from local social systems, depending on what century or even decade one chooses to examine. The most recent decline of state-directed irrigation began in the eleventh and twelfth centuries and localized irrigation arrangements persisted in varying strength through the advent of British control at the end of World War I.[5] Since World War I, state direction of irrigation has steadily increased but local initiative is still important.

We do not know the size of the population which subsisted on grain crops grown during those periods in the last four hundred years when irrigation-based agriculture proceeded entirely without benefit of state control. It is clear, however, that local canalization continued and perhaps even prospered during this period. The effectiveness of cultivation by locally directed irrigation in southern Iraq must not be underestimated for this kind of cultivation may well have preceded and continued long after the advent of "high" civilizations with outstanding urban expressions in Mesopotamia.

A Technical Description of
the Government Canals in the Daghara Area
from which the El Shabana Tribe Takes Water[1]

The Daghara canal is part of the Hindiyah Barrage Canal systems, that is, it depends on the Hindiyah Barrage for its command level. The Hillah canal is the old course of Euphrates before what is now the Hindiyah branch had deepened and widened itself, leaving the Hillah channel almost high and dry. The Hindiyah Barrage was built primarily to remedy the effect of the change. The original Hillah canal head regulator was constructed in 1912–13 by Sir John Jackson Co. but proved unsuccessful. Work on the new Hillah canal head regulator was commenced on the 20th of April, 1932 and completed in October, 1933. The normal full supply level during the high rotation of the Hillah Canal is R.L. 31.40 — .50 (i.e., from 31.40 to 31.50 gage reading level, relative measurement) with an average discharge of 150 cu.m/sec. (cubic meters per second), while the normal supply level during the low turn (summer season) is about R.L. 30–40 ms. with an average discharge of 40 to 50 cu.m/sec. The Hillah canal is about 104 kilometers in length. It branches into the Daghara, Diwaniyah and Hurriyah canals. The gross area within the irrigation boundary of the canal is about 1,000,000 mesharas of which a total commanded area of about 860,000 mesharas is actually under cultivation, including garden areas. There are also ten pump installations on the canal for irrigation purposes, irrigating about 10,000 mesharas which are mostly planted in gardens. The Diwaniyah branch leading off from the tail of the Hillah is the old course of the Euphrates, its length from head to tail (at Gat'ah, the Abu Sukhair bifurcation in the Shaymiia area) being approximately 124 kilometers. The main towns on the banks are Khan Jadwal, Diwaniyah, Imam Hamza and Rumaitha. In 1942, the number of pumps on the Diwaniyah branch totalled 160, total horsepower 5,784. The average lift is 6 meters, and the total protected area estimated at 430,000 mesharas, about half of

163

which is cultivated yearly with shitwi crops. Also an area of about 180,000 mesharas, irrigatable by flow in the Rumaitha area at its tail, brings the total protected area to 610,000 mesharas, but no canal system existed at Rumaitha in 1941. Rotation of water takes place between the Diwaniyah branch and all others, the Daghara being provided only with drinking water during days of low supply. The full supply at Diwaniyah head is 40 cu.m/sec.

THE DAGHARA BRANCH

The Daghara branch is about 77 kilometers long. Main towns along the banks are Daghara, 19 kilometers from the head; and Bedair, 77 kilometers from the head. The Daghara head regulator was built at the same time as the Diwaniyah canal head regulator. During high rotation, there is an average discharge of 22 cu.m/sec.; at low turn, just enough for drinking. Due to the silting up of the Daghara, the discharge at its head has declined from 35 cu.m/sec. in 1928 to 13 cu.m/sec. in 1940, with gauge reading of 22.85. It has thus become necessary to gradually raise the supply level to obtain the required discharge . . . Cultivation on the canal has been reduced commensurately with the reduction in required discharge during the last 15 years, by putting the area which used to be irrigated from the left bank on to a recently-dug canal known as the Hurriyah Canal. Thus deterioration of the channel due to silting has not as yet contributed to any appreciable reduction of the total area under cultivation. The present area depending on flow from the Daghara is estimated at 165,000 mesharas, while the pump area is about 35,000 mesharas. In 1942, there were 12 pumps on the Daghara, with a horsepower of 434. The average lift of 3 meters makes the total 200,000 mesharas.

THE HURRIYAH CANAL OR LEFT DAGHARA CANAL

The Hurriyah Canal takes off from the left bank of the Hillah Canal immediately upstream from the Daghara head, and irrigates the lands situated on the left bank of the Daghara branch to a distance of 25 kilometers from the head. It consists of a main channel of about 6 kilometers in length, and two branches, the northern branch, 18 kilometers long and the southern branch, 24 kilometers long. Work on the canal was started in 1935 and completed in 1942 at an estimated cost of ID 22,000. Both the main and northern canals were completed and opened in 1937, and the southern branch opened on December 12, 1942. The area commanded by the canal is as follows: main canal: 3,000 mesharas; northern branch, 57,000 mesharas; southern branch, 38,000; total: 98,000 mesharas. The full supply design of the head regulator is 9 cu.m/sec., but in fact it passes 11 cu.m/sec.

Estimated total average of areas cultivated yearly (shitwi — winter cultivation):

on the Euphrates	1,140,000 mesharas
on the Tigris	550,000 mesharas
on the Zab	50,000 mesharas
on the Diyalah	470,000 mesharas
total winter crop land under cultivation in Iraq	2,210,000 mesharas

Estimated total crop areas in Daghara region:

Winter crops (shitwi)	130,000 mesharas
Summer crops (sayfi)	
Rice 7,000	
Other 15,000	22,000 mesharas
Total land under cultivation (winter and summer) in Daghara area	152,000 mesharas

Selected Examples of Irrigation Problems Brought Through Formal Petition to the Office of the Daghara Irrigation Engineer and the Office of the Daghara Mudir Nahiya, 1952–57

CASE I

Sayid Nam'a ibn Sayid Hassan wished to move his pipe to another location. The engineer wrote to the mudir nahiya because other men are on this same pipe. The mudir nahiya replied that he had found the other men had no objection to this move.

CASE II

The shaykh of the El Shabana protested the practice of cleaning the north branch canal by machinery and taking contributions from the tribesmen to pay for this. The users at the tail of the north branch are large owners who are not members of the El Shabana and who pre-ferred to pay; the El Shabana preferred to contribute their labor to cleaning by hand. The latter course was followed.

CASE III

The Irrigation Directorate informed the users of the south branch that they must clean the canal. This took 500 men 20 days to remove ap-proximately 20,000 cubic meters of mud. This has to be done about every four years.

CASE IV

A group of ten Sada composed of brothers and paternal male cousins wished to have another group of Sada removed from the first group's pipe. The latter group also petitioned for an individual pipe. The request was not granted.

CASE V

El Hakam and El Ghrush, two shabbas of the El Shabana, filed a joint petition which included the signatures of from 30 to 40 men, asking that they be provided with (a) more water, and (b) individual pipes for each shabba. This same request has been made for five years but has never been granted for technical reasons related to the position of the land and the available water supply.

CASE VI

The engineer noted a series of petitions protesting the closing of the Hurriyya canal for purposes of cleaning. He remarked that this is typical every time the question of closing canals for cleaning comes up: the users at the head of the canal protest the cleaning and those at the tail request it. This is because the users at the head of the canal are not suffering from lack of water as the deposit of silt, though decreasing the total amount of water entering the canal, has resulted in the water level remaining stable near the head. However, because the deposit of silt is less toward the tail, the users near the tail have experienced a fall in water level and thus cannot fill their canals and receive their apportioned supply.

CASE VII

The irrigation engineer discovered that El Hillalat were stealing water from the government canal near their land. He informed the mudir nahiya, and through police action the mudir nahiya forced the El Hillalat to cease. A year later, after he had inspected their situation, the irrigation engineer increased their supply even though they had been receiving the amount to which they were technically entitled. He said that he did this because the Hillalat cultivators held farms from about 10 to 40 masharas in size and about 50 families lived on this land. Since the normal supply of water was sufficient to irrigate only one third of this land, this meant that some families were totally unable to cultivate. He said, "This decision was not from a technical point of view; it simply seemed fair and necessary." The chief engineer from the district agreed.

CASE VIII

The El Shidayda shabba of the El Shabana petitioned, claiming an uncle of the shaykh was taking more water than he was entitled to from a pipe which they all share.

CASE IX

Khadim el Abays of El Hamid and Raba el Raʿad of El Gharanim (not of El Shabana), who had previously asked for a separation of their water supply by two pipes, requested that their pipes be joined again, realizing, said the engineer, that a greater volume of water results from one fifteen centimeter pipe than from two seven-and-a-half centimeter pipes.

CASE X

Khadim el Jarid and Flayya el Hafid petitioned because they wished to have the canal which they share with 15 other men from their shabba cleaned, and the other men refused to contribute to the work. The petitioners are near the tail of the canal and those who refused to work are near the head. The mudir nahiya and the engineer sent for all the men of the shabba and asked them to choose a tribal muhakkim (judge) to decide their dispute. The men chose a wakil of the shaykh. This man refused to act as muhakkim on the basis of an excuse which showed, said the engineer, that he simply did not want to be involved. Another muhakkim was selected—a respected man from the Elbu Salih shabba of the El Shabana. An agreement was made to clean the canal in question. The engineer said that the mudir nahiya may have threatened jail to force such an agreement.

CASE XI

The users of the "shaykh's canal," including Shaykh Mujid and 13 other men, protested the closing of the canal for purposes of cleaning. The engineer noticed that all those protesting were upstream users; after finding that the users downstream on this private canal (three men) wished to have the canal cleaned because of a shortage of water, the engineer closed it, warning the petitioners that if the canal were not cleaned at this time, he would close it again and they would be short of water before the end of the agricultural season.

CASE XII

In October, 1956, it was necessary again to clean the south branch of the canal. The engineer knew that the last time this was done the El Shabana had been left to distribute the cleaning distances for each man according to tribal custom, and that certain problems had stemmed from this; individuals had protested to the government that they had received more to clean than was fair. For this reason, the engineer asked the mudir nahiya to call representatives from the El Shabana section to his office to find out if they wanted to continue to have the area per man assigned by the shaykh or if they wanted the government to assign cleaning according to the proportion of water taken by individuals and subgroups. All appeared at this meeting except a tribesman who had urged the engineer to assign the cleaning shares in the future! When the men assembled, all claimed that they wanted to clean the canal according to tribal custom, in spite of the engineer's suggestion that he would be willing to make the assignments. According to the engineer, the tribesmen distribute cleaning responsibilities according to the size of the pipes. This, he claims, is unfair to the small owners because the amount of water increases by the square of the pipe diameter. The engineer agreed that the men could continue to clean according to tribal wishes, provided they did not petition during the time of the cleaning. They did not petition. However, in 1957 a large group of small owners came to the engineer and said they wanted to clean the canal according to the amount of land cultivated (as the engineer had suggested) rather than according to the size of the pipe. The engineer agreed.

CASE XIII

Two small owners from El Jami'yyin petitioned, protesting that a fakhd of the Elbu Salih (both groups are from the El Shabana) was ditching water across their land and, because of salination and water-logging, ruining it for cultivation. The men from the Elbu Salih claimed that they had been taking water in this way for ten years. The case was not settled in the irrigation office and the engineer believes that the eldest brother of the El Shabana shaykh resolved the problem between these men.

CASE XIV

The men from the Elbu Najim fakhd, Elbu Ubayd shabba, had been petitioning for three years to be allowed to take water from the Hur-riyya canal. Their land lay between the Daghara and Hurriyya canals. This shabba had one major supply pipe from the Daghara, but to reach the land of the Elbu Najim, the water must pass through the land of the Elbu Muhammad fakhd. This latter group had reduced the total flow of water so that their land would not be so waterlogged. The Elbu Najim therefore had no water for cultivation, but petitioned to be given water from the government canal (El Hurriyya) lying closest to their land. The engineer could not permit this as the El Hurriyya canal water was fully scheduled and because the Elbu Ubayd had a full quota of water from the Daghara. The Elbu Najim could ask the government to force the Elbu Muhammad to give them their share of water, but they would not do this, preferring to let land stand idle.

APPENDIX IV

Tables

Table 1. Land and population.

	Tenants on large holdings	Tenants on medium holdings	Farm owners	Communal Farms	Owners on date orchards	Tenants on date orchards
Total gross area	575,800[a]	350,300	201,400	64,800	9,900	28,000
Waste lands	301,500	171,500	112,800	26,600	100	3,100
Farm lands	274,300	178,800	88,600	38,200	9,800	24,900
Average size fertile holding	66	53	32	32	5	13
Total population[b]	24,520	21,587	18,546	7,158	14,308	14,554
Population density per sq. km.	17	25	36	44	571	210
Average no. persons per holding	5.9	6.4	6.7	6.0	7.3	7.6
Percentage total farmland	44.6%	29.1%	14.4%	6.2%	1.6%	4.1%
Percentage total population[a]	24.4%	21.4%	18.4%	7.1%	14.2%	14.5%

Source: A. P. G. Poyck, Farm Studies in Iraq, composite of Tables 4.3 and 4.4, p. 35.
[a] one meshara equals 0.62 acres.
[b] Agriculturalists only.

Table 2. Cropping pattern in mesharas of land.[a]

	Land owned per family	Land farmed as tenants	Winter crops	Summer crops	Orchards	Fallow land	Waste or idle lands	Land not annually fallowed (%)
Large holdings	—	66	32.6	4.6	0.4	33	—	2
Medium holdings	—	53	29.7	4.7	0.3	23	—	20.6
Farm owners	48	6	22.3	2.3	1.7	14	16	31.6
Communal farms	36	12	24.4	2.4	0.6	20	4	—[b]
Owners on date orchards	8	8	5.0	1.0	4.0	5	2	—[b]
Tenants on date orchards	19	—	6.0	1.0	7.0	6	—	—[b]

Source: A. P. G. Poyck, Farm Studies in Iraq, composite of Tables 4.12 and 4.19, pp. 57, 65.
[a] In every category of holding a small amount of land is cropped every year, both winter and summer (from 4.7 to 1 meshara) which accounts for the discrepancies between cols. 1 and 2 and cols. 3 through 7.
[b] No data available for communal farms. Of course date orchards cannot be fallowed.

Table 3. Average yields of crops in kilos per meshara and percentage of total farmland devoted to selected crops.

	Tenants on large holdings		Tenants on medium holdings		Farm owners	
Wheat	214	14.2%[a]	221	14.9%	128	9.9%
Barley	224	30.2%	223	38.2%	174	47.1%
Broad beans	175	—[c]	208	—	—	—
Cotton	202	—	208	—	132	—
Orchards (dates)	903	0.4%	843	1.0%	710	4.4%
Rice	278	3.6%	268	5.9%	211	8.5%
Winter fallow		49.1%		39.0%		31.2%
Summer fallow		93.3%		87.4%		85.1%
Rotation factor[b]		.58%		.74%		.84%

Source: A. P. G. Poyck, *Farm Studies in Iraq* adopted and composited from Table 4.6, p. 40, and Table 4.7, p. 48.

[a] Note that percentages will not total 100% because a) not all data are given and b) table includes both summer and winter crops, though summer crops are only a small fraction of total (see "Summer fallow").

[b] Rotation factor: $R = \dfrac{\text{mesharas crop harvested per year}}{\text{gross meshara farmland}}$.

[c] No data available.

Appendix IV

Table 4. Average number of livestock per farm.

Regions	Horses	Mules	Donkeys	Cows	Calves	Sheep	Lambs	Goats	Kids	Buffalo	Poultry	Average number of mesharas per farm unit
Large holdings	0.8	—	1.8	2.1	1.1	12.2	3.8	2.0	0.6	0.1	4.6	66.0[a]
Medium holdings	0.5	0.1	1.3	1.7	1.0	9.6	3.1	1.4	0.3	—	4.8	53.0[a]
Farm owners	0.7	—	0.8	1.3	0.7	6.2	2.2	0.8	0.3	—	4.3	48.0[b]
Communal farms	0.7	—	1.0	1.5	0.9	8.5	2.9	1.8	0.6	—	3.9	36.0[b]
Owners of date orchards	0.1	—	0.8	1.5	0.6	2.2	—	1.4	—	—	4.7	8.0
Tenants on date orchards	0.5	—	0.8	1.3	0.6	4.5	—	—	—	—	2.9	19.0[a]

Source: A. P. G. Poyck, Farm Studies in Iraq, Table 4.13, p. 59.
[a] These are tenant farms within the landholding.
[b] This does not include rented land.

Table 5. Income per farmer in Iraqi dinars per year by region.

	Tenants on large holdings		Tenants on medium holdings		Farm owners		Communal farms		Owners on date orchards		Tenants on date orchards	
Gross Income												
		%		%		%		%		%		%
Winter crops	77.0	46.6	77.6	48.8	43.5	43.3	50.4	44.0	19.6	26.9	12.5	16.1
Summer crops	23.2	13.9	35.2	22.1	16.6	16.5	12.6	10.9	7.7	10.5	24.5	31.6
Orchards	1.1	0.7	1.0	0.6	3.9	3.8	1.0	0.9	15.4	21.0	13.5	17.4
Meat	13.2	7.9	11.1	7.0	7.8	7.7	11.2	9.7	4.3	5.9	5.2	6.7
Milk	45.6	27.6	29.9	18.8	25.2	25.1	35.6	31.0	23.2	31.8	19.6	25.2
Wool, hair, eggs	5.4	3.3	4.3	2.7	3.4	3.6	3.9	3.5	2.9	3.9	2.3	3.0
Total gross income	165.5	100.0	159.1	100.0	100.4	100.0	114.7	100.0	73.1	100.0	77.6	100.0
Exploitation Costs												
		%		%		%		%		%		%
Seeds	10.4	6.3	12.0	7.5	7.6	7.6	8.2	7.1	2.8	3.8	3.3	4.2
Imputed costs[a]	14.7	9.0	13.7	8.6	9.6	9.6	13.6	11.8	7.5	10.1	6.5	8.2
Taxes	0.5	0.3	0.6	0.4	0.2	0.2	0.1	0.1	—	—	0.4	0.5
Hired labor	0.2	0.1	0.8	0.5	1.5	1.5	0.9	0.8	2.1	2.9	0.3	0.3
Hired services	7.9	4.7	7.5	4.7	5.0	4.9	5.3	4.6	0.4	0.5	0.9	1.1
Rent	53.1	31.4	61.7	38.7	5.1	5.1	11.7	10.2	6.2	8.4	19.5	25.1
Total costs	86.8	52.3	96.3	60.4	29.0	28.9	39.8	34.6	19.0	25.7	30.9	39.4
Net income	78.7	47.7	62.8	39.6	71.4	71.1	74.9	65.4	54.1	74.3	46.7	60.6

Source: A. P. G. Poyck, *Farm Studies in Iraq*, Table 4.17, p. 64.

[a] Including depreciation of tools and work animals, and imputed charge for fodder grown on fallow land.

Table 6. Income from crops compared with income from livestock as percentages of gross income per region.

	Tenants on large holdings	Tenants on medium holdings	Farm owners	Communal farmers	Owners on date orchards	Tenants on date orchards
Gross income from crops	61.2	71.5	63.6	55.8	58.4	65.1
Gross income from livestock	38.8	28.5	36.4	44.2	41.6	34.9
Exploitation costs and rent for crops	45.4	54.0	22.5	25.2	17.6	33.6
Exploitation costs and rent for livestock	6.9	6.4	6.4	9.1	8.1	5.8
Net income:						
from crops	15.8	17.5	41.1	30.6	40.8	31.5
from livestock	31.9	22.1	30.0	35.1	33.5	29.1
Total net income	47.7	39.6	71.1	65.7	74.3	60.6
(Percentage of net income from livestock)	(66.8)	(56.0)	(42.1)	(53.4)	(45.6)	(47.0)

Source: A. P. G. Poyck, Farm Studies in Iraq, Table 4.18, p. 63.

176

Table 7. Tenant on large holding compared with farm owner with respect to income and subsistence levels.

	Tenant on large holding	Farm owner
Average net farm income	78.7 ID	71.3 ID
Average value of food consumed	52.9 ID[a]	55.1 ID[a]
Percentage income for food purchases	67%	77%
Average calorie-intake per day per capita	1,947	1,827
Value of food derived from farm produce	39.6 ID	45.6 ID
Percentage home-produced food of total food consumed	75%	83%
Percentage marketed of disposable production	52%	36%

[a] Average family size for tenant is lower than for farm owner; correspondingly the per capita average value of food consumed is 8.95 ID and 8.25 ID respectively.

Source: A. P. G. Poyck, *Farm Studies in Iraq*, Table 4.26, p. 71.

Table 8. Family size, land, and income.

	Size of family	Labor force per farm[a]	Cropped land (mesharas per farm)	Fallowed land (mesharas per farm)	Average income in Iraqi Dinars[b] per meshara		per capita	
					Net	Gross	Net	Gross
Large holdings	5.9	2.5	37.6	33.4	1/192	2/507	13/339	28/100
Medium holdings	6.4	2.6	34.7	23.3	1/184	3/001	9/812	24/900
Farm owners	6.7	2.5	26.3	14	1/876	2/642	10/649	15/000
Communal farms	6.0	2.4	27.4	20	1/702	2/605	11/891	19/100
Owners on date orchards	7.3	2.3	10.	5	3/864	5/221	7/410	10/000
Tenants on date orchards	7.6	2.4	14.	6	2/457	4/084	6/144	10/200

Source: A. P. G. Poyck, *Farm Studies in Iraq*, composite of Tables 4.19 and 4.20, p. 65.
[a] Poyck counted every male between 16 and 50 as one labor unit, while females between 16 and 50 and all children between 12 and 16 were considered one half unit in reckoning the labor force.
[b] Note that the average per capita income figures are obtained by dividing average income per family by average family size, producing a biased estimate.

Table 9. Relation between family size and farm size.[a]

Family size	Tenants on large holdings	Farm owners
2	43 mesharas	20 mesharas[b]
3	46	11
4	49	19
5	58	20
6	67	25
7	72	37
8	77	39
9	78	44
10	82	57
11	94	82
12	100	88

Source: A. P. G. Poyck, *Farm Studies in Iraq*, p. 75.

[a] There is clearly a tendency for farm size to increase with the size of the family; indeed the rank order correlation coefficient is 1.0 between cols. 1 and 2 and .96 between cols. 1 and 3.

[b] Excluding wasteland and land farmed as tenant.

Table 10. Tenants on large holdings versus farm owners in terms of food intake, calories, and expenses.

	Tenants on large holdings			Farm owners		
	Kilos per year per capita	Calories per person per day	Computed expenses in fils per year	Kilos per year per person	Calories per person per day	Computed expenses in fils[a] per year
Wheat	10.7	91	214	13.2	112	264
Barley	46.5	431	465	32.0	296	320
Rice	24.8	231	573	30.1	278	692
Green gram	7.5	57	150	7.5	57	150
Dates	54.5	443	216	65.1	531	260
Millet	6.1	67	61	2.0	19	20
Chicken	2.4	8	240	3.0	10	300
Meat	9.9	52	693	11.3	59	791
Fish	1.3	3	260	1.7	5	340
Eggs	0.9	4	153	1.4	6	238
Ghee	5.3	128	2,666	5.1	124	2,565
Milk	17.3	31	346	15.6	28	312
Leban	47.2	39	—	79.4	69	—
Yoghurt	11.2	22	224	7.9	16	158
Vegetables and fruit	65.5	59	655	50.7	46	507
Tea	2.1	—	315	1.4	—	210
Sugar	24.7	270	1,729	15.7	171	1,099
TOTAL	—	1,936	8,960	—	1,827	8,226

Source: A. P. G. Poyck, Farm Studies in Iraq, composite of Tables 4.23 and 4.26, pp. 68, 71.
[a] One Iraqi Dinar = 1000 fils.

Table 11. Type of marriage within two fakhds of the Elbu Ubayd, a shabba of the El Shabana.

	Elbu Najim	% of Total	Elbu Muhammad	% of Total
(Plural marriages[a]	2	4.6	10	13.1)
Parallel cousin marriages	11	25.0	21	28.0
Intra-fakhd marriages[b]	11	25.0	11	14.0
Intra-shabba marriages	2	4.9	2	02.6
Intra-ashira marriages	6	14.5	18	24.0
Intra-sillif marriages	1	02.4	5	07.0
Marriages with Sada	3	06.9	2	02.6
Marriages with servants			1	01.4
Marriages with mother's relative (mother not parallel cousin)			1	01.4
Marriages with foreigners	9	21.3	9	11.0
Origin of marriage unknown			6	08.0
Total number of marriages	43	100	76	100

Data based on genealogies complete to a depth of four generations.

[a] Each category is exclusive, with the exception of plural marriage. For example, a parallel cousin marriage is not counted as an intra-fakhd marriage. Plural marriages are counted in the appropriate categories.

[b] Intra-fakhd marriage is usually defined as "male ego marries FaFaBrSon's daughter."

Appendix IV

Table 12. Type of marriage within the El Shabana tribal settlement in Daghara village

		% of Total
(Plural marriages[a]	9	10.0)
Parallel cousin marriages	37	43.0
Intra-fakhd marriages	7	08.1
Intra-shabba marriages	11	12.8
Intra-ashira marriages	8	09.3
Intra-sillif marriages	3	03.5
Marriages with Sada	3	03.5
Marriages with mother's relative (mother not parallel cousin)	1	01.2
Marriages with foreigners	16	18.6
Total number of marriages	86	100

Data based on a census of the 77 households in the settlement.

[a] These marriages are included in the appropriate categories below.

Table 13. Composition of households within the El Shabana tribal settlement.[a]

Total number of households	77
Total number of persons in households	399
Largest household (no. of persons)	11
Smallest household (no. of persons)	2
Average size of household (no. of persons)	5.1

Persons in household other than nuclear family

Husband's mother	13
Husband's father	1
Wife's mother	2
Wife's father	0
Husband's sister (unmarried, widow or divorced)	10
Wife's sister (unmarried, widow or divorced)	1
Husband's brother (unmarried)	1
Married sons and wives	11
Married daughter (husband absent)	1
Daughter-in-law (husband absent)	1
Husband's sister's son	1
Sister of brother's wife	1
Total persons in households other than nuclear family	43

Data based on a census of the 77 households in the settlement.

[a] "Household" is defined as those persons dependent on a single adult male, or in which adult males share expenses.

Appendix IV

Table 14. Occupations of men living within the El Shabana tribal settlement

		Number
Large landowner		3
Medium landowner		6
Small landowner		8
Fallah		7
Fallah and sheep herder		1
Local sheep trader		7
Sheep exporter		3
Small grain wholesaler		2
Traveling produce salesman		2
Buffalo milk producer and retailer		1
Employed by shaykh		7
personal guard	3	
servant	1	
coffee server		
in mudhif	2	
descendant of		
Negro slave	1	
Government guard		2
Porter		2
Taxi-driver		2
Worker in mud (this is defined as any man who may do building with mud, repair streets, and do other common labor)		7
Street cleaner		3
Weaver		2
general weaver	1	
weaver of abbayas	1	
Tailor		3
general tailor	2	
tailor of abbayas	1	
Jeweler		1
Ironsmith		1
Sweetcake seller		1
Mumin (religious specialists)		3
Students (in school or college away from village)		3
Local charity cases		4
support by son in army	1	
blind (support by community)	1	
blind (relative of shaykh and supported by him)	1	
part charity case, part worker in mud	1	
Working away from settlement		4
works in Basra	1	
works in Hilla	1	
works in Karbala	1	
cloth merchant in Shamiyya	1	
TOTAL		85

Data based on census of the 77 households in the settlement.

Table 15. Ownership and usage of distributory canals by shabbas of the El Shabana (listed in order of excellence of position in relation to water supply).

Name of shabba	Exclusive user of one or more off-takes	Share an off-take with another shabba	No. of off-takes
1. El Jamiyyin	X	X	[a]
2. Elbu Khaz'al	X	X	two
3. El Shidayda		X	one (part)
4. El Mujarilin	X		one
5. El Hakam	X		one
6. El Khalat	X		one
7. Elbu Salih	X		one
8. Elbu Ubayd	X		one
9. Elbu Jurayd	X		one
10. El Ghrush		X	one half
11. El Shawahin		X	one half

[a] Several, but scattered as this is shaykh's lineage.

Table 16. Formal petitions concerning water problems presented to the Irrigation Office, Daghara, by members of the El Shabana, 1953–1957.

Type of petition	Single practitioner	Group petition (members of same shabba or fakhd)	Group petition (members of same ashira)	Total
Request for additional water	9	11	4	24
Request for redistribution of water ("outside distribution problem")	0	4	9	13
Request for redistribution of water ("inside distribution problem")	0	8	6	14
TOTAL	9	23	19	51

Appendix IV

Table 17. Problems involving infraction of water regulations by members of the El Shabana, 1953–1957 (from records of irrigation engineer and mudir nahiya).

Type of infraction	Infraction on government canal	Infraction among tribesmen sharing non-government canal	Total
Water theft involving individual tribesmen	4	0	4
Water theft involving group (fakhd or shabba)	4	3	7
Water theft involving group (ashira)	1	2	3
Cutting irrigation ditch through another man's land	0	1	1
TOTAL	9	6	15

Total water thefts among members of the same fakhd or shabba	3
Total water thefts among members of the same ashira	3

Appendix V

Maps

Appendix V

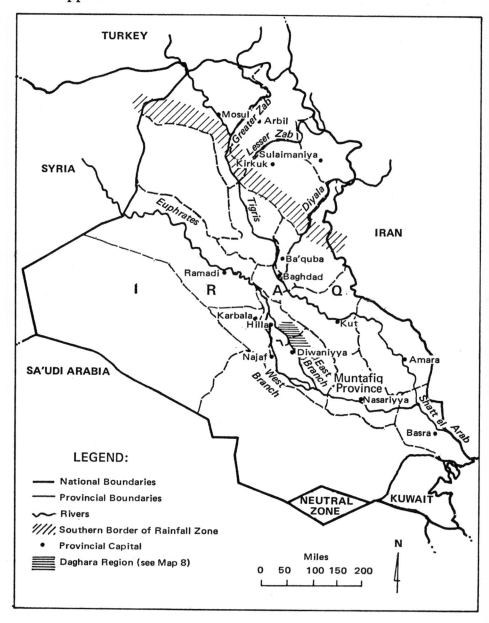

Map 1. Iraq

Map 2. Daghara area canals (British expeditionary force map of 1918)

Appendix V

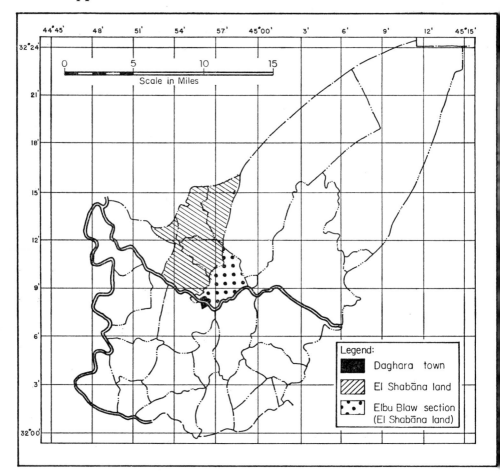

Map 3. Daghara district

190

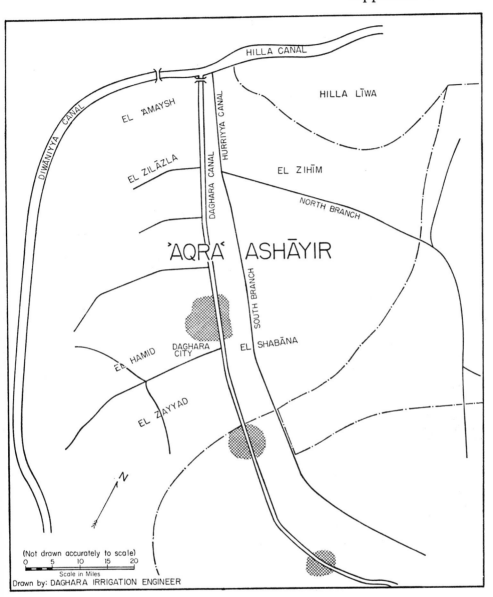

Map 4. Sketch of Daghara area showing positions of ashāyir of El
ʾAqraʿ sillif

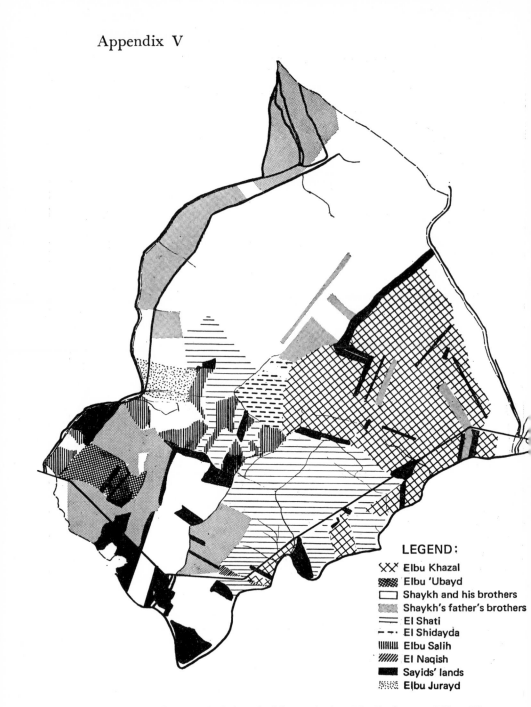

LEGEND:

XXX Elbu Khazal

Elbu 'Ubayd

☐ Shaykh and his brothers

Shaykh's father's brothers

≡ El Shati

─ ─· El Shidayda

||||||| Elbu Salih

////// El Naqish

■ Sayids' lands

Elbu Jurayd

Map 5. Land occupied by shabbas of the El Shabāna: Elbu Blaw Section

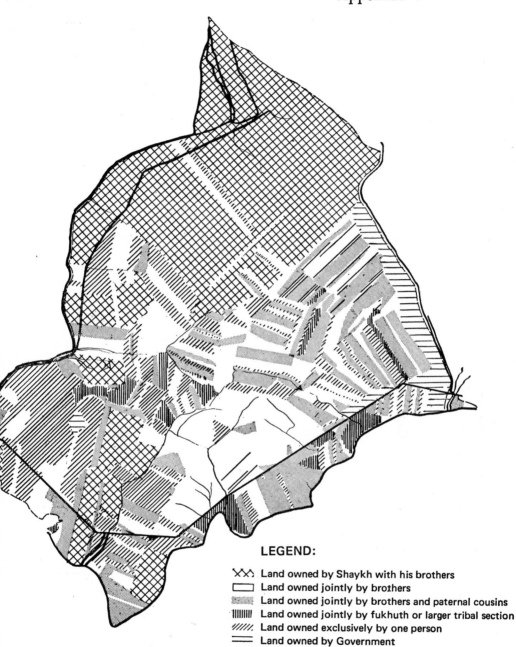

LEGEND:

XXX Land owned by Shaykh with his brothers
☐ Land owned jointly by brothers
▓ Land owned jointly by brothers and paternal cousins
‖‖‖ Land owned jointly by fukhuth or larger tribal section
///// Land owned exclusively by one person
═ Land owned by Government

Map 6. Types of land ownership among tribesmen: Elbu Blaw section
of El Shabāna land

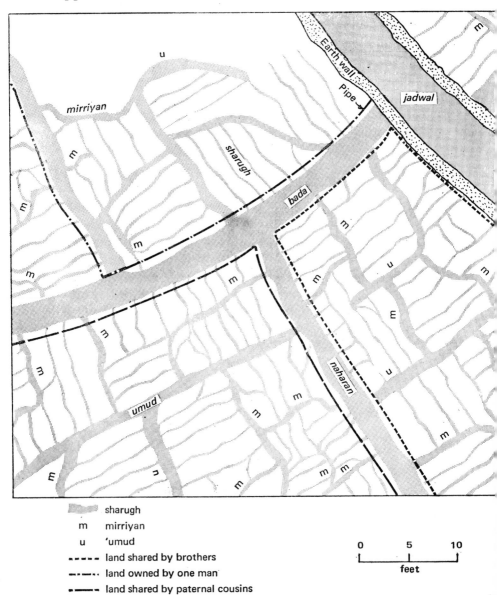

sharugh

m   mirriyan

u   'umud

-----   land shared by brothers

-·-··   land owned by one man

-·——-   land shared by paternal cousins

0   5   10

feet

Map 7. Schematic diagram of tribal irrigation system

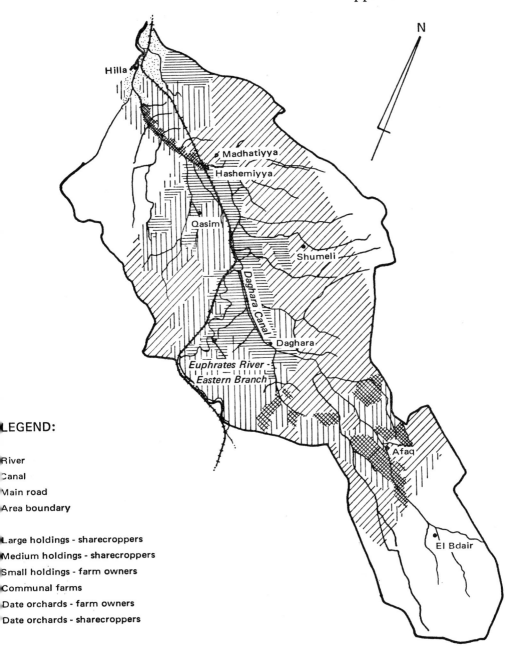

N

Hilla

Madhatiyya

Hashemiyya

Qasim

Shumeli

Daghara Canal

Daghara

Euphrates River - Eastern Branch

LEGEND:

River
Canal
Main road
Area boundary

Large holdings - sharecroppers
Medium holdings - sharecroppers
Small holdings - farm owners
Communal farms
Date orchards - farm owners
Date orchards - sharecroppers

Afaq

El Bdair

Map 8. Land tenure pattern in Daghara region

Source: A. G. P. Poyck, *Land Use,* p. 36.

Notes

NOTES TO CHAPTER I. THE SETTING: SOUTHERN IRAQ

1. Because of the silting and scouring action of the rivers, the Tigris and Euphrates have repeatedly shifted course, and the Euphrates in particular breaks into a series of shifting bifurcations south of Baghdad. Herodotus, noting this characteristic, commented that of all great rivers, the Euphrates alone appears to grow smaller as it approaches the sea.

2. Temperature reports are taken from *Statistical Abstract 1960* (Central Bureau of Statistics, Republic of Iraq, 1961).

3. Ahmed Sousa, *Irrigation in Iraq* (Baghdad, 1945), p. 12.

4. Rice-growing is thus predominantly found in the region between Amara and Basra along the Tigris and in the area around Nasiriyya on the Euphrates. The marshlands near Shamiyya and Abu Sukhair in the Middle Euphrates region are also centers of rice cultivation.

5. Shakir Mustafa Salim, *Marsh Dwellers of the Euphrates Delta* (London, 1962), p. 8. The local dialect of Arabic for example contains many Turkish morphemes, such as the suffix "chi" which indicates the doer of the action. An *arabanchi* is a man who drives a carriage or *arabiya*, a *gahawchi* is a man who makes the coffee or *gahwa*. Persian words like *cherpaya* (bed) are found. Surely one of the outstanding tasks for future anthropologists in Iraq will consist of systematic comparisons between the two valleys and of understanding these two regions in the context of the larger cultural areas of southwest Asia.

6. Great Britain, Admiralty, *Iraq and the Persian Gulf* (Geographical Handbook Series. Naval Intelligence Division. Oxford, 1944), p. 337.

7. For example, the El Harraksi are a camel-owning Arab tribe or tribal section who spend part of the year in the Daghara area. They customarily transport the grain grown by the El Shabana tribe into the village of Daghara or into the provincial capital, Diwaniyya. In return they receive a fraction of the grain transported. This relationship may account for the fact that a brother of the chief of the El Shabana is married to a daughter of the El Harraksi's chief. After the period of grain transport is over, the El Harraksi take up their tents and move back onto the desert.

8. Technically, El Shabana tribesmen considered the sharecroppers under the protection of the landowner with whom they had a contractual agreement. Sharecroppers were not expected to participate in tribal affairs, to marry El Shabana women, or to share in the payment of *fasl*.

9. A. P. G. Poyck, *Farm Studies in Iraq* (Wageningen, 1962), p. 37.

10. See Shakir Mustafa Salim, "The Role of the Guest-House in Ech-Chibay-

ish Community," *Bulletin of the College of Arts and Sciences,* Baghdad (June 1956), for a detailed discussion of the construction and use of a *mudhif.* See also Plate 6.

11. I have reserved the use of the term "hamlet" to refer to the many small settlements of cultivators scattered throughout the countryside. These settlements contain no specialized buildings other than those associated with a household, or mudhifs which are meeting places for men and where male guests are entertained. Daghara village could, because of its size and local importance, be as well called "Daghara town." I have heard local people call it both *qariya (village)* and *madina* (city). I am unaware of a term in Arabic for a collectivity of intermediate size such as is usually meant by the term "town" in English. By long tradition "madina" has usually been reserved to refer to a center which has a market place, a mosque, and a public bath. Daghara lacks a public bath. Except for these minor considerations, the use of the term "village" to refer to Daghara is entirely arbitrary and probably reflects the urban background of the writer. As an administrative and market center, Daghara village might be similar to county seats in some sections of rural America.

12. All these figures are taken from the Republic of Iraq's *Statistical Abstract, 1957.*

13. See D. M. Donaldson, *Shiʿa Religion* (London, 1933).

14. As a result of these (as well as other) contacts, the culture of southern Iraq reflects a variety of alien influences from Persia and India, as indicated earlier.

15. On February 14, 1958, I witnessed in Daghara a play commemorating events in the life of Imam Moussa ibn Jaffar.

NOTES TO CHAPTER II. ECOLOGICAL AND SOCIAL HISTORY

1. Charles Issawi, ed., *The Economic History of the Middle East, 1800–1914* (Chicago, 1966), p. 129.

2. J. A. Salter, 1st Baron, *The Development of Iraq: A Plan of Action* (London, 1955.)

3. See S. H. Longrigg, *Four Centuries of Modern Iraq* (London, 1925), chap. I.

4. Great Britain, Admiralty, *Iraq and the Persian Gulf* (Oxford, 1944), p. 433.

5. Robert M. Adams presents evidence that the western branch of the Euphrates below Mussayib consistently carried the superior amount of water from the late fifth to the fourth millennia b.c. until the present times. However, there is conflicting evidence for this, and the question will not be settled without further archeological surveys of ancient settlements in the middle and lower Euphrates area. See Robert M. Adams, "Survey of Ancient Water Courses and Settlements in Central Iraq," *Sumer,* 14, nos. 1 and 2 (1958), 101–103.

6. Great Britain, Admiralty, *Iraq and the Persian Gulf* (Oxford, 1944), p. 435.

7. J. Baillie Fraser, *Travels in Koordistan, Mesopotamia, etc.* (London, 1840), II, 105–106.

8. Fraser, *Travels in Koordistan,* III, 104–105.

9. Issawi, *Economic History of the Middle East,* pp. 129–202.

10. *Ibid.,* pp. 130–131.

11. *Ibid.,* p. 132.

12. *Ibid.,* p. 132.

13. Sir Ernest McLeod Dowson, *An Inquiry into Land Tenure and Related Questions* (Letchworth, 1931), p. 20.

14. *Ibid.,* p. 25.

15. *Ibid.,* pp. 24–26.

16. See excerpt from Saleh Haider, "Land Problems of Iraq" (unpub. thesis, London University, 1942) in Issawi, *Economic History of the Middle East,* in which is presented a comprehensive review of traditional tribal land tenure as well as a study of the Ottoman Land Code of 1858. The reader should also see Albertine Jewaideh, "Midhat Pasha and the Land System of Lower Iraq," St. Antony's Papers No. 16, *Middle Eastern Affairs* (London, 1963), for a detailed examination of his policies in this regard.

17. Jewaideh, "Midhat Pasha and the Land System of Lower Iraq," p. 130.

18. *Ibid.*

19. John Punnett Peters, *Nippur or Explorations and Adventures on the Euphrates,* (New York, 1897), II, 328.

20. F. R. Chesney, *The Expedition for the Survey of the Rivers Euphrates and Tigris* (London, 1850), vol. VII.

21. M. G. Ionides, *The Regime of the Rivers Euphrates and Tigris* (London, 1937), p. 71, offers this description of local dam-making in the "lower Euphrates area." "Huge mats of brushwood and reed are rolled round a central rope made of date palm fronds, to form a sausage-like mass called a 'badkha.' The central rope may be as large as 40 centimeters in diameter and the finished badkha 3 or 4 meters in diameter and 40 meters long. A deep trench is now dug along the bank of the river near the breach, and a heavy rope, sometimes as much as 60 centimeters in diameter, is buried in it as an anchor. To the free end of this is attached an end of the core rope of the badkha whose other extremity is held by a smaller rope also buried in a trench on the bank downstream of the heavy rope. The badkha, now lying along the bank parallel to the line of the flow of the water through the breach, is rolled into the water, partially closing off the opening and itself restrained from being swept downstream by the anchor rope, while the smaller rope at the other end keeps its tail in to shore. If the water is deep enough it floats, and is covered with palm branches resting on the shore and on the badkha itself. On top of these branches, camel thorn and earth are piled until the badkha sinks to the bottom, when a second one is rolled in on top of it. This process is continued from both banks until the breach is entirely closed."

22. Great Britain, Admiralty, *A Handbook of Mesopotamia,* Admiralty War Staff Intelligence Division Publications, vol. I, no. 1118 (November 1918), 434.

23. Ionides, *The Regime of the Rivers Euphrates and Tigris,* pp. 67, 74–75.

24. Peters, *Nippur or Explorations and Adventures on the Euphrates,* I, 228.

25. *Ibid.,* I, 228.

26. *Ibid.,* II. 63.

27. Great Britain, Arab Bureau, *British Division Administration Report, 1918–1919,* p. 121.

28. See Jewaideh, "Midhat Pasha and the Land System of Lower Iraq."

Miss Jewaideh refers to the "Daghara tribe" rather than by name to specific tribes, making the effect of the events she describes hard to relate to tribal history.

29. See Chapter IV.

30. A British source had the following to say about the position and character of the tribes along the Daghara canal: "North of Diwaniyya in the marshes of the Daghara and the khor ʿAfij are two groups of mixed tribes, known as the ʾAqra and the ʿAfij. The former live in the Daghareh in villages on the Daghareh canal, and at the end of khor ʿAfij, while the ʿAfij live in the collection of villages by the same name in the end of the khor. These people are said to be courageous and independent but are constantly feuding and inclined to brigandage." See Great Britain, Admiralty, *A Handbook of Mesopotamia*, II, no. 292 (May 1917), 153.

31. Great Britain, Arab Bureau, *The Euphrates Channels from Musaiyib to Samawah: Physical Features and Positions of Tribes* (Baghdad, 1918), p. 2.

32. Mohammed Fadhel Jamali, in *The New Iraq: Its Problem of Bedouin Education* (New York, 1934) notes "stages" in the settlement of Bedouin tribes, and places sheep-herding groups in an intermediary position between camel dependency and farming. He appears to feel that all sheep-herding or farming Arabs in southern Iraq are descendants of Bedouin nomads, and grants little antiquity to sheep-herding or farming subsistence patterns in the recent history of southern Iraq. However, apropos of our remarks concerning the alternatives of sheepherding and farming, the following quotation taken from page 67 is instructive: "It is interesting to note that even the more settled tribes are not quite as sedentary as they might be thought, for it has happened that a whole settled tribe has left its district for one reason or another and moved overnight to a new district. A dangerous neighbor or the drying up of a canal may easily provide causes for giving up a settlement and for scattering a tribe. The Khafajeh is a good example of a tribe which is beginning to reassemble after dispersal because of lack of water. Bani Saʿid of the Montafiq confederation of tribes affords a similar instance, for it has turned semi-nomadic after it was settled because of the droughts [sic] of the Shatt al Gharraf. A periodical reversion to tents is common and even . . . the villages are semi-nomadic, shifting frequently from place to place."

NOTES TO CHAPTER III.
CONTEMPORARY LAND USE AND INCOME

1. An epidemic of equine fever in 1962 wiped out most of the horses in this region and helped to seriously undermine the land economy.

2. Unlike the American prairie plow, the Mesopotamian model parts the surface but does not turn over the clods. Professor Jouette Russell has suggested that this type of plow is well suited to this land of fine soils and strong wind, where more radical disturbance of soil surface would favor dust storms —already a troublesome feature of Mesopotamian life. (Personal communication.)

3. One of the 1958 revolutionary reforms prohibits creditors from taking more grain from a farmer than an amount in excess of the basic consumption needs of the farm family.

4. The area south of Daghara, for instance, has only been cultivated over

the last twenty years, after having been abandoned for a much longer period of time owing to the decline of water from the Hilla-Diwaniyya branch of the Euphrates which feeds the Daghara, and the resulting failure of that branch to carry water to its southern extremity.

5. The local effect of post-1958 land reforms on this balance of holdings is as yet unclear.

6. Poyck, *Farm Studies in Iraq*. The company responsible for this study was Netherlands Engineering Consultants (Nedec); the survey was made from October 1958 through May 30, 1959. I left this region in May 1958. The reader should refer directly to this excellent agro-economic study for methodological statements as well as for a much fuller presentation of data than can be presented here.

7. *Ibid.*, p. 27. I did not investigate this system of land tenure. It may, however, approximate conditions of land use among tribal cultivators prior to land registration in some regions of southern Iraq, though the small amount of land in this category (as revealed by Poyck's figures) precludes the drawing of historical parallels on the basis of his evidence.

8. As may be seen from Map 8, the date orchards are near Hilla, far from the scene of anthropological research. Therefore, little comment can be offered about these last two categories, though the data are presented as a matter of general interest.

9. Poyck's classification of this region is not perfect in the sense of avoiding all problems of overlap, though it is difficult to see how any perfect classificatory system could be devised. For example, while large landholdings are compact, containing no enclaves of alien property, the same may not be said for the regions designated as "Farm-owner holdings." As may be seen in Map 6, which shows the pattern of landholdings in one section of El Shabana land, the shaykh and his kinsmen in fact own many pieces of land in and among the small holdings of their fellow tribesmen—in addition, of course, to larger holdings of land elsewhere. Many small farm owners have been obliged to sell out to larger landowners like the shaykh, and many estate owners in this region have gradually increased their holdings in the last three decades through such piecemeal purchases. Therefore, small though the pieces of land in such regions may be, they are not all owned by small-scale landowners, and Poyck's classification is thus slightly misleading.

Poyck's tables are also somewhat distorted by his apparent assumption of a one-to-one relationship between a holding and a family, the composition of which he does not define. A variety of relationships exist between landowners sharing title to the same property: an El Shabana cultivator may own some land (1) individually, (2) with his brothers, (3) with his brothers and paternal cousins, and (4) with the members of an entire section of the tribe.

Where inheritance has fragmented holdings through division of the patrimony between sons, considerable independence may develop between landownership and cultivation. Thus, inconveniently located land belonging to X may be left for Y to cultivate, perhaps for some share of the harvest, quid pro quo, in exchange for the use of a piece of Y's land conveniently situated near property which X is cultivating. Also, a man may cultivate some land with the aid of only his wife and children, while other pieces of land may be jointly cultivated with brothers or other kinsmen, the crops divided on the basis of shares of ownership. In view of these complexities, there is obviously no one standard relationship between a family and a holding of land. One imagines that the men selected in the sampling of this region in effect made their own summations of their land resources in formulating their answers to the investigators' questions. In my judgment, however, none of the problems inherent in Poyck's classification system and stratified sample seem serious enough to invalidate the results of his sampling.

10. This is called the *niren-niren* system.

11. Poyck, *Farm Studies in Iraq*, p. 38.

12. Considering that little girls practically from infancy help tend the chicks, kids, and lambs which are raised in the home, and that little boys from five on watch the family flocks and tend the cow, and that nearly all farm tasks except plowing and canal work may be done by women as well as men, one might take exception to Poyck's calculation in Table 8.

13. Poyck, *Farm Studies in Iraq*, p. 72.

14. *Ibid.*, p. 74.

NOTES TO CHAPTER IV. THE TOWN OF DAGHARA

1. Carleton S. Coon, *Caravan: The Story of the Middle East* (New York, 1951), p. 227.

2. Perhaps the fact that social Darwinism (usually coupled with certain basic ideas from Karl Marx) constituted a favorite point of discussion among the muwaddafin, indicated more about their own self-conception than could paragraphs of additional description.

3. Owning and renting shops was a profitable business for wealthier merchants and was by no means confined to their residential communities. For example, six of the shops in Daghara were owned by a man living many miles away in Hilla.

4. One man, the grown son and junior partner of the successful cloth and dihin merchant, loaned a friend ID 300 to open a cigarette and sundries kiosk at the edge of the marketplace. He received on this investment ID 20 per year until the entire sum was repaid, but this was considered an exceptionally low rate.

5. Salim, *Marsh Dwellers of the Euphrates Delta.*

6. Great Britain, Admiralty, *Iraq and the Persian Gulf*, p. 401.

7. Emrys Peters, "A Lebanese Passion Play," in *The Arab World, Atlantic Monthly* Special Supplement (October 1956), pp. 58–62.

8. See Elizabeth Warnock Fernea, *Guests of the Sheik* (New York, 1965), pp. 204–210.

9. *Ibid.*, pp. 115–117.

10. *Ibid.*, pp. 202–205.

NOTES TO CHAPTER V. EL SHABANA TRIBAL SYSTEM

1. Some years ago an issue of a popular magazine featured a cartoon showing a Cadillac in the desert and two men, presumably the driver and the owner, praying in the sand beside it. Qua cartoon, the drawing was in poor taste. However, it presented a scene frequently seen in the Near East —an apparent paradox no less significant today than in the past.

2. M. Fortes and E. E. Evans-Pritchard, eds., *African Political Systems* (London, 1950).

3. John Middleton and David Tait, eds., *Tribes Without Rulers* (London, 1958).

4. *Ibid.,* p. 7.

5. Great Britain, Arab Bureau, *Arab Tribes of the Baghdad Wilayat 1918,* (Calcutta, 1919), p. 2.

6. The Middle Euphrates valley, once dominated by the El Khaza'il confederation whose dominion was broken by Midhat Pasha, is now the scene of numerous tribal groupings, some larger than the ElAqra, others much smaller. While the description which follows rests almost entirely on familiarity with one tribe, casual contacts and conversation with other observers lead to the conclusion that the qualitative aspects of the description generally pertain to the tribes of the Hilla-Diwaniya area, but only in a much more limited degree to other regions of southern Iraq.

7. Great Britain, Arab Bureau, *Arab Tribes,* p. 2.

8. *Ibid.,* p. 3.

9. A still smaller segment, the *hamula,* will be discussed later.

10. See Raphael Patai, "The Structure of Endogamous Unilineal Descent Groups," *Southwest Journal of Anthropology,* 21, no. 4 (1965), 325–349.

11. There were a few instances noted where a man lived with his wife's father. This arrangement (called ga'adi) was agreed upon before marriage. Informants said fathers attempted to make this part of the marriage settlement when they lacked male descendants and wanted a son-in-law to look after them in old age. In return, a bridegroom accepting such an arrangement would have to pay little bride price and was the major, if not the only, inheritor of the wife's father's estate. Most tribesmen viewed such an arrangement with humorous contempt.

12. The pastoral adaptation of the cattle-owning Nuer also may result in frequent contacts between members of relatively exclusive segments. However, the fact that the El Shabana tribesmen are cultivators living together according to membership in exclusive segments does not mean the opportunity for casual contacts with tribesmen other than members of their own fakhd or shabba is lacking. Tribesmen go to Daghara village frequently and have contact with a wide range of persons on such occasions. In addition to the more formal gatherings of tribal members, my impression is that there is no lack of opportunity for intra- and even inter-ashira contacts between tribesmen.

13. The mudhif of Haji Mujid El Sh'alan is estimated to have cost more than $2500; the shaykh stated that not more than a tenth of this cost was contributed from ashiras other than the El Shabana.

14. Revolutionary political change in Iraq has not put an end to such activities. In May 1966 the rais of the El Aqra was obliged to make an arduous journey to the Shamiyya region in order to arbitrate a dispute between two ashiras of the sillif who moved there around 1919. The problem in this case involved the abduction of a young woman by a youth from another ashira. The couple had disappeared for several years but had recently been discovered in Iran by the girl's father, who killed them both. The boy's family demanded fasl, though by tradition her father was within his rights. The issue has not been resolved.

15. Great Britain, Arab Bureau, *Arab Tribes of the Baghdad Wilayat*, pp. 2–3.

16. See the photograph of a mudhif under construction (Fig. 5). This one is smaller than the one of the shaykh; it was being constructed by a fakhd.

17. Salim, *Marsh Dwellers of the Euphrates Delta*, pp. 72–82.

18. There is another group of men commonly referred to as "surkal" in southern Iraq. These men are overseers of the farming activities of fellahin employed by large landowners. The shaykh of the El Shabana employed such men; the difference between them and the surkals of the shabbas of the ashira was carefully explained, however. The latter appear to have come into existence as first the Turkish and then the British administrators required a class of persons with whom they could deal within the tribe other than the shaykh. However, surkals as overseers seem never to have been of much importance in the Daghara region, as contrasted with areas further south. See Jewaideh, "Midhat Pasha and the Land System of Lower Iraq," pp. 130–133.

19. *Sillif* means 'those who have come before,' 'ancestors,' 'forefathers'; *ashira* means 'clan,' 'kinsfolk,' from a root meaning 'pregnant'; *fakhd* means 'thigh'; and *hamula* 'to bear,' as in pregnancy.

20. See Chapter VII.

21. For example, I knew several men who regularly plowed for certain Sada without charging for it in any way; one young girl always sewed for the women of a Sayid's family without accepting payment for her work.

22. Another example of how Sada fulfill more closely the ideal cultural patterns is their attitude toward marriage. While it is said that tribesmen *should not* allow their women to marry outside their own lineage group, informants claim that Sada *never* give their women to non-Sada. Sada men can marry non-Sada women, however, and thus often have affinal ties with the group with whom they live.

23. Compare in this regard Laura Nader, "Choices and Legal Procedure, Shi'a Moslem and Mexican Zapotec," *American Anthropologist*, 67 (1965) 394–399.

24. See quotation, page 31, Chapter II.

25. The pattern of land ownership among the shaykh's lineage is an example of how land may be owned where there is a large amount held by a small group of kinsmen. The largest holdings of the shaykh's lineage are registered in the name of the shaykh and his two uterine brothers. The second largest holdings of the shaykh's lineage are jointly registered in the name of the nine sons of the shaykh's father. In fact, only the uterine brothers farm their lands as one unit; the other holdings are farmed by individuals who each take a section of the jointly registered land. This example is instructive; enough land was available for each sibling to register land in his own name, and this land would have been sufficient to provide subsistence for each sibling. Yet this was not done. The shaykh's shabba had established extensive claims to land before the registration, and, as I have noted, has been able to increase these holdings by utilizing the economic surplus which only this group within the ashira has enjoyed in recent years.

26. An independent survey of the region puts half the fertile land out of production as of 1958. Currently the percentage is said to be much higher.

27. At the same time, we might suppose that as a given fakhd further

204

segmented, its size increased. As land around it was occupied, the two seg-ments did not move far apart, but continued to cultivate contiguous lands. At this point we might expect that the term "shabba" came to refer to a social grouping of men, i.e., two fakhds as discussed above.

28. It should be added that conceivably tribesmen were using the term "shabba" relative to the El Shatti in the geographic, rather than social, sense of the term. However, since they were mentioned with shabbas when the term was clearly being used to mean social groups, I believe my interpretation is correct.

29. This was not, in fact, the case. The shaykh divided among the mem-bers of his immediate family the land he owned in excess of 1000 mesharas. On an overall basis, the redistribution of land owned by the other, much larger landowners in the region, far from being of either economic or social benefit, has actually contributed to a drastic decline in land under produc-tion—some say over one third less land is being farmed now than before the revolution. It is said that farmers abandoned their newly acquired land after the first season or two. There are a number of reasons for this. One is that no one provided seed or organized canal work, as the shaykh or his overseers had previously done. Another reason mentioned was that the rules of agrarian reform called for total cultivation of the plots of 40 meshara each, rather than allowing half to remain fallow. This, it was said, caused the land to become exhausted in a short time. It also meant that there was little or no place for grazing livestock—a major source of income, as we have seen.

NOTES TO CHAPTER VI.
THE SHAYKHSHIP AND THE DOMINANT LINEAGE

1. Doreen Warriner, *Land Reform and Development in the Middle East* (London, 1957), pp. 55–70.

2. In *Arab of the Desert* (London, 1949), H. R. P. Dickson states that the shaykhship must remain within the same family or clan. This seems to have been the expectation among the middle Euphrates tribes also and perhaps it would be fair to say that only when the struggle for this position passed outside the shaykh's lineage did succession become an occasion for political revolution.

3. Great Britain, Admiralty, *Iraq and the Persian Gulf*, p. 301.

4. Fredrik Barth has emphasized that "a pattern of father's brother's daugh-ter marriage plays a prominent role in solidifying the minimal lineage as a corporate group in factional struggle." It is difficult to understand this state-ment in the light of the example of the shaykh and his lineage given above. Where plural marriage has resulted in twelve patri-uncles, the fact that the shaykh has married one father's brother's daughter does not appear to have strengthened his relationship to the other patri-uncles with whom he was embroiled in a struggle for the shaykhship. Factionalism within the shaykh's minimal lineage appears to have encouraged marriages outside that group, so that the shaykh has strengthened his hand against his ambitious uncles by marrying a daughter of his father's brother's son (from the El Shatti group), women from other lineages of the El Shabana, and the sisters of neighboring large landowners. Such marriages have the effect of institution-alizing social relations with consequential groups both within and outside

the tribe. Barth's statement may hold where self-interest unites the members of a minimal lineage; where a minimal lineage is divided by strife, exogamous unions may be encouraged. Thus, presumably, marriages may not only form a basis for the definition of self-interest, but may also follow the lines of self-interest drawn by political and economic considerations. At the same time it is interesting to note that the eldest son of the present shaykh is married to a daughter of the next oldest brother of the present shaykh. Thus the two men who (if traditional practices hold) are most likely to succeed the shaykh are linked by marriage. The marriage is fruitful and apparently a happy one, and the relations between the shaykh's brother and his son are warm; this particular uncle was the one to whom the shaykh's son ran as a child when punished by his father. It is difficult to imagine this relationship being shattered at the death of the present shaykh. But this will not prevent the development of factionalism between other members of the shaykh's minimal lineage. See Fredrik Barth, "Father's Brother's Daughter Marriage in Kurdistan," *Southwestern Journal of Anthropology,* 10 (1954), 164–171.

5. See, for example, Jewaideh, "Midhat Pasha and the Land System of Lower Iraq," pp. 129–130.

6. In fact, there is a proverb, *kun nasīb wa la takūn qarīb,* which means "relations by marriage before blood relations." I heard this from an informant, and repeated it to another, who laughed and said: "The only good in-laws are those you would get if you married your own sister."

7. H. R. D. Dickson, *Arab of the Desert* (London, 1949), p. 52.

8. Salim, *Marsh Dwellers,* pp. 64–66.

9. But in the marshes—where among groups like the Beni Isad and parts of the Muntifiq confederation lineage stratification appears to have reached a kind of climax—adoption was a common method of affiliation among tribal units, an institution which would seem to complement the development of hierarchical distinctions among lineages. *Ibid.,* pp. 44–47.

10. *Ibid.,* pp. 62–71.

11. However, my impression is that tribal alliances and leadership played an important part in the largely successful rebellion of northern Iraqi Kurds since 1959. Furthermore, I recently have heard stories of "tribal unrest" in southern Iraq, particularly in the less accessible regions of the great marsh north of Basra. In 1967 the shaykh of the El Shabana was accused of complicity in the murder of an agrarian reform official; I am not certain whether he personally was believed to be involved (he is in his seventies now) or instead was held responsible in his capacities as a tribal leader. Finally, I suspect an approach to the analysis of contemporary national politics in Iraq which emphasized the tribal, regional, and religious origin of current civil and military leaders might yield greater understanding than preoccupation with ideology and party affiliation. Tribalism may not be of "overt importance" in modern Iraq; on the other hand this is from the perspective of a currently poorly informed outsider and intentionally begs the issue of covert importance.

NOTES TO CHAPTER VII.
CHANGING PATTERNS OF AUTHORITY: IRRIGATION

1. For details, see Appendix I.

2. See Chapter II, p. 28.

3. See Chapter II, p. 35.

4. A contemporary example of tribal disruption due to water shortage may be pertinent here. The area around Rumaytha, a town near the tail of the Diwaniyya canal, suffers from a perpetual water shortage. The irrigation engineer at Rumaytha stated that tribal units have been fragmented; not only are there no major lineages of shaykhly families, but also small groups of men (including brothers and paternal male cousins) are constantly fighting one another over water. In addition, no effective organization exists at the level of a shabba or an ashira. In 1957 Rumaytha was widely regarded by muwaddifin as one of the most lawless areas of southern Iraq. The residential expression of the tribal system has disappeared through constant jousting for better positions relative to water supply. As the minimal lineage groups continually fight, the tribal organization has lost all functioning reality.

5. I asked whether raids of expansion or raids involving the cutting of dams were *ghazu,* the well-known Bedouin raiding institution in which a man other than the shaykh may lead the raiding party to capture camels from another group. Informants said "no."

6. Following a distinction frequently made by the El Shabana tribesmen, "fallahin" is used to refer to those sharecroppers without land in the El Shabana area, who live in settlements on the shaykh's land and farm for him. In accordance with this distinction, fallahin do not participate in tribal affairs. However, about half of the more than 100 fallahin farming the shaykh's land are from the El Shabana and reside with their own tribal section.

7. *Nahar* is a cover term which might be applied to any of these waterways. It is often translated "river" but obviously this does not quite fit the usage here.

8. As noted in Chapter III, the walls (fariq) of the *lowh,* in addition to serving as water courses, may delineate subdivisions of land between corporately or individually registered owners.

9. See maps 3 and 5.

10. The supply of water in the summer is approximately one fourth of the winter supply and therefore permits much less extensive cultivation. But canals are cleaned in the spring to take advantage of whatever water may be available.

11. It is interesting to note naharan number six, named Sayid Atiyya, which is an individual canal providing water to the Sada. Four households of Sada now live with the El Mujarilin, reportedly the living descendants of two Sada brothers who were provided with land thirty years ago by the El Mujarilin. (The origin of the naharan's name, Sayid Atiyya, is not certain, but perhaps this was the name of a common ancestor of the Sada lineage group at the time the canal was dug.)

12. The latter term means "gold" and derives from a fasl payment in gold which this group received many years ago. One of their number was killed by someone from another tribe during an awna in which the entire shabba was working together in this canal.

13. Middleton and Tait, *Tribes Without Rulers,* p. 3.

14. Bichr Fares offers a description of the Arab leader which concurs with that offered both by Salim and myself.

"The elements of the honor of the shaykh can be reduced to generosity, intelligence, courage and a sense of prudence. (lit. *la mésure.*) These elements, in our days, are found in the Bedouin chief who has to be hospitable, generous, intelligent, and kind. However, it must be noted that two of these elements also appeared as a common trait among the Arabs; they were courage and generosity. Nevertheless, among the chiefs [these qualities] were boundless: courage approached temerity and hospitality was confounded with prodigality. The other two elements, prudence and intelligence, were proper to the ʿird [honor] of the shaykh: intelligence could not be divided among all the members of the group, while prudence was indispensable to those who courted power." Bichr Fares, *L'Honneur chez Les Arabes avant l'Islam* (Paris, 1932), p. 56 (translation mine).

15. Great Britain, Arab Bureau, *Arab Tribes of the Baghdad Wilayat,* 1918, p. 78.

16. *Ibid.,* p. 15.

17. *Ibid.,* p. 75.

18. *Ibid.,* p. 79.

19. Great ritain, Arab Bureau, *Administration Report of Diwaniyah District, 1918* (Baghdad, 1918), p. 199.

20. Great Britain, Arab Bureau, *British Division Administration Report, 1918–1919* (Baghdad, 1919), p. 121.

21. *Ibid.,* p. 122.

22. James Saumarez Mann, *An Administrator in the Making,* edited by his father (London, 1921), p. 251.

23. *Ibid.,* p. 252.

24. *Ibid.,* p. 231.

25. *Ibid.,* p. 219.

26. *Ibid.,* p. 275.

27. *Ibid.,* p. 246.

28. Of course, when the British government-recognized shaykhs also possessed overwhelming wealth through extensive landholdings, the shaykhs were able to exercise power through hired armed strength. This was the case in the Kut and Amara regions of Iraq.

29. Mann, *An Administrator in the Making,* p. 259.

30. See Case v, in Appendix III.

31. H. H. Gerth and C. Wright Mills, translators and eds., *From Max Weber: Essays in Sociology* (New York, 1946), pp. 296 ff. In connection with the earlier use of Weber's term "personal charisma" relative to achieving the shaykhly status, there may be some question as to whether one can speak of "charismatic leaders" occupying an institutionalized status such as the shaykhship. To conform with Weber's entire sense of the term, one might say the person who becomes shaykh behaves charismatically until he achieves that status, and then must conform to certain norms of conduct attached to that role.

32. Personal conversation.

33. Case xii in Appendix III provides one instance in which local tribesmen came to prefer the decision of the engineer to that of the shaykh.

34. There is a very practical reason why the many petitioners requesting individual water supplies are found to return the next season asking to share a pipe in the future. When a pipe of X diameter is replaced by two pipes half the diameter of the initial pipe, these provide less water than the original pipe by the square root of the difference of the two diameters. This is a fact

208

which tribesmen fail to understand when so informed, says the engineer, but they soon learn by experience.

35. Perhaps the first signs of developing rapport between tribesmen and government officials, particularly the younger ones, was their common opposition to the Iraq government prior to the July 14, 1958 revolution. Since then, with the abandonment of the "indirect rule" tribal policy and the reported formation of local political committees which include tribesmen and villagers, new patterns of local authority and leadership may well be emerging.

NOTES TO CHAPTER VIII. SHAYKH AND EFFENDI

1. R. A. Fernea, "Land Reform in Post-Revolutionary Iraq," *Journal of Economic Development and Cultural Change*, 17, No. 3 (April 1969), 356–381.

NOTES TO APPENDIX I
A TECHNICAL DESCRIPTION OF GRAVITY-FLOW IRRIGATION

1. Hassan Mohammad Ali, *Land Reclamation and Settlement in Iraq* (Baghdad, 1955), p. 30.

2. Wafiq Hussain al-Khashab notes in *The Water Budget of the Tigris and Euphrates Basin* (Chicago, 1958), p. 54, that seasons of cultivation in Iraq are customarily divided into two parts. *Shitwi* (winter) season is from December to May, when wheat, barley, beans, perennials such as citrus fruits, alfalfa, dates and deciduous fruits are grown. *Sayfi* (summer) season is between June and November, and, in addition to perennial crops, rice, cotton, and vegetables are grown in this season. In the Daghara region both winter and summer planting was earlier in the two seasons; rice cultivation took place in the Sayfi season only, as Al-Khashab suggests.

3. It is possible that summer cultivation in Mesopotamia is a comparatively recent innovation. See Thorkild Jacobsen, "Summary of Report by the Diyala Basin Archeological Project, June 1, 1957 to June 1, 1958," *Sumer*, 14, 79–89.

4. Ahmed Sousa, *Irrigation in Iraq* (Baghdad, 1945), p. 12.

5. Thorkild Jacobsen and Robert M. Adams, "Salt and Silt in Ancient Mesopotamian Agriculture," *Science*, 128 (November 21, 1958), 1251–1258.

NOTES TO APPENDIX II.
A TECHNICAL DESCRIPTION OF THE GOVERNMENT CANALS IN THE DAGHARA AREA

1. Iraq Government, Directorate General of Irrigation, *Iraq Irrigation Handbook. Part I. The Euphrates.* Compiled by Ahmed Sousa under the direction of J. D. Atkinson. (Baghdad, 1944), pp. 77–87. (This is reproduced verbatim, hence spelling may disagree with the standardized transliteration used elsewhere in this book.)

Bibliography

DOCUMENTS

Republic of Iraq. Ministry of Economics. *Statistical Abstract, 1957.* Baghdad: Zahra' Press, 1958.
——— Central Bureau of Statistics. *Statistical Abstract, 1960.* Baghdad: Zahra' Press, 1961.

REPORTS

Great Britain. Admiralty. *A Handbook of Mesopotamia.* Admiralty War Staff Intelligence Division Publications. Vol. I., no. 1118, 1916. Vol. I., no. 1118A, 1918. Vol. II, no. 292, May 1918.
——— *Iraq and the Persian Gulf.* Geographical Handbook Series. Naval Intelligence Division. Oxford: H. M. Stationery Office at the University Press, 1944.
Great Britain, Arab Bureau. *Administration Report of Diwaniyah District, 1918.* Baghdad, 1918.
——— *Arab Tribes of the Baghdad Wilayat, 1918.* Calcutta, 1919.
——— *British Division Administration Report, 1918–19.* Baghdad, 1919.
——— *The Euphrates Channels from Musaiyib to Samawah: Physical Features and Position of Tribes.* Revised to October 1, 1918. Baghdad, 1918.
Great Britain. Colonial Office. *Report by His Britannic Majesty's Government to the Council of the League of Nations on the Administration of Iraq.* (Great Britain Colonial Office Handbooks, 1920–1926. 1927–1932.) London: H. M. Stationery Office.
——— *Special Report by His Majesty's Government in the United Kingdom of Great Britain and Northern Ireland to the Council of the League of Nations on the Progress of Iraq during the Period 1920–31.* ("Great Britain Colonial Office Publications," no. 58) London: H. M. Stationery Office, 1931.
International Bank for Reconstruction and Development. *The Economic Development of Iraq.* Report of a Mission organized by the International Bank for Reconstruction and Development at the request of the Government of Iraq. Baltimore: The Johns Hopkins Press, 1952.
Iraq Government. Directorate General of Irrigation. *Iraq Irrigation Handbook: Part I. The Euphrates.* Compiled by Ahmed Sousa under the direction of J. D. Atkinson. Baghdad: Iraq State Railways Press, 1944.
——— *Report on the Control of the Rivers of Iraq and the Utilization of Their Waters by the Irrigation Development Commission.* Baghdad, 1951.
Musil, Alois. *The Middle Euphrates — A Topographical Itinerary.* American

Bibliography

Geographical Society Oriental Expeditions and Studies, no. 3. New York, 1927.

Permanent Committee on Geographical Names for British Official Use. *First List of Names in ʿIraq (Mesopotamia)*. Revised ed. London: Royal Geographical Society, 1932.

BOOKS

Adams, Doris Goodrich. *Iraq's People and Resources*. University of California Publications in Economics, vol. XVII. Berkeley and Los Angeles: University of California Press, 1958.

Ali, Hassan Mohammad. *Land Reclamation and Settlement in Iraq*. Baghdad: Baghdad Printing Press, 1955.

Campbell, C. G. *Tales from the Arab Tribes*. London: Lindsay Drummond, 1949.

Charles, H. *Tribus Moutonnières du Moyen Euphrate*. Beirut, 1939.

Chesney, Francis R. *The Expedition for the Survey of the Rivers Euphrates and Tigris*. Vol. VII. London: Longmans, Brown, Green and Longmans, 1850.

Coon, Carleton S. *Caravan: The Story of the Middle East*. New York: Henry Holt and Co., 1951.

Dickson, H. R. P. *Arab of the Desert*. London: George Allen and Unwin, 1949.

Donaldson, D. M. *Shiʿa Religion*. London: Luzac and Co., 1933.

Dowson, Sir Ernest McLeod. *An Inquiry into Land Tenure and Related Questions*. Printed for the Iraqi Government by the Garden City Press, Letchworth, England, 1931.

Fares, Bichr. *L'Honneur Chez les Arabes Avant l'Islam*. Paris: Librairie d'Amerique et d'Orient, 1932.

Fernea, Elizabeth Warnock. *Guests of the Sheik*. New York: Doubleday and Co., 1965.

Fortes, M. and E. E. Evans-Pritchard, eds. *African Political Systems*. London: Oxford University Press, 1950. (First published in 1940.)

Fraser, J. Baillie. *Travels in Koordistan, Mesopotamia, etc.* Vol. III. London: Richard Bentley, 1840.

Gerth, H. H. and C. Wright Mills, trans. and eds. *From Max Weber: Essays in Sociology*. New York: Oxford University Press, 1946.

Harris, George L. *Iraq*. New Haven: Human Relations Area Files Press, 1958.

Ionides, M. G. *The Regime of the Rivers Euphrates and Tigris*. London: E. and F. N. Spon, 1937.

Irrigation Civilizations: A Comparative Study. Washington: Pan American Union, Social Science Section, Department of Cultural Affairs, 1955.

Issawi, Charles, ed. *The Economic History of the Middle East, 1800–1914*. Chicago: University of Chicago Press, 1966.

Jamali, Mohammed Fadhel. *The New Iraq: Its Problem of Bedouin Education*. New York: Bureau of Publications, Teachers College, Columbia University, 1934.

Al-Khashab, Wafiq Hussain. *The Water Budget of the Tigris and Euphrates Basin*. Chicago: University of Chicago Press, 1958.

Lloyd, Seton. *Twin Rivers: A Brief History of Iraq from the Earliest Time to the Present Day*. New York: Oxford University Press, 1945.

Longrigg, Stephen Hemsley. *Four Centuries of Modern Iraq*. London: Oxford University Press, 1925.

Longrigg, Stephen Hemsley. *Iraq, 1900 to 1950*. London: Oxford University Press for the Royal Institute of International Affairs, 1953.

Main, Ernest. *Iraq from Mandate to Independence*. London: George Allen and Unwin, 1935.

Mann, James Saumarez. *An Administrator in the Making*. Edited by his father. London: Longmans, Green and Co., 1921.

Middleton, John and David Tait, eds. *Tribes Without Rulers*. London: Routledge and Kegan Paul, 1958.

Peters, John Punnet. *Nippur or Explorations and Adventures on the Euphrates*. Vols. I and II. New York: G. P. Putnam's Sons, 1897.

Poyck, A. P. G. *Farm Studies in Iraq*. Wageningen: H. Veeman & Zonen N. V. for Mededelingen van de Landbouwhogeschool, 1962.

Salim, Shakir Mustafa. *Marsh Dwellers of the Euphrates Delta*. London School of Economics Monographs on Social Anthropology, University of London: The Athlone Press, 1962.

Salter, J. A., 1st Baron. *The Development of Iraq: A Plan of Action*. London: Caxton Press for Iraq Development Board, 1955.

Sousa, Ahmed. *Irrigation in Iraq*. Baghdad: New Publishers, Iraq, 1945.

Steward, Julian H. *Theory of Cultural Change*. Urbana: University of Illinois Press, 1955.

Warriner, Doreen. *Land Reform and Development in the Middle East*. London: Oxford University Press for the Royal Institute of International Affairs, 1957.

Wittfogel, Karl A. *Oriental Despotism*. New Haven: Yale University Press, 1957.

ARTICLES

Adams, Robert M. "Survey of Ancient Water Courses and Settlements in Central Iraq," *Sumer*, 14, nos. 1 and 2 (1958), 101–103.

Barth, Fredrik. "Father's Brother's Daughter Marriage in Kurdistan," *Southwestern Journal of Anthropology*, X, Summer, 1954, 164–171.

Fernea, Robert A. "Land Reform in Post-Revolutionary Iraq," *Journal of Economic Development and Cultural Change*, 17, no. 3 (April 1969), 356–381.

Jacobsen, Thorkild. "Summary of Report by the Diyala Basin Archeological Project, June 1, 1957 to June 1, 1958," *Sumer*, 14, nos. 1 and 2 (1958), 79–89.

——— and Robert M. Adams. "Salt and Silt in Ancient Mesopotamian Agriculture," *Science*, 128 (November 1958), 1251–1258.

Jewaideh, Albertine. "Midhat Pasha and the Land System of Lower Iraq," *St. Antony's Papers No. 16: Middle Eastern Affairs: Three*, ed. Albert Hourani. London: Chatto and Windus, 1963.

Nader, Laura. "Choices and Legal Procedure, Shiʿa Moslem and Mexican Zapotec," *American Anthropologist*, 67 (1965), 394–399.

Patai, Raphael. "The Structure of Endogamous Unilineal Descent Groups," *Southwest Journal of Anthropology*, 21, no. 4 (1965), 325–349.

Peters, Emrys. "A Lebanese Passion Play," in *The Arab World, Atlantic Monthly* (October 1956), 58–62.

Bibliography

Salim, Shakir Mustafa. "The Role of the Guest-House in Ech-Chibayish Community," *Bulletin of the College of Arts and Sciences.* Baghdad, vol. I, June 1956.

Thompson, R. Campbell. "Some Notes on Modern Babylonia," *Journal of the Royal Asiatic Society* (1923), 233–242.

UNPUBLISHED MATERIAL

Hardan, Adnan. "Agriculture in Southern Iraq." Unpublished report prepared for the Diyala Basin Archeological Project, a joint enterprise of the Oriental Institute of the University of Chicago and the Iraq Directorate of Antiquities, under the auspices of the First Technical Section, Iraq, Development Board, 1958.

Glossary

ʿabāya	a long cloak, worn by both men and women
el ʾafrād	tribesmen
ʿagūl	camel-thorn bush
ʾahl el sūq	people of the market
ʾajawīd	respected men of the tribe who are in close council with the shaykh
ʿalwiyya	term used to denote a female descendant of the Prophet; proper name of a shabba canal
ʿashīra (pl. ʿashāyir)	tribal grouping
ʿawna	aid or help
ʾawlād ʿamm	father's brother's sons
ʾawlād khāl	mother's brother's sons
bida	first in a series of irrigation canals
badkha	a dam made of brush and palm mats
baggāl	fruit and vegetable store-keeper
bayt	literally, house; household
bedawi	a nomad; Bedouin
būrī	water pipe
dakhiliyya	internal
dihin	clarified butter
dinar	Iraqi currency = $2.80
dira	tribal land or domain
dish-dash	men's ankle-length garment
dulāb	a cupboard or wardrobe
fakhd (pl. afkhad)	tribal segment
farīq	division: literally, boundary made by low earth wall
faṣl	payment to end blood-feud
fātiḥa	period of mourning after an individual's death;

215

Glossary

	literally the first verse of the Koran read at the funeral
gaʿadi	marriage in which the man agrees to live with his wife's father
ghazl	grazing on immature grain
ghazu	raid
ḥākim	judge
hamal	brushwood dam
ḥamūla	a small tribal segment
haqq el sakan wa zaraʿ	right to reside and farm
ḥaras	guard
hosa	war chant
jadwal	irrigation canal
jawba	a small canal
kraya	religious reading
lazma	type of land ownership
leban	cultured milk
lowḥ	a small area of land
madīna	city
majlis	council; court
matam	ceremony of ritual mourning
meshara	measure of land, .6 acre
misḥa	shovel; used as a unit of lineal measurement
mirriyān	a small canal
muḍīf	tribal guest-house
mudīr nāḥiya	chief administrative officer of a district (nāḥiya)
muḥakkim	witness
mumin	pious man; part-time religious functionary
mukhtār	an elected official of the market
musaʿada	help or aid
muwaḍḍifīn	literally, ones who serve; white-collar workers
nādi	club house
nahar	river or large canal
naharān	an irrigation canal
nāḥiya	smallest unit in the administative subdivisions of Iraq
niren-niren	cropping and fallowing system
nizāʿ	dispute
qadma	first payment of a faṣl (blood-feud settlement)
qariya	village
raʾīs	chief of a sillif (tribal confederation)

raqāba	legal ownership of land by the state
sad	a small dike
sarai	government offices
ṣayfi	summer crops
ṣaggāl	knife and gun repairer
sayyid (pl. sāda)	male descendant of the Prophet Muhammad
serīfa	mud and mat hut
shabba'	a tribal segment
shabba' mal mayy wa'arḍ	a section with water and land
shāhid	witness
sharīf	honest
sharūgh	small feeder canal
shawiyya	goat-and-sheep pastoralists
shawk	wild perennial plant
shaykh	chief of an ʿashīra
shitwī	winter crop
sillif	tribal confederation
surkāl	nominal chief of a shabba
sūg (sūq)	market
tapu sanad	title deed to land; Turkish term
ʿumda	adviser
ʿumud	small canal
waqt	literally, time; by local custom period from sunset to sunrise and from sunrise to sunset
wakīl	shaykh's representative

Index

Abbas, Imam, 21
Abbasid rule, 36; collapse of, 25; post-Abbasid period, 28
Abu Dahab canal, 126
Administration: British, 150; local, 57–59, 77, 142–149; general discussion, 136–142: *See also* British rule; Daghara region; Daghara town
Administrators, *see* Daghara region, irrigation engineer; Daghara town, administrators
Afaq: town of, 17, 19, 35, 119; tribes of, 90, 120
el Afrad, 55. *See also* Tribesmen
Agrarian reform, 152
Ahl el suq, 55. *See also* Market folk (ahl el suq)
Albu Sultan, 137–138. *See also* Shabana, El
Ali, Imam, 21, 70
Alwiyya naharan, 125. *See also* Canals
Amaysh, El, 82. *See also* Shabana, El
Amr, El, 82. *See also* Shabana, El
Animal husbandry, 39, 47, 89, 152; as alternative source of income, 39; exploitation cost of, 48; income from, 176; small landowner's production from, 47; statistics of, 171, 174
Aqra, El, (sillif), 34–35, 107; ashiras of, 120; description of, 80–90; jural community of, 88–90; *raʾis* of, 87–89
Arab Bureau, 80
Arabian Peninsula, 11, 21, 77
Arabs, *see* Bedouins
Ashira, see Segmentary lineage system; Shabana, El; Tribal confederation; Tribal organization; Tribe
Ashura, *see* Muharram; Shiʿa, ritual and ceremony
Atiyah Shaʿlan (Shaykh), *see* Aqra, El (sillif); Shabana, El; Shaykh; Shaykh Atiyah; Shaykhship; Tribal revolts
Atiyya naharan, 125. *See also* Canals

Authority, 1–2; central, 23, 25, 152–153; contemporary structure of, 151–153; of irrigation engineer, 148; Ottoman, 30–32; patterns of, 114–119, 129, 146; rebellion against, 151; of shaykh, 109, 134–136, 143–145, 147–153; of state, 29, 35–37; transition of, 152; tribal, 128–129, 150–153. *See also* Chapter VII; Irrigation, engineer; Daghara region, administration; Daghara town, administrators; Shaykh

Baghdad, 8, 21; administrators' attitude toward, 57–58; labor migration to, 39, 46, 50, 56
Barley: consumption of, 180; cultivation of, 6, 9, 158, 238; export of, 29; saving of, 40–41; yields of, 46, 173. *See also* Crops; Cultivation; Iraq, trade; Irrigation
Basin irrigation, 25–26
Basra, 1–2, 6, 8–9, 29, 61, 181
el Bathahtha, 34
Bayt, 82–83. *See also* Segmentary lineage system; Tribal organization
Bazil canal, 80. *See also* Irrigation
Bedouins, 11–12, 42, 115, 151; culture of, 134; relations with Daghara Arabs, 77, 104
Bell, Gertrude L., 81, 136–137
Beni Isad, 114–115
British Mesopotamian Forces, 139
British rule, 67, 106, 129; advent of, 35; description of, 136–142 *passim;* termination of (1932), 1; tribal revolt against, 29, 134
Burrimal naharan, 125. *See also* Canals

Camel herding, 12. *See also* Bedouins
Canals: field (naharan), 124–127; government cleaning and maintenance, 122–124 *passim;* government-controlled, 162–165; government-owned, 121–122;

Index

gravity-flow, 26; infraction of water 146–147; ownership of, 185; sharing of, 146–147; ownership of, 185; sharing of, 126–127; shaykh's, 129–131; "Shaykh's," 168; tribal system of, 27, 121–132, 148–149; usage and maintenance, 158–169, 185; *See also* Appendix II; Chapter VII; Cultivation; Daghara canal; Irrigation; Water

Chief administrator, *see* Mudir nahiya

Communal farms, 44–45, 50, 171–175 *passim. See also* Cultivation; Landholdings

Crops: summer (sayfi), 26, 165; winter (shitwi), 7, 9, 40, 164–165 *passim. See also* Appendix IV; Barley; Cultivation; Dates; Rice; Wheat

Cultivation, 7–10; attempts to increase, 148–149; expense of, 42; extensive, 36–37, 43, 54; increase in, 29; intensive, 42–43; irrigation-based, 26–27; methods, 40, 53–54, 152; problems of, 4–5, 25–26, 38–39; summer, 7, 38–39, 148–149, 165; tribal land claims under, 30–31; vegetables, 41–42; winter, 8, 165. *See also* Appendix IV; Canals; Chapter III; Cultivators; Irrigation

Cultivators: attitude of, 41–42; small farm owners, 14, 44–47 *passim;* shaykh's tenants, 40; statistics about, 171–180 *passim;* tenants, 14, 47–53 *passim. See also* Appendix IV; Chapter III; Cultivation; Fallow system; Landholdings; Tribal organization; Tribe

Daghara canal, 8; history and description of, 17, 33–37, 105, 119–121, 132, 160–165; improvement of, 148–149; as source of tribal friction, 121; use of, 137. *See also* Appendixes I–II; Canals; Chapter VII; Cultivation; Irrigation; Shabana, El; Water

Daghara region: administration of, 1–2, 25–26, 136–142, 143–148; changes in, 77-78; ecology of, 38; government role in, 152–153; history and description of, 9–10, 33–39; labor migration from, 50–51; occupations in, 45; pacification of, 151; tribal autonomy in, 2–3, 150. *See also* Chapter II; Settlement patterns; Shabana, El; Social organization; Tribal organization; Tribe

Daghara town, 22, 57, 68-69; administrators of, 56-60, 68, 70–73 *passim;* changes in, 74–75; description of, 17–20; expansion of, 4; government services in,

22; interpersonal relations in, 68–70; market, 56; mosque in, 29; prosperity of, 22–23; schools in, 19, 22, 74–75; social composition of, 55–57; description of, 73–75 *passim;* tribal-market relations in, 66–67. *See also* Chapter IV; Market; Marriage; Mukhtar; Shabana, El; Social organization; Tribal organization; Tribe

Daly, Captain C. K., 138, 142

Dams, 28, 33, 35–36

Date orchards, 7, 38, 45, 50; statistics about, 171–178. *See also* Crops; Cultivation; Cultivators; Landholdings; Income

Dates, 7, 29. *See also* Crops; Cultivation; Foreign trade; Income

Dikes, *see* Canals; Dams; Irrigation

Dira, 31–32, 52–53

Disputes: irrigation and water, 119–121, 129, 143–148; tribal, 139–141. *See also* Canals; Cultivators; Irrigation, Engineer; Mudir nahiya; Water

Diwaniyya City, 4, 22, 59–60

Diwaniyya district, 80–81, 138

Diyalah, 165

Dominant lineage, *see* Chapters V–VI; Segmentary lineage system; Shabana, El; Shaykhship; Tribal organization

Drainage, *see* Canals; Irrigation

Economic conditions, 28–29, 46. *See also* Chapter III

Education, 19, 22, 74–75

Effendi(s), *see* Appendix III; Chapter VII; Daghara region; Daghara town

Egypt, 7, 26–27

El Aqra, *see* Aqra, El

El Shabana, *see* Shabana, El

Elbu Abdullah, 95. *See also* Shabana, El

Elbu Blaw district, 98, 101. *See also* Land, registration; Landholdings; Maps; Shabana, El

Elbu Hassan, 95. *See also* Shabana, El

Elbu Jawad, 95. *See also* Shabana, El

Elbu Jurayd, 82, 185. *See also* Shabana, El

Elbu Khazʿal, 82, 101, 126, 185; canal, 126. *See also* Shabana, El

Elbu Muhammad, 32, 169, 181. *See also* Shabana, El

Elbu Nahud, 89. *See also* Shabana, El

Elbu Najm, 82, 169, 181. *See also* Shabana, El

Elbu Nayil, 89, 120. *See also* Shabana, El

Elbu Qlawa, 101. *See also* Shabana, El

Index

Index

Index

HARVARD MIDDLE EASTERN STUDIES

Out of print titles are omitted.

* Published jointly by the Center for International Affairs and the Center for Middle Eastern Studies.

† Published jointly by the Center for Middle Eastern Studies and the Joint Center for Urban Studies.